SEASONS
TO REMEMBER

SEASONS
TO REMEMBER

The Way It Was in American
Sports, 1945–1960

CURT GOWDY

with John Powers

HarperCollins*Publishers*

HarperCollins books may be purchased for educational, business, or sales promotional use. For information please write: Special Markets Department, HarperCollins Publishers, Inc., 10 East 53rd Street, New York, NY 10022.

FIRST EDITION

Designed by George J. McKeon

Library of Congress Cataloging-in-Publication Data

Gowdy, Curt.
  Seasons to remember : the way it was in American sports, 1945–1960
  Curt Gowdy with John Powers.
      p.   cm.
  Includes bibliographical references and index.
  ISBN 0-06-018228-8
  1. Sports—United States—History—20th century. I. Powers, John, 1948– . II. Title.
  GV583.G69 1993
  796'.0973—dc20   92-54726

93 94 95 96 97 ❖/HC 10 9 8 7 6 5 4 3 2 1

To the coaches, players, and managers of the forties and fifties, who
paved the way for the sports revolution of the sixties
—C.G.

For Eleanor, whose seasons were too few
—J.P.

Contents

Photographs follow page 106.

Acknowledgments

To Ted Williams, who was extraordinarily generous with his time and his memories

To Bobby Knight, whose tales of New York basketball coaches and West Point were priceless

To Dom DiMaggio, whose anecdotes about the Red Sox and his brothers were bountiful

To Red Auerbach, who remembers the Celtics when the green was short

To Bob Cousy, who knew Auerbach when he was Arnold

To Frank Ramsey, who played for dynasties in Lexington and Boston

To Bud Wilkinson, who made football the Oklahoma state religion

To Barry Switzer, who fed Wilkinson's monster

To Harold Keith, whose recall of OU's "forty-seven straight" is total

To Darrell Royal, who brought back his days in crimson-and-cream

To Billy Vessels, who reprised the Sooners of the fifties

To Mike Treps, who brought forth gems from his OU football files

To the late Henry Iba, who summoned forth the forties as if they were yesterday

To Bob Kurland, who knew the Iron Duke by heart

To Eddie Sutton, who keeps Iba's legacy fresh at Stillwater

To Don Haskins, who spread the Iba gospel into West Texas

To Pat Quinn, who supplied the goods on the Mikan-Kurland duels

To C. M. Newton, who told tales of Baron Rupp

To Pee Wee Reese, who revived the young Jackie Robinson

To Art Kaminsky and Janet Pawson, who brought the principals together and watched over the birthing stage

To Ed Burlingame, who nursed a soft concept into a hardcover book

To Christa Weil, who saw to a multitude of vital details

To Rick Horgan and Chris McLaughlin, who got the project across the finish line

To Jean Mulvaney, who smoothed the photo-gathering process

To the *Boston Globe*, whose voluminous files were indispensable

To Elaine LePage, who stood lonely sentinel on Weston Road

We owe sincere thanks.

Prologue:
A Simpler Time

An outfielder for the St. Louis Browns had one arm. St. Mary's College had twenty-two seventeen-year-olds on its football team. Racetracks were closed, auto racing forbidden, boxing titles frozen. World War II changed everything in America, and sports weren't immune. How could they be "normal," when nothing else was?

By the end of 1944, every able-bodied athlete between eighteen and thirty-eight was wearing a uniform. Bob Feller was shooting down Japanese planes from a battleship. Ted Williams was teaching pilots in Pensacola. Joe DiMaggio was a sergeant in the Army Air Force.

The Dodgers and Yankees and Cardinals still played the same game in the same ballparks, but the uniforms were filled with a strange collection of youngsters, old men, 4-Fs, the lame and the halt—anybody who wasn't needed for war duty.

Once the Japanese bombed Pearl Harbor, it was as if sports were suspended in time. Players began leaving for the service almost overnight and nobody knew when they'd be back. An enlistment wasn't for two or three years—it was "for the duration." That could have been four months or four years. But we knew that when they returned, nothing would be the same again.

Every month, as more and more athletes were called up, the

available roster pool grew smaller. By 1943 more than three hundred colleges—including places like Stanford and Alabama—decided that they couldn't put eleven good football players on the field and gave up the sport until the war was over. The others struggled on, using teenagers or guys who couldn't pass a military physical.

The only colleges that weren't hurting were the military academies. If you went there, you were exempt from the draft until you graduated—even if you'd already been to school somewhere else. So West Point and Annapolis became instant powerhouses. And most of the stars who'd enlisted ended up on service teams like Great Lakes, Iowa Pre-Flight, and Randolph Field. In 1944, ten service teams were ranked in the collegiate Top Twenty.

The services had baseball teams, too, and they probably would have won the major-league pennants if they'd been allowed to play for them. The Bainbridge naval station team boasted four major-league shortstops. Pee Wee Reese, who'd been the regular Dodger shortstop, was only second string on the Norfolk naval training station team. Phil Rizzuto, who played for the Yankees, was ahead of him.

The Great Lakes team, whose roster included Feller, Virgil Trucks, Johnny Mize, and Gene Woodling, won forty-eight of their fifty games in 1944. Great Lakes beat eleven of the twelve major-league clubs they played that year, and probably could have won the World Series. Actually, baseball purists will probably tell you that the *real* World Series that year wasn't between the Cardinals and the Browns, but between the Army and Navy in Hawaii.

The major-league clubs were barely minor-league caliber. By the end of the war, five hundred major-league players were GIs. So were five thousand minor leaguers. Which meant that almost anybody who wasn't in high school or in a rocking chair was unavailable.

So the number of minor leagues dwindled from forty-one to nine, but all of the major-league clubs kept playing. President Roosevelt had personally given them the green light to continue. It was a question of national morale, he said. Baseball was the American game. If there was still Opening Day, the All-Star Game, and the World Series, then people would realize that there were some things that war couldn't stop.

But it wasn't normal baseball by any means. Because of gasoline rationing, the clubs didn't go south for spring training. They worked out on frozen diamonds close to home. And because of rubber shortages, they devised a ball with a core of cork and balata from South American tree sap that was deader than a mackerel. That didn't matter, though, because most of the guys wearing major-league uniforms couldn't have hit a real baseball out of the park.

You knew that what you were seeing wasn't big time, you knew it wasn't the best. But it was still a form of entertainment. Even the best clubs, the pennant winners, were patchwork. The Detroit team which won the 1945 Series averaged thirty-five years of age. Their nickname was Nine Old Men. The St. Louis Cardinals, who won the 1944 Series, lost to Great Lakes.

The Browns, who won their only American League pennant that year, had eighteen 4-Fs plus two medical discharges in uniform. Their symbol was Pete Gray, who'd lost his right arm above the elbow after falling off a wagon as a child. But he still hit .218, made a hundred and sixty-two putouts, and threw out three runners.

"They have a rickety-looking pitching staff and an outfield that has the appearance of something discarded from the Salvation Army," *Collier's* magazine reported about the Browns as they made their pennant drive. "But these are war times and the rest of the league is no better."

Bad as they were, the Browns still finished ahead of the Yankees, who'd won seven of the previous eight pennants. All of New York's regulars were in the service now. When someone asked Joe McCarthy for his Opening Day lineup, the Yankee manager shook his head. "How could I possibly do that?" he said. "Why, I couldn't tell you who will be here next Tuesday."

McCarthy ended up putting guys named Hersh Martin, Tuck Stainback, and Mollie Milosevich in pinstripes. He even signed up Paul Waner, who had played against Babe Ruth and Murderer's Row in the 1927 World Series and was now forty-one.

"How come you're in the outfield for the Yankees?" some guy shouted to Waner from the bleachers one day.

"Because Joe DiMaggio's in the Army," Waner replied.

Waner wasn't the only old-timer to be summoned back to the diamond. Babe Herman, who was forty-two years old and hadn't played in the big leagues since 1937, suited up for the Dodgers.

Pepper Martin, who was forty and had been out of baseball for three years, became a Cardinal again. And Leo Durocher, who was managing the Dodgers, wrote himself back into the lineup as an infielder.

For those of us who were kids during the thirties, seeing those guys in uniform again was like reliving those simpler days, when it was still the Golden Age of Sports in America—and today's problems were too distant to imagine.

When I played varsity basketball for the University of Wyoming in the years just before the war, we thought we were big time, but we really weren't—not by today's standards, anyway. We didn't get any special treatment. There was no athletic dorm—three of us lived in coach Ev Shelton's house, where we paid nominal board. I had a job at the swimming pool, giving out clothes baskets for thirty-seven and a half cents an hour.

Nobody got payoffs or cars. That was unheard of in those days. No colleges got put on probation or got the "death penalty" for violating NCAA rules. That came later, with the big money. And nobody ever mentioned drugs. I'd never heard the word *cocaine*. Didn't know what it was. People said that some musicians used marijuana, but it was strange to us. For kicks, kids drank beer and got tight.

Life—and sports—was less complicated in those days. There were only sixteen major-league baseball clubs, none of them west or south of St. Louis. The National Hockey League had six teams, all of them north of Chicago. Professional football was something guys did on Sunday afternoons for a couple hundred bucks. There was no National Basketball Association. Pro basketball, what there was of it, was called "the dance-hall circuit." They'd put on a game, then have a dance afterward to attract a crowd. And college basketball was nowhere near as popular as it is now. Only eight teams made the NCAA tournament. When Oregon won the first title in 1939, they had to wire back to campus for enough money to get home from Chicago.

Ev Shelton had no assistants at Wyoming. He took care of all the arrangements on the road and did all of the recruiting and scouting. If we were going to play Utah, Ev would get in a car after we'd practiced at Laramie and drive all night, five hundred miles to Salt Lake City. He'd watch Utah play the next night, filling out his shot charts on them, then drive back to Laramie. He'd lose sleep for two nights, but that's the way it was.

We didn't fly anywhere in those days. And the driving was tough. There were no interstate highways. If you wanted to go from Chicago to Los Angeles, you took Route 66. From Miami to Boston, it was Route 1 and stoplights in a thousand small towns. Most rural roads were made of gravel. Washboard, we called them. Driving over them, your head would shake and bounce like one of those dolls with a spring. If you went to another city, you almost always went by train.

I grew up in Cheyenne, hundreds of miles from a big-league city. "Curtis," my dad would tell me, "someday you and I are going to get on a train and we're going to go to Chicago or St. Louis and see a major-league baseball game."

My dad was the chief dispatcher for the Union Pacific railroad. Five or six streamliners a day came through town, beautiful trains named after cities I only dreamed of visiting—Los Angeles, San Francisco, Portland.

When I was a boy, Jack Dempsey came through Cheyenne on his way to Chicago to fight Gene Tunney in the famous "long-count" title bout in 1927. There was a note in the paper that Dempsey would come off the train during the stopover and that he'd be happy to meet anybody who showed up.

Well, when the train stopped, about five hundred kids were lined up at the depot. Dempsey had on a white bathrobe and he hadn't shaved, but he looked like a god coming down that line. I looked up at him and Dempsey stuck out his hand.

"Howya doin', kid?"

I was almost speechless. "Hi, champ," I finally managed to say.

That's how sports heroes were in those days—approachable, yet larger than life. Radio made them that way. Radio was the theater of the mind. It supplied the words, you created the pictures. The only limits were your own imagination.

Radio was still a teenager in the years just before the war. The first sports broadcast had been done out of Pittsburgh in 1921—a fight between Johnny Ray and Johnny Dundee. There still weren't that many sports events on radio when I was growing up—the big fights, the Kentucky Derby, the college football game of the week, and, of course, the World Series. That was the one event that had a great hold on the American public.

The Series was always played in the afternoon, and the whole country sort of stopped. Everyone took long lunch hours or found ways to get out of the office and near a radio. The standing joke then was that everybody's grandmother died during the World Series.

There were no car radios in those days, and no transistors, either. Everybody had a big Philco or an Atwater-Kent or an RCA, as large as television consoles are today. You could bring the whole world into your living room, especially in the evenings, when the sky wave went down and those big fifty-thousand-watt stations with their skip signals came in from hundreds of miles away. That's how I became a USC football fan when I was a kid. I heard their games on KFI from Los Angeles.

The great announcers, guys like Graham McNamee, Ted Husing, Bill Stern, and Clem McCarthy, were more than just disembodied voices. They were creators, who set the scenes for your theater of the mind. Of course, since there were no pictures, the announcers could take great liberties with what was actually happening. That was one thing about Stern, who was known more for drama than for accuracy.

If he made a mistake calling a football game and had the wrong guy running for a touchdown, Stern would have him lateral to the right guy just before he crossed the goal line. I guess he figured the listener would never know the difference.

Once, after McCarthy had the wrong horse winning the Kentucky Derby, Stern ribbed him about it. "Well, Bill," McCarthy replied, "I guess you can't lateral a horse."

You certainly couldn't have done it on television, but television was still regarded as an experimental gadget then, something they were fiddling around with in New York. There had been a few primitive broadcasts in 1939—ball games between the Dodgers and Reds and between Princeton and Columbia and a football game between Fordham and Waynesburg. But only a handful of people saw them—it was like Alexander Graham Bell trying out his telephone—and once the war came, there wasn't much time for experimental gadgets.

That didn't mean that television would go away. Everything during the war was simply in suspended animation. You couldn't start anything new—not if it required fit young men and any materials that a fighting army or navy might need.

But once Germany surrendered in May 1945, the spell was broken. The men who played sports and the men who watched them began returning by the boatload—and attendance at sports events soared. It was as though you'd been denied dessert for four years, then somebody handed you a big dish of chocolate ice cream.

More than eleven million fans—a record—saw major-league baseball that summer. Even though the racetracks had been closed until the middle of May, more than a billion and a half dollars were bet by year's end—and that's when two dollars could buy you a pretty good dinner.

After four years of war, the American public was eager for "normal" things, like watching Joe Louis fight Billy Conn for the heavyweight title again or sitting in the bleachers and arguing whether DiMaggio or Williams was the better hitter. People figured that once everybody got back from overseas, sports would be back to "normal." But I think everybody knew deep inside that sports would never be normal again.

Kids who'd gone off to the Marines at seventeen instead of going to college would be enrolling as twenty-one-year-old freshmen. Television, air travel, and night baseball were on their way. And Negroes, as they were called then, would soon be playing in the major leagues.

Maybe it took the war for people to realize that it was absurd for the national pastime to practice segregation. If a man could wear a uniform for Uncle Sam, he should have been able to wear one for the Yankees. Yet for decades, the owners, the press, and millions of Americans had accepted the idea that major-league baseball was a white man's game.

Black players were restricted to Negro League teams like the Homestead Greys, the Kansas City Monarchs, and the Pittsburgh Crawfords. Or else they barnstormed, driving hundreds of miles night after night to play in ramshackle old ballparks.

There were fabulous players on those teams, guys like Satchel

Paige, Josh Gibson, and Cool Papa Bell, who was so fast that they said he could turn out the light and be in bed before the room got dark. They would have been Hall of Famers if they'd been allowed to play in the majors. But even during the war, when clubs were desperate for anybody who could play, they bypassed blacks entirely.

When Bill Veeck tried to buy the Phillies in 1945 and put a black team on the field, the commissioner himself stepped in and saw to it that the Phillies were sold to another group which was offering only half of what Veeck was.

By the fall of 1945, though, the color barrier was coming down. Branch Rickey, who ran the Dodgers, signed Jackie Robinson, a twenty-six-year-old infielder who'd played for the Monarchs, had been a star halfback at UCLA, and had served as an infantry lieutenant during the war.

He clearly had the skills to be a major leaguer, but what convinced Rickey was that Robinson also had the character to stand up to the physical and verbal abuse he was destined to take from resentful white ballplayers.

So Rickey signed Robinson and sent him to Brooklyn's farm club in Montreal. By 1947, Robinson would be playing in the World Series—and the World Series would be on television.

Nothing would change sports the way television did. It would pump in immense sums of money, enriching owners and players alike. It would have its negative side, too. Television devastated baseball's minor leagues: Why would you want to see a game of Class B ball when you could see the Giants play the Dodgers? And it all but killed off boxing, especially the neighborhood clubs that were the sport's lifeblood.

I don't think anybody could have foreseen those things in 1946, but they knew things weren't going to be the way they'd been before the war. Pro athletes were starting to realize that they ought to have some bargaining power with the owners, that they didn't have to take whatever was handed to them.

That year Danny Gardella, an outfielder with the Giants, had taken baseball all the way to the Supreme Court. He was challenging the right of an owner to essentially bind players to his club for life through the reserve clause in the contract. Gardella ended up settling for sixty thousand dollars and his unconditional release and the reserve clause stood until 1976. Even challenging it was viewed as un-American somehow. Rickey said that those who opposed the clause "lean to Communism." And he was considered one of the more liberal owners.

Even though they were starting to assert themselves after the war, the players were still whipsawed by the owners. There were no unions, no free agency, no guaranteed contracts, no pension plans— and no agents. Owners wouldn't have talked to them anyway. I remember Ted Williams telling me that he'd never send a lawyer up to see Tom Yawkey, who owned the Red Sox.

People ask now, why did the players take that stuff for so long? Simple—because they loved to play. Every American boy grew up dreaming of wearing a big-league uniform. When you were already in heaven, who'd quibble about money?

Once, when I was drinking with Bobby Layne, the old Lions quarterback, I asked him why the pro football players didn't ask for more money. Layne reached over and grabbed me by the shirt.

"Hell, I'd play for nothing," he growled. "I love it."

After four years of death and deprivation, Americans were delighted to have the luxury of playing and watching games again. As amazing as the turnstile count had been at the end of 1945, it was dramatically higher in 1946.

Baseball attendance jumped to nearly nineteen million, and ten clubs—even the last-place Giants—drew over a million. Golf, tennis, and auto racing all attracted record crowds. So did college football, which had six years worth of players crammed onto its rosters.

Once the wartime spell had been broken, nothing was the same again. College basketball was now enthralled with the big man, seven-footers like Bob Kurland and George Mikan. And college football had changed, too. With the war over, the lure of West Point had diminished. With the GI Bill guaranteeing every serviceman a free college education, every school now could put together a powerhouse.

The first warning shot of the new age was a telegram that the students at South Bend sent to Red Blaik, the Army coach. THE WAR IS OVER, it said. AND THE MEN ARE BACK AT NOTRE DAME.

SEASONS
TO REMEMBER

1

Black Knights and Our Lady

 They weren't very imposing by modern football standards. Glenn Davis stood only five feet nine inches tall. Doc Blanchard weighed just over two hundred pounds. But during the war—and before television—they were giants.

Until I went up to Michie Stadium to watch Army play Oklahoma in the autumn of 1946—the first big football game I ever broadcast—Mr. Inside and Mr. Outside lived mostly in my imagination. I'd created them from Ted Husing's radio broadcasts, from black and white clips in the Movietone newsreels, from the cover of *Time* magazine.

If Blanchard and Davis were larger than life, so were the football teams they played on. Army had losing seasons in 1940 and 1951, but in the decade between, they were the stuff of fantasy.

There was a romance to West Point that reached its peak in the forties, especially during the war. The Plain overlooking the river, the Gothic architecture, the corps of cadets with their immaculate gray uniforms and straight backs. And the football team, with its black jerseys and gold helmets.

"I want an officer for a secret and dangerous mission," General George Marshall had said during the war. "I want a West Point football player."

They were the Black Knights of the Hudson and their most magical days came in 1944 and 1945, when Army took people apart every Saturday. Of course, most folks forget how it was back then, when virtually every able-bodied twenty-one-year-old was in a military uniform somewhere.

They forget that those Army varsities were facing teams which were pasted together with 4-Fs and teenagers. What they remember were those incredible scores: Army 69, Pitt 7; Army 59, Notre Dame 0; Army 83, Villanova 0.

The teams that Blanchard and Davis played on would have been great in any era. But toward the end of the war, they were completely overpowering. To people like me, sitting at home in Cheyenne and listening to Army's games on radio, the Cadets were mythic figures. And Blanchard and Davis—the Touchdown Twins— were pretty close to gods.

Blanchard was Mr. Inside, the rampaging fullback who knocked aside tacklers as though they were bowling pins. And Davis was Mr. Outside, the slippery halfback who had more gears than a race car. Each of them won the Heisman Trophy, which goes to the best college player in America.

Davis might only have weighed a hundred and seventy pounds, but I don't think that America has ever produced a better natural athlete. Red Blaik, who coached at West Point for eighteen years, said that Davis was the best athlete he'd ever seen. A dozen major-league ball clubs were after him—the Dodgers offered Davis a blank contract. He set the academy record on their grueling fitness test, which included everything from chin-ups to a three-hundred-yard run. He played varsity basketball, too.

And that story about him playing two sports against Navy on the same afternoon is true. After he scored a couple of runs in the baseball game, Davis jumped in a car, laced on track shoes, and won the 100 and the 220.

By forties standards, Blanchard was a steamroller—six feet, two hundred five pounds. He threw the shot for the Army track team and ran the 100 in ten seconds flat. "Have just seen Superman in the flesh," coach Ed McKeever cabled someone back in South Bend after West Point destroyed his Notre Dame team 59–0. "He wears Number 35 and goes by the name of Blanchard."

Together, he and Davis formed the most devastating combination in college football history. If you tried to clog the center of the line to stop Blanchard, Army would get the ball to Davis on the outside and let him run wild. And if you tried to cover the ends to pen Davis in, Army would cut Blanchard loose inside, bucking and crashing.

"Every time I get knocked on my back, Davis or Blanchard goes by," said Notre Dame's Frank Szymanski after Army demolished the Irish in 1944. "And every time I look up, somebody's putting a new 6 on the scoreboard."

If times had been normal, neither Blanchard nor Davis would have ended up at the Point. But the war—and the new football eligibility rules—changed everything.

Even if you were already playing for another college—as Blanchard was at North Carolina—you could transfer to West Point and get three more years of eligibility. You were exempt from the draft until you graduated. Then you went into the service as a second lieutenant. Who could pass up a deal like that?

Not Blanchard. He'd already been drafted in 1943 and was sitting at an Army base in New Mexico, waiting to be shipped overseas. So he jumped at the chance to go to West Point. Davis was headed for Southern Cal on a Navy scholarship. Army got him by promising to take Davis's twin brother, too.

By 1944, when the war had been going for nearly three years, West Point had the best two teams in the country—its plebe-sophomore squad and its first-class squad. Blaik rotated them, to make sure everyone got a chance to play. But it didn't matter which squad was in the game. Army just rolled over everybody.

Their 1944 team, which gave up only five touchdowns, averaged fifty-six points a game—a national record that still stands. The 1945 varsity outscored its opponents 412–46. Both teams were undisputed national champions. When you're scoring a point a minute on people like Notre Dame, you're not going to get much of an argument from anybody.

Naturally, there was a lot of criticism about the way Army was running up the scores. But Blaik wasn't purposely trying to do it. He had such superior talent that he couldn't help it.

His 1945 team, which rubbed out Notre Dame 48–0, scored all

of its touchdowns standing up. Blaik couldn't ask his players to fall down or fumble. So West Point rolled on.

When the 1946 season started, the Cadets had won eighteen in a row by an average score of 50–4. But by then the world had changed—literally. The war had been over for nearly a year and servicemen had been coming back to campuses for months.

They were back at Oklahoma, too, where I was broadcasting Sooners games for KOMA in Oklahoma City and where Jim Tatum was running a continuous tryout camp. Everybody was welcome—returning lettermen from the 1945 team, guys who'd played there before the war, incoming freshmen. And guys who'd played for anybody else, anywhere. Oklahoma was creating a football team from scratch.

They'd had a break-even season in 1945 with a ragtag, pickup varsity. The war had only been over for a few weeks, so anybody old enough and healthy enough to play football was still in the service. So the Oklahoma team—almost anybody's team that year, really— was still filled with guys who wouldn't normally have been varsity material.

The Sooners had ended up losing five of their final eight games in 1945, including a 47–0 defeat at home to Oklahoma State, which was then called Oklahoma A&M. It was the worst beating in school history, all the more embarrassing because it was laid on by the guys from Stillwater.

So Snorter Luster, an old Sooner letterman who'd been coach during the war, had quit because of poor health. What he meant was that the fans were driving him nuts because he kept losing to A&M and Texas.

Oklahoma people didn't have a whole lot to feel proud about back then. The Depression and the Dust Bowl days had created this feeling of inferiority. So the board of regents decided that a good football team at OU would give folks around the state something to rally around. And there'd never been a better time to build one.

Because thousands of servicemen were back on campus, there were no transfer restrictions. Freshmen—some of them twenty-two years old—were eligible, too. So it turned into a real meat market. There were stories of colleges offering cash and cars and other inducements to get guys to enroll.

The *Saturday Evening Post* did a big story that fall on what it called "football's black market." As a case history, the magazine used Shorty McWilliams, who'd been the fullback behind Blanchard and Davis the year before. McWilliams had played a year at Mississippi State while he was waiting to be accepted at West Point. After the war was over, some Mississippi State booster reportedly offered him fifteen thousand dollars in cash, a car, a three-hundred-dollar-a-month summer position, and a job after he graduated.

Well, there was a great uproar about the idea of McWilliams leaving the academy. Some people called him a draft dodger. Others said that West Point had no right to hold him there. McWilliams ended up going back to Mississippi State on a scholarship.

But he wasn't the only guy being chased. Buddy Young, who'd played for Illinois before he went into the Navy, got offers from more than two dozen colleges while he was still in the service. The going black-market rate for a top player—especially if he'd been on a big-time varsity before the war—was five figures. That was triple what the average working guy was making in a year.

The postwar rules were simple—no rules at all. A returning serviceman could go back to his old school or any school he wanted. Uncle Sam would pay his way on the GI Bill. And he could try out anywhere he wanted—no strings attached. Some players visited several campuses to try out. Many of them weren't even enrolled.

That was a terrific arrangement for a guy like Tatum, who'd never had much patience for recruiting handbooks or eligibility restrictions. He'd coached at North Carolina before he went into the Navy and been with the Iowa Pre-Flight Seahawks and the Jacksonville Fliers during the war.

So Tatum knew who the players were. All he had to do was round them up. "Tatum was hired at lunch," somebody joked, "and by supper he had a backfield and half a line."

Tatum literally turned up at train stations and bus depots to lasso guys like Jack Mitchell, who'd played quarterback at Texas before the war. He got George Brewer to transfer from Texas Tech, Jake McCallister from Alabama, Charlie Sarratt from Clemson. He signed up a couple of guys from Marquette.

Eight of the guys who played on Tulsa's 1945 Orange Bowl squad ended up at Norman. Tatum even had guys who were still in high school come down and scrimmage. If you were a player and stopped by Norman for as much as a sandwich in the spring of 1946, Tatum found a way to get you into uniform for a tryout.

It wasn't as though Norman was at the center of the universe, especially back then. It was a sleepy town of about twenty-seven thousand people that was twenty miles south of Oklahoma City and had begun as a switching point for the Santa Fe Railroad.

"It is not claimed for this city that she will ever be a great metropolis," the Norman *Transcript* conceded in 1893. "But it is one of the most desirable places of residence of which the mind can conceive."

The OU campus, about thirty modest brick and collegiate Gothic buildings, was laid out on a prairie on the town's southern end. OU has more than twenty thousand students now, but there were only about ten thousand then. And Owen Field, the red-tile football stadium, seated just thirty thousand, as compared to seventy-five thousand today.

But Tatum was a hell of a recruiter and he wasn't stingy with the cash, either. He had money from the Athletic Council, which had no official connection to the university. It gave out scholarships, paid for recruiting and bowl trips—and provided some "extras," too. Tatum also signed up some "sponsors," rich businessmen from Oklahoma City who'd get to visit the Sooners dressing room after games and hand players a little something.

Well, when I drove down to Norman that spring of 1946 in the KOMA station wagon, there must have been four or five hundred guys working out. The campus looked like a boot camp, with dozens of guys arriving with suitcases, fresh off buses and trains.

Calisthenics were a mob scene, with a thousand arms and legs thrashing around. There were two contact scrimmages a day that spring, then a summer session. It was all wide open, like a pro camp.

Finally Tatum and his staff drew up a list of fifty-six players for fall drills, but even then the roster was fluid. The handout printed up by the sports information office listed not only everybody who was on hand, but anybody who was "expected." Six of the eleven players who started the opening game weren't even on the roster at the beginning of August.

There were no fresh-faced recruits, either. Most of the players were twenty-three, twenty-four, twenty-five years old. Joe Golding, Oklahoma's best running back, was twenty-six. A lot of them had seen combat. But they all had one thing in common—white skin. The Southwest and Southeastern Conferences were segregated then, and they stayed that way for at least another decade.

OU played in the Big Six, but it might as well have been a southern school. Back then, there was an unofficial law that prohibited blacks from living in Norman or even from being on the streets after sundown. Oklahoma's first black player, a running back named Prentice Gautt, didn't enroll until 1956.

Almost all of the players were homegrown, too. They lived in places like Muskogee and Pawnee and Eufaula. Only ten or so came from outside of the state and almost none of them from outside of the Southwest.

Maybe twenty of them had been Sooners lettermen before they went in the service, but they were starting from scratch in Tatum's new offensive system—the Split T. Most of the players were used to the single wing or the A formation. What Tatum was teaching was the forerunner of the Wishbone.

The Split T got its name because backs were arranged in a T behind the quarterback with the line split, spaced out by a couple of yards. The split spread out the defense, sometimes making holes for the backs with the line barely having to block at all. They might just brush block, moving somebody out of the way and then heading downfield to block there.

It was a quick-hitting offense that paralyzed defenders because they had to stay at home, nailed down. The key was the quarterback, who had to be a better runner than passer. He had several options on every play. He could hand off to a diving back, who might get through one of those big gaps and into the secondary.

Or if the quarterback faked to the back on the dive, he'd start down the line of scrimmage, keeping his eye on the defensive end. If the end crashed toward him, the quarterback would pitch out to a trailing halfback, who would get outside for a long gainer. But if the end held his position to guard against the outside play, then the quarterback would tuck the ball under his arm and turn upfield.

The beauty of the Split T was its simplicity. There were only seven or eight plays, like the dive tackle, quarterback keep, quarterback pitchout, and variations off of them. Now and then there'd be a pass, but not often.

The Split T had its dangers, though. Like the Wishbone, it was a high-risk offense because a lot of tackles were made at the point of the pitchout or the handoff. So there were a lot of fumbles. It took a long time for the Oklahoma players to get comfortable with the system. The quarterbacks, especially, weren't used to all the "feinting and feeding" they now had to do.

Every day was a new day with the Split T, but Tatum and his staff did a great selling job it. Tatum was a big, strapping guy who had played tackle for Carolina in the thirties. He was pretty gruff, and I never got as close to him as I wanted to. As a rule in those days, you got closer to the assistants than you did to the head coaches, who didn't want to be bothered too much.

So I became pretty friendly with a young assistant named Bud Wilkinson, who was responsible for the offense and had been working closely with the quarterbacks. He was wide open with me about the Split T philosophy. He'd take me aside and explain what they were trying to do.

Tatum concentrated on the other side of the ball, and his legacy to the game was what became known as the Oklahoma defense. It was a five-man line, with the two ends dropping off to form a five-four-two defense. The Sooners became famous for it, and it was widely copied.

Though we didn't know it until later, OU was much better that year than people thought. They were big and mature and physical. Maybe by today's standards Tatum's team wasn't all that impressive, but for that time they were pretty imposing.

They had a fine grasp of the game, too. Six of them went on to become head college coaches—Darrell Royal at Texas, Jim Owens at Washington, Jack Mitchell at Kansas, Wade Walker at Mississippi State, Dee Andros at Oregon State, and Warren Giese at South Carolina.

But in September 1946, what was going on in Norman was just a rumor most everywhere else. All people knew was that the Sooners were coming off a .500 season with a new coach, a new system, and a bunch of people who hadn't played football for anybody in a while.

If that OU team had played Army in November, when they had half a dozen games under their belts, I'm convinced they would have beaten them. But nobody even gave them a chance in September.

West Point was still West Point. They were coming off back-to-back unbeaten seasons. They still had Blanchard and Davis. And in their opener, they'd walloped Villanova 35–0 in a downpour.

The point spread wasn't as popular in those days but it was still published and the Sooners were made thirty-six-point underdogs. Some of their younger guys were in awe of Army. But some of their older service veterans, like Wade Walker and Myrle Greathouse, had supreme confidence.

They'd literally been fighting for their lives in the war. Homer Paine was in an anti-tank unit in Europe. Eddy Davis stepped on a Nazi land mine. Dee Andros won a Bronze Star at Iwo Jima for wiping out Japanese machine gun nests. Compared to combat, football was child's play to them.

"No way Army's going to beat us thirty-six points," they told Royal, who was a freshman running back that year. "They'll be lucky to win."

But there was one thing that bothered the Oklahoma guys. They'd heard that Army had these new Riddell plastic helmets instead of the usual leather ones. If Blanchard and Davis had them, they wondered, then why couldn't they?

So Tatum promised his players that he'd get them Riddells. When the days went by and the helmets still weren't there, the players began jabbing Tatum about it. Then one day a big truck showed up at the practice field, with Tatum perched high up on a bunch of boxes.

"The helmets are here, boys, the helmets are here," he shouted as the driver went along the sidelines. Then Tatum started opening the boxes and flinging the helmets out on the field as the players grabbed for them.

Jack Mitchell, the quarterback, got one so big that he could spin it around on his head. So he went to Tatum and complained about it.

"Aw, strap it up tighter," Tatum told him. "You're lucky to have one."

Now, Oklahoma hadn't played a game east of the Mississippi in four years. Almost all of their games were against the other Big Six teams and the Texas schools.

But West Point didn't travel much. Their football team didn't get any special privileges, so the players couldn't afford to take many days off from classes. If you wanted to joust with the Black Knights, you had to go where they were. They'd travel to Philadelphia to play Penn and Navy, and they'd cross the river to play Notre Dame at Yankee Stadium. But most people had to play them at Michie.

So the Sooners chartered two DC3s, prop planes, and flew to New York. "If one crashes," Tatum figured, "we'll still have enough to play the game." He was a kidder that way. A lot of people would take Tatum seriously, but it was usually tongue-in-cheek.

Tatum tried to keep his team calm before the game, but he was a bundle of nerves inside. When he couldn't open a metal door that was blocking the tunnel leading to the field, Tatum went nuts.

"They did this on purpose, to get us excited," he shouted, jumping up and down. "But it won't work. We won't get excited. If I just knew who did this, I'd . . . Now, don't get excited."

Well, Saturday was one of those glorious end-of-September days that you get in the Northeast when the foliage is starting to turn but the air is still warm. And West Point, of course, is one of the most beautiful places in the country, with the plain and the view out over the river.

Michie Stadium seats forty thousand now, but it had room for fewer than twenty-five thousand then and the stands weren't very high. From my broadcast booth, I could almost reach out down below me and touch the Army team. Their bench was right beneath me.

I'll never forget how the Black Knights looked when they came out in that bright sunshine, wearing those fabled black jerseys and gold helmets. I had my field glasses on them, looking for numbers 35 (Blanchard) and 41 (Davis).

But Blanchard had hurt his knee in the Villanova game and wasn't playing. All he did was go out for the toss to see who got the ball first. Oklahoma sent out three captains to meet him. One writer wisecracked that they had to send out three guys just to cover Blanchard during the toss.

Nobody knew what Oklahoma had, including me. But we found

out soon enough. The second time Davis carried the ball, on a reverse, Plato Andros wrapped him up in a bear hug. Then Norman McNabb grabbed Davis from behind and dropped him after a yard. Then Giese forced him out of bounds for no gain. Andros told me later that he couldn't believe how easily he was able to get through the Army line.

Davis just couldn't run the ball. He was used to getting over a hundred yards and three or four touchdowns every game, but he ended up with only nineteen yards that day. At the end of the first quarter, Davis had gained only five yards and the Sooners had held Army scoreless.

Nobody could believe that Oklahoma had played them this tough. "Those in the stands sat goggle-eyed," the Associated Press reported the next day, "as the big Oklahoma line, as tough as the Army mascot and twice as stubborn, hurled the Cadets back on their heels."

By now, everyone began to sense that Army might be in for something. I could see the tension starting to build on the Army sideline. Blaik was pacing up and down and getting very animated. Years later, he could recount every moment of that game from memory. Of course, that wasn't unusual for Blaik. Bobby Knight, who coached basketball at West Point before he went to Indiana, told me that he had lunch with the Colonel when he was ninety-one, and that he could recall every game he'd ever coached or played in as though it had happened the day before.

Suddenly, Oklahoma was ahead. McNabb blocked a punt and Bill Morris fell on the ball in the end zone for a shocking touchdown. Except for the two thousand fans who'd come up from Oklahoma, the stadium was silent.

For a while, it seemed as though Oklahoma would take the lead into the locker room. Then Arnold Tucker took over. He was a terrific athlete who wound up getting the Sullivan Award for best amateur in the country that year. Well, Tucker threw a couple of passes to Davis that got the ball down to the OU five. Then he tossed a quick pass to Hank Foldberg, his big end, in the end zone, and with forty-five seconds to go before the half, the game was tied.

Even so, it was a tremendous upset in the making. The mighty Black Knights were being played off their feet by a six-touchdown

underdog from the prairie. I was imagining what was happening in
the other stadiums around the country when they announced the
halftime score—Army 7, Oklahoma 7. What a roar must have gone
up. It was the first close game Army had had in three years.

Well, it didn't take the Cadets long to score when they came
back out. Barney Poole blocked Oklahoma's first punt and Army got
the ball on the fifteen-yard line. Ug Fuson, their big fullback, went
over from the two a few plays later and it was 14–7.

Meanwhile, Tatum was running up and down the sidelines,
totally absorbed in the game. He was such a perfectionist that he
tried to do everything himself. Tatum didn't trust the trainer to tape
the ankles, so he wanted to tape the key guys himself. But he did
such a poor job on Charlie Sarratt that Sarratt had hurt his ankle.

Sarratt was standing with his dirty foot in a bucket of ice water
when Joe Golding broke loose on a nice run. Sarratt stood up to
watch and pulled his foot out of the bucket. Tatum came by,
grabbed the bucket, and took a long drink.

Nobody told him that Sarratt had had his foot in it, and Tatum
hadn't noticed. He was completely caught up in the game. At one
point he was so engrossed in trying to find McNabb, who was man-
ning the phone to the press box, that he went right past him three
times. Didn't even recognize him.

"Where the hell have you been?" Tatum yelled when he finally
noticed McNabb.

"Right here, Coach," McNabb said with a shrug.

Well, Mitchell drove the Sooners all the way back to the Army
four and they seemed certain to tie it up. But Tucker picked off a
pass to stop them.

Then, just as the fourth quarter began, came the play they're
still talking about at both West Point and Norman. It was the ulti-
mate Split T nightmare—the pitch that goes haywire. Oklahoma
fumbled ten times in that game and lost five of them, but none like
this one.

Dave Wallace was only thirteen yards from the Army goal when
he started down the line and pitched to Royal, the trailing back. But
the ball hit the ground and Tucker caught it off the bounce and ran
eighty-five yards for a touchdown.

Royal still insists he can still see the ball coming off the ground. The next week, Bud Wilkinson reran the films for me and you could see Royal was right. But the officials thought Tucker had recovered the ball in the air, so they let the score stand.

Well, that finished the Sooners. The final score was 21–7—no disgrace for a bunch of guys who hadn't played football in three or four years and who'd never played a game together. When I went into the OU dressing room later, I thought there'd be some elation because they'd given Army its first real test in three years.

But the atmosphere was gloomy. The Oklahoma players really thought they'd had the better team, that they should have beaten Army. They felt they'd missed a real chance to make some football history.

Still, OU had outplayed the Black Knights in their own stadium and put on a great show. In fact, the Sooners nearly went unbeaten for the rest of the season. They lost by seven points to Bobby Layne's Texas team, but Oklahoma was on the Texas two-yard line with a chance to tie the game when the gun went off. Then they lost in a great upset to Kansas in the rain, when the KU kicker braced the ball with a mound of mud and booted a long field goal.

But Tatum's men beat everybody else, including a sweet 73–12 flogging of Oklahoma A&M up at Stillwater. That was a huge symbolic victory for the Sooners. They had only beaten A&M once since the war began and had taken a horrible drubbing from them at Owen Field in 1945. Now their coaches could go into any high school in the state with a recruiting edge over the Aggies. Which side of those seventy-three points did you want to be on?

So OU went to their first postseason game in eight years and demolished North Carolina State in the Gator Bowl. That was the start of what Barry Switzer later called the Monster, the great Oklahoma football creation. And it all began that afternoon on the shore of the Hudson.

The Army dynasty began crumbling that day, too. It was the first indication anyone had that the Cadets were mortal again. A week later Cornell scored twenty-one points at Michie Stadium. No visiting team had done that since 1940.

Then Army went out to Ann Arbor and only edged Michigan by

a touchdown. They'd beaten them by three touchdowns the year before. If anybody needed evidence that the war was truly over, it was there in the scoring statistics every Sunday morning.

"Small wonder Blaik can't sleep," sportswriter Tim Cohane—the man who'd coined the Black Knights nickname—wrote in a poem for the New York *World-Telegram*. "For Army's former legion is now but a brigade."

So the whole country got fired up about the Army–Notre Dame game at Yankee Stadium a month later. Tickets had been sold out for months, and scalpers were getting two hundred dollars apiece, back when that was a month's pay for most people. By some estimates, bettors across the country waged as much as forty million dollars on the outcome.

The newspapers were calling it the game of the century. But for the two coaches, it was more than a game. It was a crusade. There weren't two better coaches in America than Blaik and Frank Leahy—or fiercer competitors. They may have respected each other as equals, but they wanted to demolish each other.

And their rivalry wasn't confined to the football field. Once, when Leahy was visiting West Point, he and Blaik were scheduled to play golf. It was raining, and Blaik suggested they call it off. But Leahy insisted, so they played in a downpour and Leahy lost by a stroke. Then he went home and practiced a full year for the rematch.

That was Leahy for you. Preparation, preparation, preparation. "There are no shortcuts in life," he told his squads a thousand times. "Pay the price, pay the price. Strive for perfection daily."

With his bow tie, his thick eyebrows, and his hair parted down the middle, Leahy looked like a grammar instructor from the Victorian era. He talked like one, too. That year Ziggie Czarobski, Notre Dame's All-American tackle, had skipped spring practice. This is how Leahy put Czarobski on public notice that he'd better come back in shape: *If Zygmont does not return in September in the most perfect condition, we shall be obliged to ask him to disassociate himself from our group.*

Leahy put his players through the torments of hell during practice. He observed every detail from a thirty-foot-tall wooden tower, with microphones hooked up to loudspeakers down on the field.

His players—lads, he called them—weren't just preparing for a football game on Saturday. They were defending the honor of the Blessed Virgin. "Lad, lad," he'd call to a downed player. "Leap to your feet and resume the struggle for Our Lady."

Playing for Blaik at West Point wasn't an afternoon's recreation, either. Even during the war, when the Cadets were blowing everybody away by ten touchdowns, Blaik drove them like mules. He'd been that way since his days at Dartmouth, where one of his players dubbed him "that metronomic drill devil" after Blaik made them run the same basic plays dozens and dozens of times.

And the better the player was, the harder Blaik pushed him. In 1958, his last year at West Point, Blaik had his best player since Davis—Pete Dawkins. Dawkins was a fabulous running back, the last Army player to win the Heisman Trophy. Well, midway through the season Dawkins injured a calf muscle. One day, Blaik walked into the training room as Dawkins was doing some leg raises on a two-by-four, trying to rehabilitate the muscle.

"Get up, Pete, get up on that leg," Blaik ordered Dawkins. "Get up on it, Pete."

If you knew Dawkins, you knew that he had an extraordinary work ethic and a high pain threshhold. It was obvious that Dawkins was punishing himself on that two-by-four, but Blaik kept pushing, pushing, pushing. "Get up, Pete."

Finally, Dawkins turned around, exasperated. "Damn it, Colonel. I can't."

Well, Blaik finally walked away, realizing that Dawkins had reached his limit. But he wasn't going to be satisfied until Dawkins had given every ounce of effort that was in him. The Colonel believed in the Spartan approach—sacrifice and simplicity. No nonsense, no wasted time.

If you went into Blaik's office, you didn't stay long because there was no place to sit. There was a desk, Blaik in a chair behind it, and a big picture of Douglas MacArthur behind him. If you had to talk to the Colonel, you made it brief and to the point. The funny thing was, Blaik didn't have to be that way at West Point. If you weren't organized, disciplined, motivated, you never went there in the first place—or you didn't last long.

Blaik's players were in awe of him. Once, when the Cadets were far ahead, Blaik ordered his third team to take it easy. Well, one of his linemen somehow ended up with the ball and nobody between him and the end zone. Just before he was about to cross the goal line, the lineman looked back at Blaik on the bench—and put the ball down on the one-yard line. You took what the Colonel said literally.

His assistant coaches, whom Blaik drove for eighteen hours a day, were in awe, too. Vince Lombardi, the immortal coach of the Green Bay Packers, said that Blaik was the finest coach who ever lived. He was certainly the most thorough. One year during the war, Blaik sent one assistant to Annapolis just to observe Navy's practices and compile a report. When the assistant sent back word that he couldn't possibly see everything that Blaik wanted to know about, the Colonel sent down ten more men to help him—one for each position.

Leahy and Blaik would have treated that 1946 meeting as Armageddon even if the teams had never played before. But those whippings Army had laid on Notre Dame during the war made things even more intense—especially because Leahy hadn't been around for them.

Even though he had a wife and four children, Leahy had joined the Navy and spent two years in the Pacific as a lieutenant aboard a submarine. While he and most of his players were ducking depth charges and bullets, Blaik's "draft dodgers" had been beating up on Notre Dame's teenagers.

So Leahy wanted to win that game with West Point more than anything—and he was licking his chops at the idea of playing the Cadets with a real varsity. All week in practice, Leahy had his players chanting: *"Fifty-nine and forty-eight, this is the year we retaliate."*

Even though Army had won twenty-five straight games, the Irish were actually favored by a couple of touchdowns. But it was obvious from the start that the squads were all but even. Every snap of the ball, every tackle was vital, and emotions ran high.

"Livingstone, you son of a bitch," Johnny Lujack yelled after Bob Livingstone, one of the Irish defensive backs, missed a tackle. Well, Leahy just tore into Lujack for his profanity, saying he'd promised Lujack's parents that he'd get a good Catholic education.

Then Livingstone missed a tackle on the next play, too.

"Lads," Leahy informed the players on the bench, "I fear that Jonathan Lujack is right about Robert Livingstone."

Actually, Notre Dame came a lot closer to losing the game than they did to winning it. Their best drive was stopped on the Army four-yard line. But Blanchard broke free late in the game and dashed down the sideline, headed for a touchdown. Lujack, the only man between Blanchard and the goal line, had to bring him down by the ankles to save the day.

So the game ended in a 0–0 deadlock. It was much ado about nothing–nothing, as one sportswriter put it and nobody on either side was very happy. "I suppose I should be elated over the tie," Leahy said. "But I'm not." Neither was Blaik. "There is no jubilation in this locker room," he observed.

It seemed only a matter of time until Army would lose—and it almost happened in the season's finale against Navy. The Middies had lost seven in a row, were twenty-eight-point underdogs and trailed 21–6 at halftime. But with ninety seconds to play, it was 21–18 and Navy had a first down inside the Army three-yard line.

If the Middies had converted any of their three extra points, they could have won it from there with a field goal. Instead, they were hit with a delay-of-game penalty, had to try a lateral on the next play, and watched the clock run out on them. So Army ended up 9–0–1, Davis won the Heisman, and Blaik was voted Coach of the Year.

But because of their close shave with Navy, the Cadets lost the national title to Notre Dame and haven't won one since. The next year, with Blanchard and Davis gone, West Point finally did lose— by a point to Columbia.

Now, Columbia was an Ivy League team and they'd lost two games in a row before they met Army, but Blaik was still worried. Lou Little, who'd been at Morningside Heights since 1930, was a terrific coach, known for getting the most out of his material.

He was the son of immigrants and he was born Luigi Piccolo— "Lou Little" in Italian. Yet Lou was anything but little. He stood six-feet-one, weighed over two hundred pounds, and had a prominent Roman nose. And, until he ruined it by screaming from the sidelines and had to resort to using a bullhorn, Little had a voice you could hear across the Hudson River.

His won-loss record was anything but glittering—from 1937 through 1956, Columbia had only five winning seasons. But Little's teams always gave you a Saturday's worth of worry. They were always in great shape and always well drilled. "Oh, my, my, my, my, my," Little would say in distaste from beneath his cap and pince-nez glasses whenever a player missed an assignment.

Columbia's players had to execute perfectly, because they were usually overmatched physically. So Little often had to resort to deception and trickery. When the Lions shut out Stanford in the 1934 Rose Bowl—still one of the greatest upsets in football history—they scored the game's only touchdown on a spinner-reverse play called KF-79. Stanford didn't know that Al Barabas was the man with the ball until he was sprinting down the sideline. The next morning, a San Francisco sportswriter quoted from the Bible: *Now Barabbas was a robber.*

Before the war, Columbia had always played Army tough. In 1943, when all of his best players were in the service and his team was headed for a winless season, Little still held off the Cadets until halftime with what he called his "Japanese Navy Defense": "Never come out and fight," Little explained.

This time, Blaik was afraid his team would be overconfident. They were unscored upon in four games that season and they'd demolished Columbia 48–14 the year before. Well, after Friday's practice up at Baker Field, where Columbia played, Blaik took his coaching staff into a nearby grove of trees for a talk.

"We're not ready to play this game," Blaik told them. "And it's my fault and it's your fault that these kids aren't ready."

Well, Army actually scored the first two touchdowns. And after Rip Rowan ran eighty yards for another one, the Cadets led 20–7 at the half. But Blaik was still worried. "I did everything possible to wake my players up at halftime," he told me years later. "Even though we led by a couple of touchdowns, I knew we were in real trouble."

Columbia had already scored once and had been stopped on the goal line another time. And they had a great passer in Gene Rossides and a fantastic end in Bill Swiacki, who later played for the New York Giants. "He catches passes the way the rest of us catch the common cold," said Bill Heinz of the New York *Sun*. "He knows where he gets some of them and the rest he just picks up in a crowd."

Well, in the fourth quarter, Swiacki grabbed one ball for a touchdown as he was stretched out horizontal to the ground. The Army players swore it wasn't a legal catch, but the officials disagreed. Then Swiacki caught another pass on his knees at the three-yard line. Lou Kusserow ran in for the touchdown and Army was beaten.

Well, that loss stuck in Blaik's craw until the day he died. Years later, we relived the game on *The Way It Was*, a nostalgic sports show I hosted on PBS. We'd take a famous event, like Bobby Thomson's "shot heard 'round the world" in 1951, and bring back the key players to watch the crackly old black and white films and share their memories. We were filming in a studio in Los Angeles and Blaik came over from Palm Springs, where he'd retired.

"Colonel, they say it's hard to get you off the golf course to go anywhere these days," I told him. "Why did you come over here to do this?"

"Curt, I still think that Swiacki trapped those passes, that the ball hit the turf before he caught them," Blaik said. "So I wanted to take a look at them one more time for my own satisfaction."

In the forties, coaches didn't have the sophisticated game films they do now. So Blaik had run the newsreel films back and forth, back and forth for hours, until he was convinced that Swiacki never made those catches legally.

Now Rowan, who'd had the big touchdown run for Army, was sitting next to Blaik. The Columbia guys were Swiacki, Rossides, and Kusserow. The funny thing was, Kusserow had wanted to go to West Point. He'd only enrolled at Columbia so he could spend a year getting his math grades up, then transfer. But he loved Columbia so much he decided to stay.

Well, Kusserow had had a couple of drinks before he got to the studio. After we'd watched the films and began taping, I asked Blaik whether he'd been afraid of the Columbia game. Just as he'd begun to answer, up piped Kusserow.

"I *shtill* say that Lou Little was the greatesht coach in the hishtory of college football."

"Cut!" our producer said, and walked over to Kusserow. "Don't interrupt Colonel Blaik," the producer told him. "He's trying to explain something."

So we did it again from the top. I asked Blaik the same question, and he began answering again.

"I *SHTILL* say Lou Little—"

"Cut!"

By now they were going to kick Kusserow off the show. We finally told him that he had to keep his mouth shut unless we asked him something. All he could do was nod.

Well, we never did settle the question of who the better coach was. And Blaik still believed that Swiacki trapped the balls. But the score still stands. And the only people more disappointed than the Army players that day were the guys at Notre Dame.

They were playing Iowa on the road that day, and when the Army score was announced over the loudspeaker, some of the Irish players dashed their helmets to the turf in disgust. "God, how we hated Columbia for doing that," Johnny Lujack said, years later. "It took the edge off the game for a lot of people. They said, well, if Columbia can beat Army, anybody can."

The Irish had been counting on ending Army's streak themselves in two weeks, when the Cadets would visit South Bend for the first time ever. "Our entire season was dedicated to the destruction of the Army football team," Lujack said. "There is no denying that. We wanted to win that game by a 60–0 score."

Notre Dame hadn't lost since they'd tied the Cadets. They hadn't even been challenged. They were ranked first in the country that week, and Army was only ninth. But when Leahy met Blaik before the game, he tried to bluff him into believing that Army would win.

"Earl, I believe your players will be very happy after this is over," Leahy told him. "I do not see any way that you can fail to defeat Notre Dame this afternoon."

"Oh, Frank," Blaik said, shaking his head. "Save the poor-mouthing for somebody who believes you." Sandbagging was Leahy's style. To hear him tell it, his teams never had a chance in any game they played.

Before the first game he coached at Boston College in 1939, Leahy told a tale of woe to Billy Sullivan, who was the school's publicity director and later owned the New England Patriots.

"William, I am quite worried about this football team that we meet today," Leahy said. "They do not have a man under two hundred and ten pounds on their offensive line and their backs have speed. Boston College could easily be beaten today, William. Oooooh, it could happen."

"Get beat by Lebanon Valley State?" Sullivan said in disbelief. Final score: Boston College 45, Lebanon Valley State 0. Leahy's team ended up playing in the Cotton Bowl that year. The next year, before BC went undefeated and beat Tennessee in the Sugar Bowl, a Boston newspaper ran this headline: LEAHY FEARS IDAHO. Final score: Boston College 60, Idaho 0.

The media and his coaching rivals soon learned to discount much of what Leahy said. "Any time Frank Leahy admits that he has a team populated by cripples, dim-witted children and assorted humpty-dumpties," mused Jimmy Cannon in the New York *Post*, "you can safely sit down and write that he won't be beaten all season."

Now, Notre Dame was favored to beat Army by several touchdowns that day. But Leahy was taking nothing for granted. His fight talk to the squad that day was probably the most emotional of his life. He brought it all back—the terrible beatings during the war, the Army draft dodgers, the scoreless tie at Yankee Stadium.

"You must redeem the honor of our school, which has suffered," Leahy told his players. "Now I ask you, in the sacred name of Our Lady, to go onto that field and shake down the thunder. Go and persevere. Our Lady demands it."

Terry Brennan—the man who eventually succeeded Leahy as coach—ran back the opening kickoff for a touchdown, and the Irish ended up romping 27–7. When the final gun went off, Leahy and Blaik met at midfield, shook hands, then walked off the gridiron ten feet apart, without saying another word to each other.

That marked the end of the Notre Dame–Army rivalry for ten years. Blaik was convinced that the Irish had become too powerful, that his Cadets couldn't stay on the same field with them. So Army dropped them. The Cadets kept winning, though. Over the next three years, they only lost one game—to Navy at the end of the 1950 season. The only thing that stopped them was the West Point honor code, which wiped out the football team in 1951 after a cribbing scandal.

Anyplace else but the academy, they would have expelled merely the students who'd been caught cheating. But West Point's code says that cadets not only won't lie, cheat, or steal, but that they won't tolerate anyone who does. So anybody who knew that his classmates were cheating and didn't turn them in was considered guilty, too. That meant all but one of Blaik's players, including his own son, Bob.

Naturally, the Colonel was devastated by the scandal. For a while he thought he should resign. But he decided not to after he talked to MacArthur, who had been superintendent of the academy when Blaik himself had been a cadet. "Never quit under fire," MacArthur told him.

So Blaik stuck it out, but the Army program was ruined for two years. The dynasty was now at South Bend. Leahy's varsity went undefeated for four years and won three national titles. Recruiting became almost unnecessary. Everybody wanted to go to Notre Dame. "I took a young lad and stood him in front of Our Lady up on that Golden Dome," Leahy conceded, "and I didn't really have to say all that much."

The only thing that halted the Irish was the school itself. Some of the faculty members had grown concerned that the university was getting a reputation as a football factory. So Notre Dame cut its scholarships almost in half and the Irish came down to earth. Their record in 1950 was only 4–4–1, their worst since 1933. Leahy was beside himself.

When Notre Dame had hired him and given him a ten-year contract, Leahy had vowed that the Irish would go undefeated for the next decade. "Ooooh, I meant to go undefeated," he said, after he'd retired. "I saw no reason in the world why we should not aim toward that horizon. Was not the University of Our Lady worthy of such a sacrifice? I thought so. I could have gone through those ten years without losing a single game. It could have happened."

Leahy might have talked about losing and worried about losing, but he never thought his teams should lose. "Frank, it's not possible to win every game," his wife told him once.

"Where is that written, Floss?" Leahy demanded to know. "In the Bible?"

Losses just tore Leahy apart, and now there were a couple every season. "Coaching burns out a man's insides," he concluded. By 1953, the tension was ruining his health. Finally, during a showdown with Georgia Tech at South Bend, Leahy felt chest pains and had to be helped into the dressing room at halftime.

People thought he had suffered a heart attack, and a priest gave him the last rites of the Catholic church. Turned out it was just acute pancreatitis. The next morning, when Leahy woke up to find the Irish had won by two touchdowns, ending Tech's thirty-one-game unbeaten streak, he still upbraided his assistant coach. "What the hell happened with Georgia Tech's belly series?" Leahy demanded.

Leahy was back on the sidelines the next week, and the Irish ended up unbeaten. But that was Leahy's last season at South Bend. Odds are his health might have forced him to stop coaching anyway. But what happened during their tied game with Iowa certainly hastened Leahy's departure. Just before halftime, with the Irish threatening to score but out of time-outs, tackle Frank Varrichione suddenly collapsed with a scream on the grass, holding his back.

Well, the officials stopped the clock with two seconds left to tend to the "injured" Varrichione, and Ralph Guglielmi threw a touchdown pass as the gun went off. Varrichione wouldn't talk about what happened after the game, but most folks accused Leahy of having his player fake the injury to get a free time-out. Forest Evashevski, the Iowa coach, wrote a sarcastic poem about it for the college newspaper:

When the one great scorer comes to write against your name,
it's not whether you won or lost,
but how you got gypped at Notre Dame.

Notre Dame was embarrassed by the uproar. "This has become a problem that is rapidly growing out of hand," wrote Father Hesburgh, the university president, to his adjutant. So Leahy was nudged into resigning for health reasons. "It's over, Floss," he told his wife. "It's over." Meanwhile, down in Norman, the Monster was growing.

2

The Oklahoma Monster

 Barry Switzer, who won three national championships at Oklahoma, called it the Monster. Once upon a time, OU football was a simple Saturday pastime, played in a thirty-two-thousand-seat stadium. Today, it's probably the state's number two industry, right behind the oil business.

The Sooners, their crimson-and-cream uniforms, their chuckwagon mascot, and their fight song ("Boomer Sooner") are known all over America. And around the state, they're the main topic of conversation from August until February.

The norm in Norman is 12-0 and a national title. And 8-3—especially if it includes a loss to Texas—is considered a losing season. Every man who's coached at Oklahoma since the war—from Chuck Fairbanks to Switzer to Gary Gibbs—has had to feed that Monster. And every autumn, it just comes back bigger and hungrier.

Bud Wilkinson didn't create the Monster, but he kept its belly filled for seventeen years. Under his quiet direction, Oklahoma won eighty-three percent of its games, three national championships, fourteen conference titles, six major bowl games, had winning streaks of thirty-one and forty-seven games, and was ranked among the Top Ten eleven straight times.

I was there when the Monster was just beginning to toddle, at the end of the 1946 season. Jim Tatum's team had won eight games and crushed North Carolina State in the Gator Bowl. Then, suddenly, Tatum was gone.

Maryland had made him an offer which Oklahoma couldn't— actually, wouldn't—match. Tatum wanted a ten-year contract at fifteen thousand dollars a season. He also wanted OU to fire its athletic director and sports publicist. So the university, which wasn't thrilled with Tatum to begin with, let him go.

Tatum had never worried much about what was and wasn't allowed around a college program. That might have been fine in 1946, when the rules were loosened to accommodate returning veterans. But it was clear that Tatum's style was going to get OU in trouble before long.

The breaking point came after the Gator Bowl when George Cross, the university president, went over the financial report and noticed six thousand dollars for "Miscellaneous." He'd told Tatum that it was against NCAA rules to give his squad any gifts, but Tatum had ignored him and offered his players either a gold watch or a hundred and twenty dollars in cash.

Now, a hundred and twenty dollars was a couple of weeks salary for a working man in those days, so the OU players took the cash. It turned out that Tatum had also overspent his budget by more than a hundred thousand dollars.

So the university didn't fight to keep him. OU simply promoted Wilkinson, who was the man that Cross and the regents had wanted in the first place. Wilkinson had coached the quarterbacks and centers up at Iowa Pre-Flight, where Tatum had been line coach. When Tatum went to Oklahoma for his interview, he'd asked if he could bring Wilkinson along.

Well, the OU people had been more impressed with Wilkinson than with Tatum. He was everything Tatum wasn't—soft-spoken, affable, and good with the media.

Bud was a new coach for a new era and his teams reflected everything he believed in. They were well prepared, smart, disciplined, poised, and quick. And they revered Wilkinson, who was old enough to be their big brother.

He was only thirty-one years old when he took over as head coach, but Wilkinson had the worldliness of a middle-aged professor. By the time he arrived at Norman, he'd already earned his master's degree in English and served as hangar deck officer on the aircraft carrier *Enterprise* during the war. And Wilkinson's football credentials were impeccable.

He'd played on Minnesota's three national championship teams in the mid-thirties, first at guard, then as quarterback in the single wing. Nobody was better at sizing up the defense at a glance, then changing signals and producing a long gainer.

Wilkinson was a thinking man's football coach, always open to innovation, and his players at Oklahoma took to him immediately. All but two of them were veterans like himself, some of them with wives and young children. They hadn't gone to college to find themselves. They were there to get their degrees and start earning a living. They loved football, but it wasn't going to pay the bills.

So Wilkinson played down the rah-rah stuff. He didn't bother with a curfew. And he kept his practices crisp and short—just around two hours. But Wilkinson and his staff would spend eight hours getting ready for those two.

I'd never known a football coach, before or since, who spent as much time preparing for Saturday as Wilkinson did. Everybody looked at game films then, but nobody dissected them the way he did, running the projector back and forth for hours.

"Hey, watch this," Bud would tell me, pointing to something he'd freeze-framed. "See how they trap? Look at how this guy is out of position."

Coaching was his profession, and Wilkinson dressed like a professional on game day—gray flannel suit, button-down shirt, red necktie, snap-brim hat. He spoke quietly—I don't think I ever heard him shout—but there was never any doubt about what he wanted done.

His players nicknamed him the "Great White Father," as though Wilkinson were some sort of blond god. No question, he was charismatic, a tall and handsome man who commanded attention merely by entering a room. When he and Bear Bryant walked through the lobby together at college football conventions, heads would turn.

Bud contributed to that Great White Father image by keeping himself a little bit apart from his players and using his assistants to crack down on them. Gomer Jones, a down-home country type of guy, handled the linemen and the defense. If you messed up on the practice field, it was Gomer who threw his cap on the ground and got in your face. And Port Robertson supervised the study hall and handed out the discipline. It was him, not Bud, who called you a peahead, who made you run the stadium steps in the September heat.

Wilkinson approached you like a professor would, his voice always calm and rational. If he could see that you were having a rough time of it, Bud would put an arm around your shoulder and invite you to his office for a chat.

If there was something bothering one of his players, Wilkinson wanted to know about it. I remember the game at Texas Christian in 1948, when Oklahoma was struggling to move the ball and Bud decided to take out Darrell Royal and put in Lindell Pearson, his big sophomore running back.

The decision made perfect sense. TCU had a big rough team, full of brawny kids from West Texas. Royal was only about a hundred and seventy pounds. Pearson weighed over two hundred. You needed power to run the Split T effectively, and Royal was getting banged around by those bigger TCU guys.

Well, Pearson ended up scoring two touchdowns. On one of them, he ran thirty-eight yards, stiff-armed the safety, and crossed the goal standing up. Oklahoma won by three points. After the game, Wilkinson and I went out to get something to eat in Fort Worth and I could see that he was sort of disturbed.

"What's the matter, Bud?" I asked him. "You won the game. You should be happy."

"Well, a funny thing happened after the game," he said. "Darrell wasn't happy about his playing time and I had to call him aside for a private talk. 'Darrell,' I told him, 'I needed some weight in there, some power. That's why I played Pearson. He has forty pounds on you and he can move some of those guys. But don't worry. You're important to us.'"

Now, most coaches of big-time programs wouldn't worry whether one of their players had bruised feelings, certainly not after a win on the road. But Wilkinson did. A dozen years later, when Royal was coaching at Texas and I was broadcasting their big

Thanksgiving game with A&M, I reminded him about that TCU game.

"I don't know whether you know it or not," I told him, "but Bud was really upset that *you* were upset because you'd been removed for a sophomore."

Royal nodded. "How many times have I been confronted with that same situation now?" he said.

Nobody in the game was a better communicator than Wilkinson was, especially in the dressing room. His halftime talks were models of understatement.

Billy Vessels, who won the Heisman Trophy in 1952, told me that some of Wilkinson's best talks were very low-key. There'd be none of this "Go out there and get 'em" stuff. When Wilkinson got through, there'd be complete silence in the dressing room. Then he'd turn around and walk out and his players would storm after him.

He knew just how to manipulate his team's psyche. Probably Wilkinson's best motivational job was before the 1956 game with Texas. Now, the Sooners had won thirty-two consecutive games and were headed for their second national championship in a row. They'd beaten Kansas State 66–0 the week before, and the players were in high spirits when they arrived in Texas on Friday.

Well, Wilkinson canceled practice and called a team meeting. He looked discouraged, ready to concede. "It's no disgrace to be beaten by a team as strong as Texas," he told his players. "Even when they beat you tomorrow, remember you're still Oklahoma. So be sure to hold your heads up high."

Suddenly, the OU players were worried. They decided not to go out to a movie that night and stayed in their rooms, memorizing their assignments. The next morning at breakfast, Wilkinson told them the same thing. "Keep your heads up. No disgrace to get beat by Texas." Well, the Sooners tore out of the dressing room that afternoon and buried Texas 45–0.

When Wilkinson got mad—which was almost never—it had the effect of a thunderbolt. "Men, take off those OU jerseys," he ordered them a couple of weeks later, when the Sooners were losing by two touchdowns at halftime up in Colorado. "You don't deserve to wear them." Final score: Oklahoma 27, Colorado 19.

The season before, when Oklahoma was losing at halftime to Maryland in the Orange Bowl, Wilkinson had ripped into his squad. "Sit down," he ordered. "I've never seen anything like this in all my life. If you guys don't get busy and start playing football, you're going to get the hell beat out of you."

None of the Sooners had ever heard Wilkinson use a cuss word. They sat stunned as Wilkinson stalked out of the room and stayed out. Final score: Oklahoma 20, Maryland 6.

Yet five weeks into the 1947 season, lots of Oklahoma folks wanted Wilkinson fired. The knock on him was that he was too soft-spoken, too nice, to be effective. Some people wanted Tatum back. What they meant was that Wilkinson's team was 2-2-1 and that they'd lost to Texas by twenty points. The carping got so bad that Wilkinson's wife, Mary, stopped going to games because she couldn't stand to listen to what the fans were saying in the stands.

I heard those complaints firsthand. As part of my job, KOMA arranged for me to give speeches about OU football at fifty luncheons around the state. I spoke to every civic and business group there was. The idea was to promote our broadcasts, and I'd be up there with a blackboard, showing how the Split T worked.

And every time, somebody in the audience would raise his hand and ask the question: "What do you think about Wilkinson?" And before I could answer, I'd hear the muttering: "Aww, he's too young. Get rid of him and get someone experienced in there."

"Look, the guy just came in," I'd argue. "Sure, he's young, but he's got a good mind. He knows football as well as anybody."

Truth was, Oklahoma was locked into a brutal schedule in those postwar years. The Big Six (Colorado and Oklahoma State hadn't yet made it the Big Eight) wasn't the top-heavy conference it is now. Missouri was a strong team then and Kansas was to go to the Orange Bowl in 1948. The season-ender with Oklahoma A&M was a civil war. And Texas was, well . . . Texas.

But the most important game of the 1947 season—and what Bud later considered the most important one of his career—was the game at Missouri against his old mentor, Don Faurot. Tatum had beaten the Tigers handily the year before, but they were undefeated in the conference now.

The result turned on the kicking game, which Wilkinson always believed was a key to victory. The Sooners broke a fake-handoff punt return seventy yards for a touchdown and Royal pinned Mizzou against its goal line twice with coffin-corner punts. OU won 21–12, then beat Nebraska by a point on a freezing afternoon at Lincoln and finished the season by stuffing their rivals from Stillwater.

So the heat was off Wilkinson—until the following September, anyway. The Sooners had won their final five, ended up 7-2-1, tied Kansas for the conference title, and were ranked sixteenth in the country. But as far as the fans were concerned, Wilkinson was still on probation.

"What do you have to *do* down here?" he asked me after the 1947 season. Bud, of course, wasn't an Oklahoman, and I'm not sure he understood how important it was to people there to have something to rally around.

Wilkinson had grown up in an upper-middle-class home in Minneapolis. His father was a real-estate mortgage dealer, his mother a model. He came from the prosperous heartland of America.

But Oklahomans, who'd had it especially rough in the thirties, still felt put down by the rest of the country. Even after the war, the stereotype of the flat-busted Okie, leaving his repossessed farm in a beaten-up car with his family crammed inside and the mattress on the roof, still lingered.

So Oklahomans were desperate to dispel that "Grapes of Wrath" image. Football was the best available means. Tatum had given them a taste of glory in 1946. Now Wilkinson had provided them with another. His 1948 team, which went 10-1 and won the Sugar Bowl, served a full meal to the Monster.

Oddly enough, the 1948 season began with a loss at Santa Clara. They don't play football anymore, but they were a Top Twenty team then. Still, the Sooners had them in hand by ten points at the half. Oklahoma teams didn't blow leads like that, but this one did. Santa Clara threw a couple of long touchdown passes to a Oklahoma kid named Hall Haynes and ended up winning 20–17.

Well, Wilkinson was beside himself afterward. When I went down to the dressing room, he was sitting with his face in his hands, looking as though he were about to cry.

"Boy, that was a tough one to lose, Bud," I said, putting my arm around his shoulder.

"Sure was," he admitted. "Hell, we probably won't lose another game for three years."

Bud called it on the nose. Oklahoma won their final ten games that year, all eleven in 1949, and their first ten in 1950. Their next loss was in the Sugar Bowl to a Kentucky team coached by another young innovator—Bear Bryant.

What Wilkinson sensed from the first day of fall practice of 1948 was that he had a terrific team, the best at Norman since the 1938 Orange Bowl squad. He still had his war veterans, plus two classes of fresh recruits. So the battle for positions that year was fiercer than it had ever been. Oklahoma had five full teams and they fluctuated from day to day. Nobody's spot was secure. You had to earn it all over again every day.

The challenge began on the first day of double sessions in September. To beat that awful, sticky heat that came off the turf in waves, the players were up at five-thirty in the morning and got in two hours of practice before breakfast. There was a nap, team meetings, lunch, another nap, more meetings, and another two-hour session before dinner.

If you weren't putting out every minute you were on the field, there'd be two or three or four other guys at your position who were. After fighting for your life against your own teammates day after day, playing Nebraska was comparatively easy.

Wilkinson was a master motivator and his most effective tool was the depth chart. If you'd played poorly on Saturday—or worse, had been lackadaisical in practice—Wilkinson would quietly drop you a team or two on the chart. Few players wanted—or dared—to ask him why.

Depth was Wilkinson's best weapon. He used it to wear out opponents and he used it to keep his own players sharp and hungry. If two guys were vying for the same position, Bud saw to it that they roomed together. Your competition literally slept in the next bed.

OU had so much talent that Wilkinson had the luxury of rotating teams. This was still in the single-platoon days, when everyone played both offense and defense. Wilkinson's guys played both sides of the ball, too, but he always had a fresh team ready, and his second string wasn't much weaker than his first.

Whichever way you chose to play against them, the Sooners had an edge. If you left your tiring starters on the field, their reserves were more than a match for them. If you went to your substitutes, theirs probably were better than yours.

That's why Oklahoma was a great second-half team, especially playing at home in the autumn heat. They simply ground you down. That 1947 team came from behind in eight of its ten games.

But the most impressive thing about those OU varsities was how few mistakes they made, how cool they were in the closing minutes if the game was on the line.

That was the Wilkinson style, inspired by his old coach at Minnesota, Bernie Bierman. Wilkinson admired how efficient Bierman was, how little time he wasted. That's the way Wilkinson was at Oklahoma. He only wanted two hours a day from you once the season started, but he wanted two hours of perfection.

His squads always knew exactly what he wanted them to do because he kept things simple. The offense he used had only four basic plays. But the Sooners ran them to perfection because they could run them in their sleep.

Wilkinson believed that you played the way you practiced. He could tell you on Thursday if his team was going to win on Saturday, just by how they'd looked during the week. So he wanted guys with a work ethic, guys who understood that nothing came easily. He found plenty of them inside the Oklahoma borders.

The people Wilkinson recruited came from small towns and farms, many of them, and they would have walked to Norman barefooted for a free education and a ticket to the good life. That's why Wilkinson urged them to major in useful subjects like geology and petroleum engineering and made sure they graduated. Nine out of ten of his players did, year in, year out. Check the list of guys who own drilling companies in Oklahoma today and you'll see a hefty number of Sooner football lettermen.

Wilkinson wanted athletes, but they had to have brains and character, too. Bud had played at a big-time school and he knew that forty-four of his fifty-five guys wouldn't be playing as much as they thought they should. So he wanted people who could sit on the bench and wait their turn and not complain. One bad apple, he believed, could spoil a whole team. He didn't want any bad actors.

Bud wanted smart kids—not necessarily Rhodes scholars, but bright enough to make snap decisions on the field. That's what you needed to make the Split T function—players who could choose among several options in a split second, guys who could pick up on all the audibles OU used. But you also needed speed.

Wilkinson was a nut on speed and quickness. I'd see him at practice with a stopwatch, lining up his players and timing them over forty yards. Bud's teams may not have been big, but they were like whippets, even the linemen. Wilkinson went for those Southwest kind of guys, lean and leathery, who could run. And he put his fastest guys on defense, made them linebackers and corners.

The Oklahoma squads of the seventies and eighties—those of Chuck Fairbanks and Switzer—beat you by turning a football game into a footrace. Wilkinson's teams did the same thing. In the midfifties, when hurrying Tommy McDonald was carrying the ball and the Sooners were in the middle of their forty-seven-game streak, the Sooners operated at seventy-eight rpm when everybody else was at forty-five.

Wilkinson called it his "fast recovery" offense and he was forty years ahead of the pros. As soon as the whistle blew, his Sooners would dash into the huddle, quickly decide on a play, then run back before the defense had a chance to regroup. Sometimes he even used what he called a "go-go" offense with no huddle at all. The quarterback simply called the play at the line.

Operating at normal speed, OU was still too fast for most folks in 1948. A week after the Santa Clara game, the Sooners ran wild over Texas A&M. But the victory that marked the turning point of Oklahoma football, the one that gave the vital jolt to the Monster's electrodes, was the one over Texas.

Maybe you have to live along the Red River to understand what the Oklahoma–Texas game means to people there. It's a turf war, a reunion, and a carnival all in one. And the game itself is unbelievably intense. Darrell Royal, who played in the game for Oklahoma and coached it for Texas, once called it an "old-fashioned, country, jaw-to-jaw, knucks-down gut check." And he was understating it.

Then, as now, the game was played in October on relatively neutral ground—the Cotton Bowl is halfway between Austin and Norman—while the Texas State Fair was going on outside. But nobody was neutral.

You were either wearing crimson or burnt orange, you were either an "oily" or a rancher, and if you lived in one state and played for the other, you had some explaining to do. "Being from Texas and playing for Oklahoma," a Longhorn fullback once said, "is like playing for Nazi Germany."

I've never seen any scene to match that Friday night in downtown Dallas. It's like Times Square on New Year's Eve—except nobody seems to go to bed. The honking motorcade along Commerce Street goes on forever. And the two old hotels on either side—the Baker and the Adolphus—are packed solid.

I used to have to drive down from Oklahoma City on Wednesday to secure the rooms we'd reserved, because they would have been long gone by Friday. By the time I got there, they would have already cleared the furniture out of the lobbies of both hotels to make room for the crush.

In 1948, Oklahoma hadn't beaten Texas for eight years. And the 1947 loss stuck in every Sooner craw because of a controversial touchdown just before halftime. Actually, the Cotton Bowl clock—which both teams had agreed would be official—had already run out. But Jack Sisco, the referee, had ruled that Texas had called time out with three seconds left.

So Texas had gotten one more play and scored a touchdown, even though the OU players claimed that Bobby Layne's knee had touched the ground. The Longhorns ended up winning 34–14, after disgusted Sooner fans littered the field with bottles. To this day, Oklahoma people call it the "Sisco game." And the State Fair now serves all its beverages in paper cups.

There were no halftime touchdowns and no bottles in 1948. OU dominated Texas from the start, won 20–14, and rubbed out bad memories that went back before the war. That was the start of the Wilkinson legend. Week after his week, his Sooners were trampling people, and the same people who'd wanted Bud's scalp the year before were now calling him a genius.

It didn't take long for the rest of the country to discover what was going on in that sleepy college town south of Oklahoma City. Seven weeks into the season, NBC Radio sent down Bill Stern to do Oklahoma–Missouri as its national game of the week.

As far as the polls were concerned, it was a bigger game than OU–Texas had been. Missouri, which had just upset Doak Walker's Southern Methodist team, was ranked ninth in the country. Some people thought OU wouldn't stand a chance—including Bill Stern. When he said so on his coast-to-coast broadcast on Friday night, claiming that Oklahoma didn't belong on the same field as Mizzou, the Sooners had all the motivation they needed.

They just destroyed Missouri, 41–7. And the play that broke it open—a quarterback spinner—was vintage Wilkinson. Oklahoma had never used it before. His players thought the spinner was crazy and never dreamed he'd call for it in a game. But it worked like magic. Jack Mitchell—General Jack, his teammates called him— faked a handoff, spun around completely, and ran thirty-five yards through a gaping hole for a touchdown.

That was the kind of thing that made Wilkinson different from other coaches. He was generally conservative and liked to keep things simple. But he was an innovator, too. He always had two or three surprise plays ready—not trick plays, just things he'd never done before. Wilkinson would work on them in practice, then spring them when he felt the time was right.

That's where he differed from Bierman. Bernie was an old-school type of guy who stuck with the single wing even after people began stopping it. Once Wilkinson sensed that teams might have figured out how to thwart the Split T, he devised a trap system, just in case. The quarterback spinner ran off the trap.

Wilkinson was one of the first coaches to put an assistant in the press box to provide an overhead view of the game. He graded his players' performances from game films long before others did.

Probably the most innovative thing Wilkinson did was his weekly letter to the alumni during the season. He knew that only thirty thousand fans could see the home games and only a couple of thousand could follow the team on the road.

So Wilkinson re-created the game for the alumni, to make them feel they had a stake in Sooners football. He knew that the alums were a priceless resource to his program. They lived in every town in the state and all over the Southwest. They could tip him off about potential recruits and even do some of the recruiting themselves. And they'd be happy to give money to the program if they felt they had a stake in it.

The letter was a simple thing. Harold Keith, OU's longtime sports publicist, would talk to Wilkinson on Sunday morning and write the letter under Wilkinson's byline. Wilkinson would read it that afternoon and the letter would be mailed Monday morning.

It was a straightforward, honest letter. If the game was a mismatch, Wilkinson would say so. If the Sooners had played badly, he'd say that, too. It didn't take long for the letter to become must reading for the OU alums. It was a great public relations tool for Wilkinson, and it helped bind the alumni and the school together.

Bud was years ahead of his time in understanding how to sell his program to the public. He knew how important radio was, how it's the theater of the mind.

In those pretelevision days, most Oklahomans followed the Sooners by listening to my broadcasts. KOMA had a network that went all over the state, maybe thirty or forty stations. We had a fifty-thousand-watt signal, and at night it just boomed all over. And our sponsor was Oklahoma Gas & Electric. You couldn't get more homegrown than that.

Well, that 1948 season was pure magic. Every Saturday brought a new delight. The Sooners scored six touchdowns in eighteen minutes against Nebraska. They crushed Kansas—whom they hadn't beaten in three years—by a count of 60–7. They held off Oklahoma A&M with three goal-line stands in the rain. Then it was off to New Orleans for the Sugar Bowl and a date with third-ranked North Carolina and Charley "Choo-Choo" Justice, their great tailback. When Oklahoma won 14–6, the state went crazy.

Wilkinson could have signed a lifetime contract on the spot after that game. But he did something that still puzzles me. He went up to Wisconsin to interview for the coaching job there. I couldn't understand why Bud would do that. Wisconsin hadn't won in years. He'd have to build from scratch in the Big Ten, which was the toughest conference in the country.

Well, Wilkinson called me long-distance from Madison.

"I'm getting on a plane," he informed me. "Can you pick me up at the airport? I want to talk to you."

When Bud got in, we went to Bishop's Restaurant in Oklahoma City for a late dinner.

"What the hell were you doing up in Wisconsin?" I asked him. "My God, with the material you've got at Oklahoma? You've got this thing rolling. You told me that to develop a team, you had to get a winning tradition. Now you've got it. You're probably the best team in the country. You've got all these guys coming back next year, a great freshman class coming up . . ."

Wilkinson shrugged. "Well, I was reared in the Big Ten," he said. "I was just curious to see what Wisconsin had to offer. I really wasn't serious about it. I just wanted to investigate it. I think a fellow should investigate things."

I kept shaking my head. "I'll never understand it, Bud," I said. "Why would you leave the situation you've got here? Whoever comes in behind you will inherit the fruits of your labor."

The funny thing was that the regents had already agreed to raise Wilkinson's salary from ten thousand dollars to fifteen thousand— more than the university president himself was paid—and give him a five-year deal. The Wisconsin people were only offering twelve thousand.

It wasn't as though Wilkinson needed leverage. He'd won ten in a row—no Oklahoma coach had done that in a decade. He'd claimed two conference titles, won a bowl game, beaten Texas—and kept those folks up in Stillwater quiet. And the university had already taken a giant leap into the future. Urged on by President Cross, the regents had voted to spend a million dollars expanding Owen Field from thirty-two thousand seats to fifty-five thousand. The Monster needed elbow room.

The Sooners were big time now and the Okie stigma finally had been erased. Wilkinson didn't have to scour obscure corners of the state to sweet-talk players into coming to Norman any longer. The players came to him. That was the fruit of the winning tradition that Wilkinson had talked so much about. And it came full flower in 1949, when the Sooners went 11-0 and destroyed Louisiana State in the Sugar Bowl.

Wilkinson never said it publicly, but I think he believed that 1949 team was the best he ever had. Some purists consider it the greatest varsity of all time. It was a marvelous squad, the last hurrah for the servicemen like Wade Walker, George Brewer, and Stanley West who'd played on Tatum's team in 1946.

That Sooner team averaged thirty-six points a game, hung up five shutouts, and played only one close game—the rematch with Santa Clara. After they'd shredded LSU, one Tennessee columnist likened them to an engineer battalion harvesting stumps. That team did have a relentless precision to it, and I saw it from the opening kickoff of the opening game up at Boston College.

The game was supposed to have been played on a Friday night at Braves Field. I'd broadcast the Yankees that afternoon in Washington, then zipped up to Boston in a low-level bomber that was piloted by a friend of mine who needed to get his hours in.

It was a rainy, murky evening and I got to the park shortly before kickoff—and found it dark, with the gates locked.

"Must be at Fenway Park," I concluded, so I told the cabbie to drive across town. But Fenway was dark, too. So I went back to Braves Field.

"Hey, kid," I asked some youngster who was hanging around outside. "What happened to the game?"

"Called it off," he shrugged.

Normally, football games don't get postponed unless a hurricane blows through. But severe thunderstorms had left the field under water, so Wilkinson and Denny Myers, the BC coach, met an hour before the 8:30 kickoff and agreed to put off the game for a day. Each guy figured he'd get the advantage that way. BC had a great quarterback in Butch Songin, who later played for the Patriots, and Myers was hoping he'd pass the Sooners dizzy. And Wilkinson had the Split T, which BC had never seen. So both teams wanted a dry ball and good footing.

Well, on Saturday, George Thomas ran the kickoff back ninety-five yards for an OU touchdown and BC never recovered. Oklahoma ran wild with the Split T, put four BC players in the hospital, won 46–0 and went on from there.

Wilkinson had his program on automatic pilot now. He knew what his squad could do because he'd coached some of them for four years. By Thursday, when the practice week was done, Wilkinson would have his staff and their wives over to his house for a drink or two. If the team had practiced well—and they almost always did—Wilkinson was convinced they'd play well.

He always amazed me by how accurately he could call a game before it was played. "They'll give us some trouble in the first half," Bud might say, "but we'll take them in the second." Or, "We've got to get off to a good start. Have to score a couple of times in the first quarter, then they'll fold."

Wilkinson never let his players know how confident he was, though. If anything, he worked them harder and worried more before games with the weaker teams. Playing Kansas State terrified him because he was afraid his players would take a victory for granted. Getting them up for Texas was no problem. Some things took care of themselves.

Whenever the Sooners were facing a tough Saturday, Wilkinson became a minimalist. He stuck with the basics, just a few plays he knew would work. Bud believed that you won the big game by making fewer mistakes than the other guy.

That's why he stressed defense—because it was always there for you. Whether you were playing in a sauna in Norman, a near-tornado in Kansas, a downpour in Dallas, or snow up in Nebraska, defense was a predictable thing.

But tough Saturdays were becoming rare around OU by the time I left after the 1949 season. The Sooners won their first national championship the next year, and didn't lose more than two games in a season until 1959. And with every victory, the Monster grew. The Sooners had stopped being a college football team. They had become the state talisman.

That famous quote by a college president—"I want to build a university of which the football team can be proud"—was made by Cross himself. And he wasn't joking. Cross had gone up to the legislature in 1951, a few months after the Sooners had won their national title, looking for more money for the school budget. When some cynical lawmaker asked Cross what he wanted it for, he uttered The Quote.

Well, it was reprinted all over the country and some folks thought it was a classic case of misplaced emphasis. But virtually nobody in Oklahoma batted an eyelash. That's how important OU football had become in only five years.

Oklahoma had—and still has—no professional sports teams. Both by choice and by default, the Sooners are the state's NFL, NBA, and major-league baseball franchises all wrapped up in a crimson pom-pom. So an actual losing season—more losses than victories—is literally unthinkable. The Sooners have had only two since the war, and none at all since 1965.

OU didn't have any losing seasons under Wilkinson until 1960. So the expectations were impossible. What passed for perfection—11-0 and the Sugar Bowl—became the standard after Wilkinson did it once. The Sooner fans, who'd been grateful for anything in 1946, had become totally spoiled.

Since they had so few losses to complain about, they began griping about narrow victories. One Saturday toward the end of the forty-seven-game streak, fans called up the *Daily Oklahoman*, the biggest newspaper in the state, grousing that the Sooners had beaten Kansas State by only thirteen points.

Finally, the sports editor hung up on yet another howling voice. "I wonder how much rice a Chinaman can eat," he said. Ever since then, the rabid OU fans have been called Chinamen.

They've given the Monster its relentless appetite—and they've done their share to get OU in trouble with the NCAA several times. Oklahoma was one of the first colleges to have booster clubs. A guy named Big Boy Johnson, who lived in Norman, started it in 1947, Bud's first year. The Touchdown Club, it was called. They raised money for recruiting and, for a while, even gave out scholarships.

As the Sooners kept winning, the number of boosters kept growing. The pathway from the stadium to the athletic dorm was nicknamed the "Million-Dollar Walk" because so many oil-rich fans would be lined up, supposedly stuffing money into players' hands after victories.

That kind of stuff got OU put on probation twice—once for the 1955 and 1956 seasons and again in 1960. But it didn't hurt them on the football field. The Sooners won national titles both in 1955 and 1956. They didn't lose another game until Notre Dame shocked them near the end of the 1957 season.

That was the end of the forty-seven straight and the return of the real world to Norman. In 1959, OU lost three games for the first time in Wilkinson's years there. The next year the Sooners went 3-6-1—their worst record since 1931, when they'd lost to the Honolulu Town Team.

People who hadn't beaten OU in years were getting even all at once. Colorado beat them for the first time since 1912, Iowa State for the first time since 1931, Missouri for the first time since the war. Texas handed the Sooners their worst flogging in the series since 1941. "They all just want to beat our brains out, every team we play," an Oklahoma guard told one of the local writers. "They just can't wait to play us. Nobody can wait."

The Big Eight wasn't Oklahoma and the Seven Dwarfs any longer. Every game was a struggle. There were several reasons. That long winning streak had created some complacency. The probations hadn't helped. And the rest of the league was catching up. Oklahoma's success had forced everybody to get better if they wanted to survive.

By then, Wilkinson had lost a little of his edge, too. How many victories, how many titles, how many bowl games were enough? Folks who'd visit his house began noticing that Wilkinson wanted to talk about other things. He'd always been well-read and curious about the world beyond football. Now he seemed caught up in politics. Bud became a close friend of President Kennedy and advised him on national physical fitness.

Maybe it was coincidence, maybe it wasn't, but after Kennedy was assassinated, Wilkinson called it a career. He coached two more games, then went in and told Cross he couldn't get into the "proper frame of mind" to prepare for football games anymore.

Instead, he ran for U.S. Senate in 1964. Talk about an underdog. Wilkinson was running as a Republican in a state that was eighty percent Democrats in a year when Lyndon Johnson was destined to retain the presidency in a landslide.

Yet Wilkinson made a fight of it, losing by only twenty-one thousand votes in the middle of that LBJ tornado. He probably could have come back to Norman and resumed coaching, but Bud had had enough of the Monster. The next time he took a coaching job, it was with the St. Louis Cardinals of the NFL—where the pressure was less.

Gomer Jones, who took over after Wilkinson resigned, was fired after two years and eleven losses. Jim Mackenzie upset Texas and Nebraska—then died of a massive heart attack after a year on the job. Chuck Fairbanks lost four games two years in a row and saw people driving around with CHUCK CHUCK stickers on their bumpers. Switzer won his three national titles, then resigned under pressure after some of his players ended up on police blotters and questions were raised about OU recruiting.

By the time Switzer left the job, the Monster was as big as Godzilla. Bud Wilkinson, who lives in St. Louis now, must look at it in awe.

3

The Duke and the Baron

 They were the Baron and the Iron Duke—and both of them were royal dictators. "Nobody talks back to me," said Adolph Rupp, who had the last word at Kentucky for forty-two years. And nobody at Oklahoma State ever called Henry Iba "Hank." His first name was Mister.

Rupp and Iba were the twin giants of college basketball in the forties and fifties. Iba was the first coach to win back-to-back national titles. Rupp won four—plus eighty-two percent of his games. Iba won with defense, Rupp with offense. But they won, year after year, 1,642 games between them. And when they were done, their schools named arenas after them.

Iba grew up playing basketball in coveralls up in rural Missouri, when the game was played outdoors on dirt courts. One day, after his high school team had lost a game 64–14, an astounding score back then, Iba concluded that there were two ways to win games: score more points than the other guy or allow fewer. Allowing fewer, he decided, was better.

When Iba came to Stillwater in 1934, Oklahoma State hadn't had a winning season in seven years. Their team the year before had given up thirty-six points a game. To Iba, that was absolutely sinful.

His first team allowed just twenty-four a game—and made the opposition sweat and strain for every one.

That was Iba's style, and it paid off immediately. His Aggies went 16-8 the next year, then 20-3, then 25-3. Playing them soon became a nightmare, because they didn't need to score to beat you. A couple dozen points was enough for Iba.

When I was playing for Wyoming, we met Oklahoma State (it was A&M in those days) in the All-College Tournament at Oklahoma City. That was the first time I ever saw Iba up close. When we walked into our locker room at halftime—behind, of course—he was out in the corridor. Iba was wearing an immaculate tan suit, a brown shirt, and matching tie and highly polished brown shoes, nervously smoking a cigarette and studying the stats.

I thought we had better material than they did, but the Aggies still beat us 46–35. They just took the game away from us. They wouldn't let us go where we wanted to on the floor. They wouldn't let us drive down the middle. Anytime we tried, someone in an orange and black jersey was blocking the way. "Where do you think *you're* going?" the Aggies would say. They just strangled us.

That was Iba's secret. He knew that teams have off nights on offense, especially on the road. You're playing in strange surroundings, hundreds of miles from home in front of fans who are hooting every move you make. The backgrounds are different, the backboards and rims aren't what you're used to.

But Iba believed that great defense could be there every night, that it should never change. You stopped your man from where he wanted to go. You kept him from getting good shots. If you played for Iba, you pressured the man with the ball, you sagged in the lane, and you kept the ball out of the pivot.

Iba's teams always played tight man-to-man defense. They fought through picks and slid through screens. If you managed to get by one Aggie, there'd always be another coming over to set up a roadblock.

"Help him, help him," Iba would shout, and everybody would sag and cover and make you kick the ball back out. Nobody ever went down the middle against the Aggies. If you drove into the paint, somebody would be there to put his nose in your belly button. And nobody ever got loose down low. That was a cardinal sin, the way Iba saw it.

If an Aggie let his man get under the basket and score, he was out of the game and he knew it. He'd start for the bench before Iba even sent in a sub for him. That's the way it was and all of Iba's players understood that.

Frustrating as it was to try scoring on the Aggies, it was even worse when they had the ball. They'd pass it a hundred times if they had to, waiting for the high-percentage shot. Iba hated wild, off-balance shots. He'd yank you right out of the game if you took one.

He didn't even like bounce passes, because they were risky. His players passed from chest to chest, so they could either shoot or pass again. But Iba's guys always took their time. "Think, and then act," was his credo. "Never act and then alibi."

Of course, there was no shot clock back then, so the Aggies could take as long as they pleased. Rival fans hated that. They called them the Slowpokes, and said they came from *Stall*water. Iba didn't mind. "If you're just out there running loose," he said, "you're not a good basketball team. We aren't going up and down the floor unless we're going with the ball."

That's why Iba never got many high school hotshots. They didn't want to go to a place where a entire team only scored forty points. But with Iba's system, you didn't need stars. You just needed workers.

That's why he almost never recruited players. Iba wasn't much good at it, and he thought it was demeaning. He believed he shouldn't have to beg a boy to come to Oklahoma A&M. If the boy didn't want to be there in the first place, Iba didn't want him. As far as Iba was concerned, it was a privilege to play for the state university. He hadn't recruited you. He had invited you.

So Iba had tryouts instead. He'd invite a hundred prospects to Stillwater for three days of workouts, and he'd pick the ones he liked. He'd offer them a scholarship and a spare-time job. For an Oklahoma kid who'd lived through the Depression and the Dust Bowl, that was a hell of a deal.

All Iba wanted in return was complete dedication whenever he had you on the court. He believed that there were no shortcuts, that there was a price you had to pay to win. As far as Iba was concerned, there was no such thing as too much practice.

Ask anyone who ever played for him and they'll never tell you it was fun. Rewarding, satisfying, maybe. But never fun. "Any player who says it was fun is lying," said Don Haskins, who played for Iba before his coaching days at Texas Western.

Practices lasted for hours. Repetition, repetition, and more repetition. And if Iba didn't like the way a game had gone, he'd order the whole squad back on the floor for practice and work them until midnight if he had to. Everyone dreaded vacation weeks. Nobody got to go home, not even for Thanksgiving or Christmas. Iba would have them practicing three times a day, for three hours each time.

And it wasn't shooting practice, it was defense. The worst thing was, the players had to come back and put on the same sweaty uniforms they'd had for the first practice. Even now, at Stillwater, there are three practices on the first day of workouts. Eddie Sutton, who played for Iba in the fifties, does it to honor him. "Hell, son," Iba told Sutton, "you ought to have four."

It never occurred to any of the Aggies to complain—certainly not to complain to Iba himself. They were in awe of him. I called him Hank, but almost nobody else did. To his players, he was strictly Mr. Iba—even after they'd graduated.

"How come you still call him Mr. Iba?" I once asked Missouri coach Sparky Stalcup, who'd played for Iba at Maryville Teachers College before he'd coached at A&M. "You're a big-time coach now."

"I wouldn't call him anything else," Stalcup told me.

Neither would anybody else at A&M—not after a sophomore named R. C. Cox got a little too familiar at practice one day. "Is that the way to shoot that shot, Hank?" Cox asked Iba after he'd sunk a set shot.

The gym went silent as a tomb.

"Son," Iba told him, "you don't know me well enough to call me Hank."

Well, Cox turned scarlet with embarrassment.

"I'm sorry, Mr. Iba," he said. And that's how it started. Not one of his players ever called him anything but Mister.

He looked like an Iron Duke. Iba was six-foot-four and imposing, with his hair slicked back and parted right down the middle. He always wore a tailored suit and a four-in-hand necktie. He was the best-dressed coach I ever knew. And he had a voice you could hear halfway across town—especially if you were doing something wrong.

"Now, cut that out," Iba would boom—and you did.

If you came to Stillwater, you played basketball Mr. Iba's way. You kept the ball out of your basket. That's the vision Iba had of Bob Kurland, the man who brought those two national titles to Stillwater. Not as a man who could score forty points a game—but who could prevent forty.

If Kurland had been born fifty years earlier, P. T. Barnum would have put him on exhibit in his American Museum and charged admission to see him. Kurland stood six-foot-eleven and three-quarter inches in a day when a big man was six-foot-six. Even when I played, people that size were considered freaks, unsuited to basketball.

Big men in those days were made to feel self-conscious, almost ashamed of their height. They'd stoop and shuffle, trying not to call attention to themselves. They were considered clumsy and uncoordinated, so coaches didn't even bother recruiting them. It would have been too much work making them into players.

When I played at Wyoming, just a couple of years before Kurland turned up at Oklahoma A&M, our tallest player was Milo Komenich. He was just under six-foot-seven. Our power forward was six-foot-five. Everybody else on the team was six-foot-three or under. The Oregon team which won the 1939 NCAA title was nicknamed the Tall Timbers, because they had three guys who were over six-foot-four.

So people were astounded when Iba went up to St. Louis to recruit Kurland. Iba never recruited anyone, rarely took players from outside Oklahoma, and had never used a big man. Certainly nobody of Kurland's size. The first time I met him, I glanced at legs that just kept going up. *My God*, I thought. *I've never seen a man this tall.*

Kurland was six-foot-six when he was thirteen, six-foot-nine by the time he was seventeen—and still growing. He played for a suburban high school, but nobody had really recruited him. Kurland had thought about going to the University of Missouri to study engineering, or possibly attending one of the universities in St. Louis.

Then one day his coach asked him if he would come to Sunday dinner at Ruggerio's, a famous Italian restaurant on Dago Hill, and meet Iba. Iba asked Kurland if he'd like to come to Stillwater for three days to try out—no guarantees. In those days, coaches could still do that. After the tryouts, Iba took Kurland aside.

"I never coached a boy your size before," Iba told him. "You're pretty awkward. I don't know if you can play college basketball or not. But if you come here and stay eligible, I'll take care of you."

So Kurland got a scholarship—it was thirteen dollars a year at A&M in those days—plus a job sweeping out the gym. And Iba set about developing him into a player. Now, Kurland literally couldn't run when he got to Stillwater, but Iba spent hours and hours working on his footwork, teaching him how to spin off the post.

Any other coach but Iba might have written off Kurland as hopeless. During one session, Kurland missed the hoop, the backboard, and everything else with his first hundred hook shots. His next hundred weren't much better. But Iba kept him shooting, six hundred times in all, until Kurland found the range.

Anyway, it didn't matter to Hank whether Kurland ever became a scoring machine or not. What he saw in Kurland was a defender who would completely change the way the game was played.

The assumption back then had been that the big man would be an offensive weapon. That's why the three-second rule was put in—to prevent huge centers from camping under the basket and flipping in shot after shot. Nobody worried about goaltending—until Iba unveiled Kurland in 1942.

All of a sudden, here was this seven-footer who looked like an alien, batting away shots just before they dropped into the hoop. You could run a perfect play and take a perfect shot and it wouldn't mean a thing.

Well, opposing teams were furious. Phog Allen, who coached Kansas, called Kurland a "glandular, mezzanine-peeping goon" and insisted that the basket be raised from ten to twelve feet. Bruce Drake, who coached Oklahoma, claimed that the only reason the Aggies beat his team was because Kurland took twenty-two shots out of the basket.

"It is practically impossible to beat a team whose giant raises his defensive umbrella over your goal," Drake wrote that year in a story for the *Saturday Evening Post*.

So when A&M went down to Norman to play OU when Kurland was a sophomore, Drake had the NCAA send an official down to sit atop a platform he'd rigged behind the basket, to make sure Kurland wasn't putting his hand over the rim.

Well, that game turned into a joke. The sight of some guy up above the basket, peering down at every shot like a private eye, ended up spooking the OU shooters even more than Kurland did. The Aggies won, 14–11.

It was true that Kurland made things a lot easier for A&M. In fact, Iba changed the way he'd always played defense to take advantage of him. Instead of man-to-man, the Aggies now played a diamond zone, with Kurland as the "goalie."

Dr. Naismith never figured on a goalie when he'd posted his rules on the bulletin board back in 1891. There weren't any seven-footers at his YMCA in Springfield. Naismith was more worried about somebody sticking a hand up through the basket to knock a ball out or moving the rim itself. The idea that somebody might actually swat away a ball as it was coming down never occurred to him.

Basketball was supposed to be a game of skill, of moving and passing and shooting. But with a seven-footer out there, you could put up a perfect shot and . . . *BANGO* . . . it'd be batted away. To lots of folks, that wasn't basketball. I didn't think so, either, and I talked to Hank about it.

"It's not against the rules, and we're going by the rules," Iba told me. "I've got him and I'm going to use him. What would you do if you were a coach?"

Now, Kurland wasn't the only guy who was goaltending. There were at least half a dozen college players who were six-foot-eight or taller who were doing the same thing. The way things were during the war actually encouraged it.

By the time Kurland was playing, the war had already been going for a year. A lot of the top college players had already enlisted, or soon would. That left guys like Kurland, who were too tall to serve in any of the armed forces. Kurland couldn't have squeezed himself into a plane. He couldn't have walked through a ship with-out banging his head. And he would have been a walking target as a soldier.

So Kurland and anybody else over six-foot-six were exempt from the service, but they were ideal for a basketball varsity. Most teams had a big man by 1942—but nobody had one like Kurland.

Otis Wile, who was A&M's sports publicist, called him "Foothills," and you should have heard the reaction whenever he walked onto the court. As soon as Kurland appeared, the fans would throw things on the floor. And when he batted away that first shot, you wouldn't believe the catcalls. It got so vicious, they'd have to stop the game.

We began hearing about another big guy up in Chicago who was having the same impact. George Mikan had been cut from the high school team at Joliet Catholic because the coach said he needed glasses and nobody with glasses could play basketball. Col-lege coaches ignored him the same way they'd ignored Kurland—except for Ray Meyer at DePaul.

Meyer took one look at Mikan's six feet ten inches and two hun-dred forty-five pounds and decided there was terrific raw material there. The only thing missing was coordination. So Meyer worked Mikan the same way Iba worked Kurland: drilling, drilling, drilling, getting all those arms and legs to work in synch. Meyer trained Mikan the way you would a fighter—skipping rope, shadowboxing. And before long, he was a basketball player who could dominate.

Well, Mikan got the same reception when he walked on the floor that Kurland did. "I was a freak," he said. "I was like the fat lady in the circus or the tattooed man."

The difference was that Mikan was an offensive weapon. His glasses might have given him the look of a physics major, but Mikan had amazing strength to go along with his size. Once he developed a hook shot which he could launch from either side with either hand, Mikan was all but unstoppable.

The dimensions of the lane helped him, too. Even though the three-second rule was already on the books in 1936, the lane was only six feet wide. So even if Mikan had to move out of it, he was still within easy range of the hoop.

If Mikan got a shot off, there was no hope, so coaches double-

and triple-teamed him, trying to deny him the ball at all costs. Mikan got shoved, whacked, elbowed, and scratched, but he still got his points. He was as dominant at one end as Kurland was at the other.

When Mikan and Kurland met head-on five times, it was like a couple of *Tyrannosauri rex* clashing in a prehistoric forest. The ground shook. And basketball was never the same. The era of the big man had arrived and Dr. Naismith's rules were suddenly obsolete. Needless to say, the whole country was waiting for them to meet. It finally happened at the National Invitational Tournament in New York at the end of the 1944 season.

A&M and DePaul met in the second round, but the Kurland–Mikan duel ended up being a letdown. The Aggies led by seventeen points in the first half, but then foul trouble and the limited-substitution rules of that era ruined them. Kurland ended up fouling out, A&M was left with only four players on the floor and DePaul ended up winning, 41–38.

Still, the public's appetite had been whetted, and the next year the anticipation was even greater. Both Kurland and Mikan were All-Americans now, and Oklahoma A&M and DePaul were the two best teams in the country. They played once—at Chicago—about a month from the end of the season and DePaul won by a basket. Then they went their separate ways until after the two big tournaments.

DePaul ripped through the NIT, and Mikan put on an astonishing show. He scored a hundred and twenty points in three games and literally beat Rhode Island State all by himself. Rhode Island scored fifty-three points and Mikan scored fifty-three points, a record for Madison Square Garden.

The Ram players shoved him and hacked him from start to finish. They did everything but fog his eyeglasses. Yet they didn't come close to stopping him. DePaul won 97–53, in a day when most college teams didn't score ninety-seven points in a week.

And Oklahoma A&M, using Kurland like some giant windmill, breezed through the NCAA tournament, knocking off Utah, Arkansas, and NYU, as Kurland scored twenty-two of the Aggies' forty-nine points in the title game. He'd become a hell of a scorer by now. By the time he was a senior, Kurland led the nation. One night at Gallagher Hall, Iba turned him loose on St. Louis University and Kurland scored fifty-eight points, even though he was being covered by Ed Macauley, who went on to a great pro career with the Celtics and Hawks.

So the public was eager for what was billed as the Battle of the Goons, with the unofficial national title on the line. It came a week after the NCAA tournament in a benefit game for the Red Cross at the Garden, and a sellout crowd of more than eighteen thousand people turned up.

Before the game, the DePaul players knelt around Meyer and prayed. "Men, the Lord can do some marvelous things," Iba told his Aggies in response. "But I'll be darned if He can put the ball in the basket."

This time, Iba wasn't going to take any chances of the game getting away if Kurland fouled out again. So he used some of his team defensive concepts—the sagging and helping—and tied Mikan into knots. Mikan ended up fouling out with just nine points after only fourteen minutes.

Once Mikan was gone, Kurland was free to terrorize the other DePaul shooters. They ended up missing eighty of their ninety-six shots and Oklahoma A&M won 52–44.

Now, you'd think a team that had just done what the Aggies had would have been the obsession of the state. But their games weren't even being carried on radio back home.

"You've got a national championship team here," I told Ken Brown, who was station manager of KOMA, where I was working in Oklahoma City. "There's a lot of interest in basketball."

Brown agreed, but he shrugged his shoulders. KOMA was a CBS affiliate which carried blockbuster programs like Jack Benny and Fred Allen in the evenings. The station couldn't cancel them to carry a local basketball game.

"Well, then, what if we record the games and play them at ten-fifteen, after the news?" I suggested.

Back then there was no such thing as tape. We literally cut a groove in these big platters and played them over the air. So that's how we covered basketball, and the broadcasts were an instant hit for hundreds of miles around.

KOMA had a skip signal at night that went up into twenty-six states. You could hear us on both sides of the Mississippi. We were amazed at the response we were getting. People would call us before the news and tell us not to give the score—they wanted to hear the game as though it were live.

We ended up doing both A&M and Oklahoma games. For me, it was like being the United Nations observer at a civil war. I was caught right in the middle.

The two universities were only sixty-five miles apart, but they might as well have been on opposite sides of the earth. OU was an oil school, A&M an agricultural school. OU people thought A&M people were hicks. A&M people thought OU people were snobs. I was the voice of both teams. I couldn't win.

"Let me ask you something," Iba's wife, Doyne, asked me one night, when I was eating chili at their house. "Why don't you like us?"

"What do you mean, *like* you?"

"I don't mean us," she said. "Why don't you like the Aggies?"

"What makes you say that?" I said, puzzled.

"Well, we heard your broadcast the other night, and you said . . ."

When I'd go down to Norman, Bruce Drake would start in on me. "Hank Iba can't do anything wrong, huh?"

I was caught in between, and I finally realized there was nothing I could do. Nobody's neutral in a civil war—especially if he's on both sides.

Iba was funny about OU. He'd never refer to it as the University of Oklahoma. "We're going down to play that place south of Oklahoma City," he'd say.

"What do you think of Bruce Drake?" I'd kid him.

"Good coach," Iba would say—and that's all he'd say.

Drake was a hell of a coach, actually. He made the Hall of Fame, just as Iba did. And in 1947, he took OU to the NCAA finals, where they lost to that great Holy Cross team that had Bob Cousy on it. To get there, the Sooners knocked off Texas by one point on a shot from halfcourt by Kenny Pryor at the buzzer.

That was a fabulous Texas team, too—a small and scrappy squad led by Slater Martin, who later starred with the Minneapolis Lakers, that was nicknamed the Three Mice and Two Rats. When that long shot went in, Drake swung his pocket watch around and around on its chain, sailed it up toward the rafters, and watched it shatter on the floor.

Drake always had tough teams at Oklahoma. He used what he called a "shuffle offense" that relied on picks and screens and intricate passing. And he had more tricks up his sleeve than anybody—especially for A&M and Kurland.

Having the guy up on the platform was just one of his ideas. Drake also sent out a guy on stilts to warm up, then had his smallest guard tip off against Kurland.

He was a master of psychology, and his OU squads always gave Iba trouble, even if they seldom beat them. Even thinking about Oklahoma used to irritate Hank.

One day Bud Wilkinson, who was building a football dynasty at OU, asked me how he could meet Iba. "I don't know him, but I'd love to talk with him about coaching," Wilkinson told me. "Can you introduce me to him?"

I thought the two greatest coaches in Oklahoma history would be delighted to get together and swap theories. But when I mentioned it to Iba, he wasn't too interested. Nothing personal against Wilkinson. It was just that place south of Oklahoma City.

Of course, Iba was idolized around Stillwater because he gave folks there a reason to hold their heads up around OU people. Once Wilkinson began coaching down at Norman, the Aggies stopped beating Oklahoma in football. But as long as Mr. Iba was around, A&M was going to have the Sooners' number in basketball.

Hank had literally built the gym they played in, Gallagher Hall. Until 1938, the Aggies had used either the armory or a cramped gym on campus. Well, Iba had only been there for a couple of years when he began talking about building a huge new arena. It would have a playing surface of more than eighteen thousand square feet—by far the largest in America. It would seat nine thousand people. It would have a floor made of white maple an inch and a quarter thick. And it would cost four hundred thousand dollars.

Now, this was in the middle of the Depression in a state where four hundred thousand dollars could have bought you a small town at that time. A lot of people thought Iba was crazy, building an arena that size in a town of less than twenty thousand people. They nick-named it Iba's Folly, but Hank ended up with the last laugh.

Gallagher Hall was soon jammed for every game, and it became one of the toughest road pits in America. From the first center jump until the final whistle, there was a constant roar which never stopped. You couldn't beat the Aggies there, and most teams from back East wouldn't even try.

Long Island University was the only eastern school to play there, and they regretted it. Iba talked Clair Bee into coming to Stillwater in 1949 and the Aggies beat his team 55–33, just gave them a real lacing.

Well, Bee came over to Iba's house afterward to visit. He'd already had a few belts before he arrived and Iba poured him a couple more.

"Goddamn, I don't know why I ever let you talk me into this," Bee told him. "We never got such a beating as we got here. We don't belong here in hick country. What am I doing sitting here?"

It took a hell of a team to come into Gallagher Hall and knock off one of Hank's varsities, but DePaul did it in December 1945. This time, Kurland and Mikan were on the floor from start to finish, and Mikan won the decision, outscoring Kurland twenty-five to eighteen.

Well, I went over to Hank's house that night and he was very agitated. The Aggies hadn't lost a game at Gallagher in two years. "Ahhh, we're going to get 'em in Chicago," Iba said.

Which they did. In the middle of the season, A&M went up there and played in front of twelve thousand people at Chicago Stadium. Mikan scored nineteen points to Kurland's ten, but Kurland spent most of the night feeding his teammates. A&M ended up winning 46–38, but the effort drained so much out of them that Bowling Green—who had their own seven-footer in Don Otten—upset them the next night.

That was the last time the Aggies lost all year. They won their final eleven games of the regular season, cruised to the NCAA finals, and beat North Carolina to retain their title. No team had ever done that—and the Aggies haven't won an NCAA title since.

Of all the college coaches I've known, Iba was the best in projecting a public image and in handling his players. He helped them even after they'd graduated.

But it didn't take Rupp long to match what Iba had done. His 1948 and 1949 teams were national champions, and his 1951 team was, too. Only the NCAA stopped Kentucky—by putting them on probation for the 1952–53 season. The next year, Rupp went undefeated, with a team so dominant that the Celtics drafted three members of the starting five—Frank Ramsey, Cliff Hagan, and Lou Tsioropoulos.

Red Auerbach always loved players from winning programs, and that was the Baron's obsession. "Courage and heart are fine," he once told Pat Riley, who played for Rupp before he went on to coach the Lakers and Knicks in the NBA. "But the only thing that counts is winning."

Maybe that's why Rupp defended his players, even after it was found that some of them had fixed games in the late forties. "The Chicago Black Sox lost games on purpose," Rupp said. "These boys just shaved points." Most folks couldn't see the difference, but Rupp did. Kentucky had still won the fixed games. That's what counted.

Rupp loved winners in any arena. When I was broadcasting the Red Sox, Rupp showed up out of the blue at Fenway Park one day in September 1960. He was in the area, Rupp told me, giving a clinic on Cape Cod, and decided to come up and watch Ted Williams hit. "Ah have a hobby," he told me. "Ah like to see the best there is in any field. Ah've seen Caruso, ah've seen all the great Broadway stars, ah've seen the great conductors. But ah've never seen Williams."

Winning as often as he did made Rupp plenty of enemies, but he never minded that. In fact, he used to joke that after he died, he'd be asked to coach both the Heaven and Hell teams. "I'd rather be the most hated winning coach in the country," he said, "than the most popular losing one."

To the citizens of Kentucky, Rupp was a god. When Bear Bryant left UK for Alabama after taking their football team to three major bowl games, people said it was because Bryant was jealous of Rupp. Actually, the men were good friends. They had offices two doors apart from each other. But it was obvious to Bryant that basketball was king at Kentucky, and was always going to be.

Once, when the great pianist Arthur Rubinstein was supposed to practice for a concert he was giving on campus, Rupp prevented it. His own practice, he said, took precedence.

And Rupp's practices were closed. The gym was his schoolroom. You weren't allowed to walk into a professor's schoolroom while he taught, Rupp reasoned. Why should his schoolroom be any different? No distractions were tolerated. He wanted the complete attention of his players.

In Rupp's schoolroom, only one voice was heard. "It is generally understood," Rupp said, "that no one is to speak unless he can improve upon the silence." Most of Rupp's players would have been terrified to say anything anyway.

Frank Ramsey, who was one of Rupp's captains, told me that Rupp was really a pussycat when you got to know him. If you needed something from him, especially after you'd graduated, Rupp would always come through. But when they were playing for him, most of the Kentucky kids never saw that side of him.

C. M. Newton, who played for Rupp and is now the university's athletic director, told me that Rupp was a complete dictator. He could go in any direction—he could charm you, scare you, threaten you—but you stayed scared of him.

Rupp could be very sarcastic, especially if he saw something sloppy. Once, when I was in Lexington to broadcast the college Game of the Week for ABC, Rupp invited me to watch his squad practice.

Well, when one of his players threw the ball away on a fast break, you could hear Rupp all over the gym. Boy, did he give it to them. "That's *raht*, boys," he drawled. "Piss-poor on national television. That's *raht*. You boys will look great."

Yet Rupp never had any trouble getting players. It was an honor to be good enough to be humbled by the Baron. Rupp used to brag that he never had to recruit, that every kid in the state dreamed of wearing the blue-and-white uniform.

If a top player went anywhere else, Rupp was baffled. "Ah don't understand how a boy will not accept a scholarship to play basketball at the University of Kentucky," he once told me. "Ah think it's the biggest mistake of his life."

For years and years, there was no other place to play college basketball, certainly not in the South. Kentucky won twenty-seven conference titles during Rupp's years there and went to the NCAA tournament twenty times. Folks down there will tell you that Rupp pioneered basketball in the South, because he won so many titles that he forced the other schools to build up to his level.

They might have hated the Baron in Georgia and Alabama and Mississippi and Tennessee, but they admired him. Kentucky set the standard everybody else had to follow. When the Wildcats were running the floor and clicking on all cylinders, they were beautiful to watch. Bob Cousy once said he'd rather watch Kentucky practice than other teams play.

At the end of his career, I saw Rupp at the NCAA regionals at Athens, Georgia. He wasn't well then. He had trouble walking and his vision wasn't the best. But when Rupp walked out onto the court in his brown suit—he *always* wore a brown suit to games—everybody in the field house gave him a standing ovation. They knew what he meant to southern basketball.

If the university hadn't had a mandatory retirement age of seventy, Rupp would have kept going until cancer finally killed him in the late seventies. He was a rich man by then, from his investments in Hereford cattle and tobacco, but basketball was still his life. Once Happy Chandler, who'd been governor of Kentucky and baseball commissioner, asked Rupp why he kept coaching after he had nothing left to prove.

"Why, Adolph?" Chandler wondered. "Do you want to die on the bench?"

"I can't think of any place better," Rupp replied.

4

The Pinstriped Dynasty

 Babe Ruth had just been laid to rest. Joe DiMaggio was in the twilight of his career. And a seventeen-year-old kid named Mantle was making a hundred and forty dollars a month playing shortstop in Class D ball.

When I came to New York in 1949 to broadcast the Yankees alongside Mel Allen on WINS, the club was in transition. The Yankees had just finished third in the league, Bucky Harris had been fired as manager, and the lineup was about to be shaken up and rejuvenated.

In the next sixteen seasons, the Yankees captured the pennant all but twice and won the World Series nine times. The summer of '49 was the turning point, when the Berras and the Colemans and the Bauers began taking over and a fifty-eight-year-old rookie named Stengel made his imprint.

I was a rookie in 1949, too, just up from the Texas League. I'd been broadcasting Oklahoma City games for seventy-five dollars a week when a telegram arrived from George Weiss, the Yankees' general manager, asking whether I was interested in the number two radio job.

Back then, the ball clubs brought up their announcers the same way they did the players—from the minors. What I didn't know was that Weiss had sent the same telegram to three hundred announcers across the country. That gave the Yankees terrific bargaining power—not that they needed it. Ever since the days of Ruth and Gehrig, they'd been baseball's glamour franchise. How could you turn down the Yankees? And how could you turn down New York, especially in 1949?

The war was over, prosperity was back, and Manhattan was the symbol of the American renaissance. It was the center of finance, of fashion, of publishing, of entertainment, of sports. If you wanted to make it, you came to New York and settled in among those eight million people.

When I arrived there and rented an apartment in the East Sixties, the elevated train still ran above Third Avenue, a suite at the Waldorf-Astoria went for seventy-five dollars a night, the *Times* cost three cents, a subway ride was a dime, and a meal along the Bowery could be had for less than a quarter.

There was no better place on earth to be than New York at night. There were literally six hundred eighty-eight theaters, supper dancing at the Plaza, and Carmen Cavallaro and his orchestra "on the cool Astor roof" in Times Square. If you loved sports, you went to Gene Leone's restaurant, or to Al Schacht's, then on to Toots Shor's, where Toots himself held court. You could find DiMaggio there most nights at Table One.

In those days, before the great suburban exodus took the Dodgers and Giants with them, New York was the center of the baseball universe, too. Within the city's five boroughs, there were three major-league clubs drawing more than five million fans a year. And that was in an era of day baseball.

Somebody was playing at home virtually every afternoon. You could attend the game, go home for dinner, then walk down to the corner newsstand for the early edition of the paper and the box scores. There were still seven New York dailies in 1949—the *Times,* the *Mirror,* the *News,* the *Post,* the *Herald Tribune,* the *World-Telegram,* and the *Journal-American.*

Everybody had one or more of them under his arm. You'd walk into your neighborhood tavern for a beer and everybody would be talking baseball. As often as not, the Yankees would be at the center of the debate. You either loved them or hated them—there was no in between. But you couldn't ignore them.

The Yankees had the lore, the ballpark, and the pennants. And most of the time, they had the game's most dominant player. He might be Ruth, he might be Gehrig, he might be DiMaggio, but he was always wearing pinstripes. And the man behind the radio microphone had been there for ten years when I arrived.

Mel Allen, the Voice of the Yankees, was the symbol of the club—both for better and worse. If you couldn't get to the Stadium or the club was on the road, Allen was your eyes and ears. If you loved the Yanks, Mel was a confident, reassuring presence. If you hated them, he was a daily irritation.

Folks would tune in and hear Mel's voice: *"That brings Henrich up. Ol' Reliable. And there's a long drive to right field, going, going, GONE . . . and the Yankees win again. How about that?"* And the Yankee haters would switch off their radios and curse—*damn Mel Allen.* There'd be letters to Ballantine, which sponsored the games—get rid of Allen. Mel could never understand that, but to a lot of people he was broadcasting U.S. Steel.

The Yankees were baseball's blue-chip corporation, and their headquarters—Yankee Stadium—was the most impressive in the game. Municipal Stadium in Cleveland held more people. Comiskey Park in Chicago was older. Fenway Park in Boston had more quirky charm.

But Yankee Stadium was the most imposing ballpark of them all. It looked like a triple-decked wedding cake sticking up out of the Bronx, and everything that happened inside seemed dramatic.

I'd seen pictures of the Stadium and I'd created a ballpark in my head from listening to Allen's broadcasts from the World Series. But the first time I walked down the runway from the clubhouse and looked out at that famous upper-deck facade and the centerfield monuments and the El tracks out beyond the bleachers, I was awestruck. *The House That Ruth Built*, I thought. *Boy, this is big.*

When the Stadium opened in 1923, the *New York Times* called it "a skyscraper among ballparks." Most players would have given anything to suit up for a Series game there. After he retired, Mantle used to have nightmares in which he would hear the Stadium loudspeaker announcing his name, but couldn't get there.

Players wept when the Yankees traded them. John Blanchard, a third-stringer who would have been starting catcher for any other team in the league, was crushed when he was shipped to Kansas City. "I don't want to play every day," he said. "I want to stay here."

It wasn't that the Yankees paid generous salaries. No front office in baseball was tighter with a dollar. I found that out when Weiss offered me the job.

"We've decided to hire you," Weiss told me. "Now let's talk about money."

That's the way Weiss was. Everything was about money.

"What kind of a salary do you want up here?"

I smiled.

"What are you smiling about?" Weiss asked me.

"Look, Mr. Weiss, I'm in no position to demand or negotiate," I said. "I'd probably work for nothing to get this job. You give me the figure."

"We'll pay you ten thousand dollars for doing the Yankee games," Weiss told me. "Dan Topping also owns the New York Yankees football team in the All-American Conference. If you do their games, too, we'll pay you another two thousand."

I was a little disappointed at the amount, but I told him it was fine and I signed a three-year contract which gave me another thousand dollars the second year and another thousand or two the third.

That still wasn't bad money in 1949. The average ballplayer wasn't earning much more, and the guy in the street was making do on a lot less—like four thousand a year. When I came to Manhattan, you could buy an Oxford cloth shirt at Brooks Brothers for five bucks and eat a lamb chop dinner at Schrafft's for two. And after getting seventy-five dollars a week in the minors, ten thousand a year was a hefty raise.

"We'll see you at spring training," Weiss told me.

"Are my expenses paid to spring training?" I asked him.

With the Yankees, you never took anything for granted. They considered a World Series share as part of your salary, since the club won the pennant almost every year in those days. And the front office was the toughest in the league when it came to contract negotiations. Once, when Joe Page was warming up in the bullpen, I had the glasses on him.

"Page is up and it looks like there's something wrong with him," I said over the air. "He looks stiff and he's rubbing his left hip. I don't know if he'll be able to pitch today or not."

Right after the game was over, the phone rang in the booth. Weiss wanted to see me.

"Sit down, Curt, and tell me what you saw in the bullpen."

So I told him the same things I'd said over the air.

"These are things we want to know," Weiss said. "Now, Joe claims there's nothing wrong with his back but we think it's a sciatic condition. We've had him examined and he denies it, but I guess you caught it with your field glasses. Maybe the guys in the bullpen know it, but we want to know these things, too. They're important to us. And if you're a good Yankee, you'll report them to us."

"Mr. Weiss," I said, "are you asking me to spy on the ballplayers?"

"No, I'm not," he said. "What you saw—anybody could have seen that. But Page denies it and we're going to be battling about his salary."

That's the way Weiss was. He checked on everything. He even hired private detectives to shadow players. But the stinginess didn't come just from Weiss. It was institutional. And nobody was immune, not even the superstars.

Even after DiMaggio hit in fifty-six straight games in 1941, the Yankees tried to cut his salary. Ed Barrow, who was the general manager, said it was because there was a war on. Before the 1949 season, when it was obvious to everyone that DiMaggio was a tremendous drawing card, destined for the Hall of Fame, the front office was still fighting him about money.

DiMaggio wanted a two-year contract at a hundred thousand dollars a year. The Yankees were offering one year at ninety thousand, with attendance bonuses. The front office was afraid of breaking the six-figure barrier. They knew other players used DiMaggio's salary as a benchmark. If he was making a hundred thousand, someone half as good would demand fifty thousand.

If you had even a slight off year, Weiss would want to cut your salary for the next season. And getting a raise out of him took persistence and the nerve of a poker player. What the players didn't find out until later was that Weiss got to keep ten percent of whatever he saved from the salary budget.

Yet Weiss wasn't even as tough and tight as Barrow had been before him. One year Tommy Henrich wanted a five-thousand-dollar raise.

"No, no, Henrich," Barrow told him. "You only hit .277."

"Well, what am I supposed to hit?" Henrich asked him.

"You're a .300 hitter," Barrow told him.

"You want me to hit .300?" Henrich said. "I'll hit .300 next year. But I'm not going to give myself up. I'm not going to hit behind the runner. I'm not going to move guys along. I won't do those things. If I'm just going for base hits, I'll hit differently."

"Well, we don't want to go *that* far," Barrow said.

Henrich ended up getting a two-thousand-dollar raise. Of course, the Yankees wouldn't have needed to give him an extra dime if they hadn't wanted to. The reserve clause in the standard players' contract essentially bound them to their club for life. Free agency was a still-distant dream. So virtually everybody had one-year contracts.

It was very unfair in those days. The owners were all skilled money men armed with corporate attorneys, but the players weren't allowed to have agents. Can you imagine some twenty-three-year-old pup out of the farms going in there pleading his case alone? That's the way it was with every club, but the Yankees had refined it to an art.

During the twenties and thirties, when Jacob Ruppert owned the club, he and Barrow had a technique they'd use on holdouts. Players called it the "elevated treatment."

Barrow would talk to the player in the team offices, which were on Forty-Second Street then, and send him to see Ruppert in his brewery. "It's his money," Barrow would say. Then while the player was riding the El uptown, Barrow would phone Ruppert and brief him.

"What do you boys think I am, a millionaire?" Ruppert, who *was* a millionaire, would growl when the player arrived.

Parsimony went along with the pinstripes. Babe Ruth never made more than eighty thousand dollars, and the Yankees had whittled him back down to thirty-five thousand by his final year with them. Lou Gehrig, who played two thousand one hundred and thirty consecutive games at first base, topped out at thirty-seven thousand. DiMaggio, who played thirteen years in the Stadium, made a hundred thousand in his best season. Yet when he wrote his autobiography in 1946, he entitled it *Lucky to be a Yankee*.

The front office might consider the Series share part of your salary, but then, that was the point of being a Yankee. Who else could guarantee you the World Series every year?

"What if we don't win?" Ed Lopat asked Weiss one year. "Will you make up the difference?"

"We'll win," Weiss assured him.

The front office simply figured the Series into their profits every season. That U.S. Steel metaphor wasn't that far off. The Yankees spent heavily on research and development, stockpiling players in the minors, then bringing them up according to a long-range plan.

That plan didn't include black players. The Yankees didn't have one in the lineup until Elston Howard in 1955. Of course, they weren't alone. Baseball's color line hadn't been broken until 1947 when the Dodgers brought up Jackie Robinson.

Robinson was far from a household word when Branch Rickey signed him just after the war ended. Black players like Satchel Paige and Josh Gibson were much better known. But Robinson was precisely the type of man Rickey was looking for. He was young, smart, aggressive, and disciplined enough to maintain his poise in the face of almost unbearable abuse. That was probably more important to Rickey than how well Robinson could play the game.

"Have you got the guts to play the game no matter what happens?" Rickey asked him when Robinson first arrived at the Brooklyn front office. "That's what I want to know."

Then Rickey, playing the role of the bigoted white, put Robinson through every nasty incident he might encounter—both on the field and off. He was an opposing player, colliding with Robinson at second base. "Get out of my way, you dirty black son of a bitch," Rickey shouted.

He was a base stealer, ripping open Robinson's shin with his spikes. "How do you like that, nigger boy?" Rickey snarled, smiling.

He was a hotel clerk, telling Robinson there were no rooms for niggers. He was a restaurant owner, telling Robinson he had to eat in the kitchen. "What do you do?" Rickey kept demanding. "What do you do?"

"Mr. Rickey, do you want a player who's afraid to fight back?" Robinson asked him.

"I want a player with guts enough *not* to fight back," Rickey told him.

So Rickey handed Robinson a copy of Giovanni Papini's *Life of Christ* and told him to read the chapter on nonviolence. "I get it, Mr. Rickey, I get it." Robinson nodded. "What you want me to say is that I've got another cheek."

Rickey knew that almost nobody in baseball—including many of his own teammates—wanted Robinson in the league. If Robinson was going to slug everybody who knocked him down or called him a nigger, he'd be helping the bigots make their point—that Negroes were uppity troublemakers who didn't belong in the game.

Well, when Robinson made it to the majors, he took every bit as much abuse as Rickey had predicted. Some of his fellow Dodgers circulated a petition before the season, saying they'd refuse to play if Robinson was in the lineup.

When Robinson came out of the dugout on Opening Day at Ebbets Field, baseball changed forever. Many years later Jimmy Carter told me that his mother had taken the train up to Brooklyn to see the game, because she wanted to be part of history.

Not everybody viewed Robinson's presence as history. Most of his opponents—especially the guys from the South—saw him as an intruder. When Brooklyn was playing the Phillies early in the season, Robinson heard catcalls from their dugout: "Hey, nigger, why don't you go back to the cotton field where you belong?"

It wasn't just any bench jockey shouting the slurs. It was Ben Chapman, the Philadelphia manager. And before the game had even started, the Phillies' president had told Rickey that his club would refuse to take the field if Robinson played. Later on, the Cardinals were planning to strike if Robinson played against them.

"You know why they didn't like him?" said Carl Furillo, the Dodger right fielder. "Because he could beat them. If he was a bum ballplayer, you would have seen how quick they liked him."

The Dodgers soon rallied to Robinson's side—especially once

they realized that he was going to help put a World Series share in their pockets. And his biggest defender was the captain, Pee Wee Reese, who played next to Robinson in the infield.

Now, Reese could have felt threatened, too. He played shortstop, which was Robinson's original position. And he came from Louisville. But Reese made a point of befriending Robinson, because he knew how lonely it was for him and because he admired Robinson's courage. And because, as captain, Reese realized he could make a statement to America by how he treated Robinson.

It wasn't easy for Reese. He heard catcalls, too, from fellow southerners who said he was a nigger lover. "Hey out there, Kentucky boy," one of the Braves yelled at Reese one day up in Boston. "When yo' grandpappy finds out how you up heah socializin' and fratuhnizin' with cullud folks, he's gonna cut you off from yo' mint juleps."

Well, Reese walked over to Robinson, put his arm around his shoulder, and talked to him long enough for everybody in the ballpark to see them. The point was clear: The white shortstop from Kentucky and the black second baseman were teammates and friends.

Still, it was Robinson who had to face the beanballs and the spikes and the tar-baby jokes. For a while at the beginning, he wasn't sure he could keep turning his other cheek. "I can't take it anymore," Robinson told his sister. "I'm quitting." But he didn't—and Robinson didn't fight back, even though he was sorely provoked.

That's why Rickey chose him. Some people thought that Satchel Paige should have been the first black player in the majors. He'd been a legend for twenty years in the Negro Leagues, the greatest pitcher of his day. Maybe that was why Rickey bypassed him—because Paige's time had passed.

Nobody ever knew how old Satch really was. When I was in high school during the Depression, I saw him pitch in Cheyenne for the House of David, a barnstorming team. Paige pitched everywhere in those days, including Mexico, the Caribbean, and South America, and he pitched virtually every day. He estimated that he pitched twenty-five hundred games—and won two thousand—before he ever reached the majors. At his peak, during the thirties,

Paige claimed he won sixty games a season and averaged fifteen strikeouts a game.

He made a ton of money barnstorming. Satch got a thousand dollars or more a game, with a money-back guarantee. Paige would strike out the first nine men he faced.

He'd pitch against all-white major-league All-Star teams and mow them down, great hitters like Jimmie Foxx and Hank Greenberg. Once, Paige pitched thirteen scoreless innings, head-to-head with Dizzy Dean—and won. "Satchel and me, we'd clinch the pennant by the Fourth of July," Dean mused. "And go fishin' until the World Series. Between us, we'd win sixty games."

"Maybe I'd win all sixty by myself," Paige reckoned.

One time, Paige swore, he won a game without throwing a pitch. He was summoned from the bullpen to save a 1–0 game in the ninth with the bases loaded, nobody out, and a full count on the batter. Paige took a spare ball with him, then collected the game ball from the starter.

"I just threw those two balls at the same time, one to first and and one to third," Paige told his teammates on the St. Louis Browns. "I picked off both runners and my motion was so good, the batter fanned. That was three outs."

When I first saw Satchel in 1949, he was with the Indians. He was at least forty-three by then (some folks said he was forty-three going on fifty), he'd had all his teeth pulled, and he was living on Bisodol to soothe his cranky stomach.

But Satchel still had good stuff, with pinpoint control. Satchel had lost a foot or two off his fastball, but he'd developed the most bewildering assortment of pitches in the game.

There was his trouble ball, jump ball, bee ball, hurry-up ball, bat-dodger, woobly ball, nothin' ball, and whipsy-dipsy-do, plus a screwball and a mixed bag of loopers, bloopers, and droopers. Plus the dreaded hesitation pitch. Satch would stop at the top of his windup, and he'd still have the ball in his hand as the batter was swinging. By the time the ball crossed the plate, the batter had twisted himself into a corkscrew.

Well, Will Harridge, the American League president, banned the hesitation pitch, but that didn't stop Paige. He kept baffling hitters into his sixties. I know he was still pitching in 1965 because I saw him mystify the Red Sox in Kansas City.

People were still arguing about how old Paige was. The Harvard Medical School had done a study on what made him keep ticking. "They spent more money researchin' my age than they did on the atomic bomb," Satchel said. "What's the difference if you get the job done?"

The secret, Paige said, was his rules for staying young:

Avoid fried meats which angry up the blood.

Keep the juices flowing by jangling around gently as you move.

If your stomach disputes you, lie down and pacify it with cool thoughts.

Go very light on the vices, such as carrying on in society. The social ramble ain't restful.

Avoid running at all times.

Don't look back. Something might be gaining on you.

Well, Paige held the Sox scoreless for three innings, allowed only one hit, and needed only twenty-eight pitches.

Now, any man who pitched as long as Satchel did should have been able to retire comfortably. But he was the first man to tell you that he ran through cash like it was water.

He loved tailor-made clothes and fast roadsters and women. Lou Boudreau once said that every time Satchel pitched on the road, he always left two tickets for Mrs. Paige. He had a lot of Mrs. Paiges around the country, I guess.

By the time he was out of the game, there wasn't much left in Paige's bank account. Once, when Tony Kubek and I were up in Boston doing the Game of the Week for NBC, we had Paige up in the booth to add his observations. Afterward, we invited him to have a late-night snack with us. Satchel thanked us, but said he was tired and was going to bed.

It turned out that he and Kubek were on the same plane to Chicago the next day. When Satchel reached up to put a couple of big paper sacks up above him, the bottom fell out and a mess of groceries came crashing down—eggs, vegetables, leftover pieces of steak from the night before.

Well, Paige was terribly embarrassed. Everything was laying there in the aisle. "My family needs something to eat," he explained to Kubek. "So I ordered room service at the hotel and was going to take this home."

That's how it was for Satchel. If he'd been born thirty years later, he could have had steaks and prime rib until the day he died. His best years were gone before America ever got to appreciate him.

There's no doubt that Paige had the talent to be the first black in the majors. The year after the Dodgers brought up Robinson, the Indians signed Paige, and he ended up helping them win their first pennant since 1920. So Satchel was hurt that the Dodgers had picked Robinson instead of him, but he understood.

"They'd have had to put me right into the majors and that might have caused a revolution," Paige said. "Because the high-priced white boys up there wouldn't have had a chance to get used to the idea that way."

Rickey had other reasons for choosing Robinson, though. He was in his prime, he could play every day, and he had the personality to play fiercely yet withstand abuse. When Robinson made good with the Dodgers, it opened the door for other black players. When I joined the Yankees, there were five blacks on major-league rosters—three of them Dodgers—and several dozen more in the minors.

But the Yankees weren't in any rush to sign black players. They were winning without them, and there was plenty of talent left in their farm system, which the Yankees treated like a corporate ladder.

You waited your turn, then you moved up. If the Yankees needed a player to fill an immediate need, they simply bought him from one of the poorer franchises like the Browns or the Athletics.

The Yankees approached the game as a business on the field, too, the way they had since Joe McCarthy began managing them in the thirties. The players, from DiMaggio on down, came to the ballpark wearing suits and ties and changed into pinstriped uniforms reminiscent of Wall Street. The clubhouse was a place of business. You didn't play poker there—not after McCarthy had the card table broken up with an ax in 1931.

There was a Yankee way of behaving—and *not* behaving, too. Once McCarthy noticed a new player giving a teammate a hotfoot in a train station. "You're with the Yankees now," McCarthy scolded him. "We don't do those things."

If you were a Yankee, you went out, you played, you won, and you handled yourself with dignity. When you won, you never bragged. When you lost, you never alibied. McCarthy had drilled that into them.

Even though McCarthy had left the club during the 1946 season, his influence was still strong in the Yankee clubhouse. A lot of the guys who'd played for him were still around when I got there—and they didn't want to hear any criticism about McCarthy.

I found that out during a bridge game with Tommy Henrich and Charlie Keller and another veteran, when McCarthy's name came up.

"Wasn't he a drunk?" I said.

Well, there was a deadly silence and I knew I'd committed a mortal sin.

"C'mere, kid," Keller told me after the game was over. "I want to talk to you."

He grabbed me and put me right up against the wall. "I don't ever want to hear you talk about McCarthy like that again."

"Gee, Charlie, I didn't know," I said. "I was just asking."

"He may have been a drinker, but McCarthy was worshiped by this team," Keller told me. "You'll never hear any of us say a bad word about McCarthy."

That's one of the things that made it tough for Casey Stengel that first year. For a while, the players couldn't believe that the front office would give him McCarthy's job. He hardly suited the corporate Yankee image.

Del Webb, one of the club owners, had been dead-set against hiring Stengel. "He's a clown," Webb said. "I don't want a clown managing the New York Yankees."

That had been Casey's reputation since his playing days in the National League. One afternoon in Ebbets Field, he lifted his cap in the batter's box and a sparrow flew out. After he won a game for the Giants in the 1923 World Series, Stengel thumbed his nose at the Yankee dugout as he was rounding the bases.

And his previous years as a major-league manager with the Dodgers and Braves had been unspectacular—one winning season out of nine. After a Boston cab driver knocked Stengel down, broke his leg, and put him out of action for two months, a local sportswriter named the driver "the man who did the most for Boston baseball in 1943."

But Weiss pushed hard for Stengel. Casey had won the Pacific Coast League title with the Oakland Oaks the year before, and Weiss liked what Stengel had done with the Yankees' Kansas City farm team in 1945. So the club gave him the job.

Casey didn't figure he had to apologize to anybody for being hired. "They don't hand out jobs like this just because they like your company," he said. "I got this job because people think I can produce for them."

This time, Stengel had the players to produce with. When he'd managed Brooklyn and Boston, he had a lot of journeymen. "I had two ball clubs with no bench, no pitching, no stars," Casey told me. "Now I've got the talent."

With the talent, though, came huge expectations from the front office. Bucky Harris had managed the Yankees to the world championship in 1947 and kept them in the pennant race until the final weekend in 1948. But Weiss fired him the next day. Ruppert had been dead for ten years, but his credo still stood: "I don't like finishing second."

So Stengel was under the gun—and he didn't have DiMaggio, who had undergone heel surgery over the winter and missed spring training. "Fellas," Stengel told his ball club, "Joe won't be with us for a while."

DiMaggio might have been thirty-four that year, only two seasons from retirement, but he was still the model for the way the Yankees did things. He showed up for games in a perfectly tailored navy-blue suit, went out and played with intelligence and style, and spoke modestly about it afterward. "He makes big-league baseball look simple," Stengel said. "It ain't that simple."

The elegance and ease with which DiMaggio played took a terrible toll on him. I've never seen such an intense guy. Before games, you'd see him drinking coffee and smoking cigarettes, worrying whether he'd play up to the highest standard in the game—his own.

DiMaggio was the son of an immigrant Italian fisherman from San Francisco. His teammates called him the Dago. Nowadays, that might be grounds for a lawsuit, but DiMaggio didn't mind. He knew his teammates stood in awe of him, and that the nickname was a form of rough affection. DiMaggio even referred to himself that way.

Every day, he provided a lesson in classic baseball. His outfield play was graceful and efficient, his swing perfect. And nobody was better at going from first to third. Watching DiMaggio do it, finishing it off with a fluid slide, was one of the most delightful things in sports.

"All the rest of the players runnin' the bases are lookin' to see where their feet are," Stengel would say. "But this Dago guy, he's lookin' to the outfield to see where the ball is. He knows they haven't moved second base yet."

Without DiMaggio, the Yankees were picked for third in the league. "Third ain't so bad," Stengel said with a shrug. "I never finished third before. That's pretty high up."

Even without DiMaggio, Stengel had more weapons than most managers did. Most of his bench players could have started for any club in either league. So Casey began platooning them. That was pretty unusual back then, when most skippers just wrote the same names on the lineup card every day. And not everybody was happy about this new system.

Stengel platooned Gene Woodling and Hank Bauer in right field. Woodling went against right-handers, Bauer against left-handers. They both grumbled about playing part-time because they knew it would hurt them with Weiss at contract time. But together they batted .271 with fifteen homers and eighty-nine runs batted in.

With the lineup never set, the pressure to perform was intense. You played hurt, because you were afraid to be out of the lineup for even a day. Everybody remembered Wally Pipp, the guy who played first base for the Yankees before Lou Gehrig. He took a day off in 1925 after getting beaned in batting practice, then Gehrig stepped in and played every day for the next fourteen years. Pipp never started another game for the Yankees.

When I got to New York, Snuffy Stirnweiss had been the regular second baseman for a couple of years. He played on Opening Day, then got hit on the hand in batting practice the next afternoon.

When Stengel noticed that Stirnweiss couldn't take any more swings, he yelled over to the rookie, Jerry Coleman.

"Hey, kid," Stengel shouted. "You're in the lineup." Snuffy never got his job back. The next year, he was playing for the Browns. Coleman never felt secure, either. A kid named Billy Martin was below him in the minors. When he got the job, Martin worried about Gil McDougald. Then McDougald worried about Bobby Richardson.

No matter what the position, the Yankees always had another guy in the wings. They let Tony Lazzeri go after he hit .400 in the 1937 Series because they had someone in Newark named Joe Gordon who was ready.

"I read the papers every day to see how Henrich and Red Rolfe were doing down in Triple A," George Selkirk said. "If they had gone four-for-four, you'd better believe it made me try harder."

There was always somebody hitting .300 over in Newark that the Yankees could bring up the same day if they wanted to replace you. That's how Henrich became a Yankee. One of their outfielders was sitting in front of his locker one day after New York had failed to sweep a doubleheader when McCarthy came through the clubhouse glowering. The outfielder took a shoe and slammed it into his locker.

"What the hell does he want us to do, win every game?" he muttered.

Well, McCarthy overheard him, walked into his office, and picked up the phone. "Get Henrich in here," he ordered. And when Henrich came up, they told him that story.

The pressure was especially tough on the outfielders in 1949, because nobody knew when DiMaggio would be coming back. He was still on crutches when the season began, and unbelievably frustrated. Any time DiMaggio tried to walk normally on his right heel, he felt the pain shoot through him. Late in May, he went out for a workout and had to give up. He ended up missing the first sixty-five games of the season.

Then one morning in late June, my phone rang.

"Curt, something's happened," DiMaggio told me. "When I got up this morning, I stood up and felt no pain in my heel. I walked around the room—still no pain. Then I walked around the block. Nothing."

He wanted to go up to the Stadium for some batting practice— it was an open date before a big series in Boston—so we took a cab up to the Bronx. I'd never seen DiMaggio so excited. He got into a uniform, found somebody to pitch to him, and cracked dozens of balls, one after the other. When he came in, his hands were raw and bleeding.

"You shouldn't take any more," I warned him, but DiMaggio wasn't concerned about his hands. "I can't believe it," he said. "It's a miracle."

So Stengel penciled him into the lineup—"You're the boss," Casey told him—and DiMaggio went out and had what he called the greatest series of his career up at Fenway.

Joe hit a two-run homer to win the opener, tracking down a long ball from Ted Williams with two out in the ninth to end it. He brought the Yankees back from the dead, down six runs, with two homers to win the second game. Then he topped off the sweep, hitting a three-run shot off the light tower in left.

When it was done, the Boston fans—who hated the Yankees more than anybody—gave DiMaggio a standing ovation. *Life* magazine put him on its cover.

The Yankees, meanwhile, were four games ahead of the field. My first year in the majors and I was in the middle of a pennant race. In those days, when the seasons were shorter, the franchises fewer, and television still a novelty, the pennant races seemed much more intense and dramatic than they are now.

The season was a hundred and fifty-four games, eight fewer than now, and it began later. Opening Day was April 19 in 1949 and the final game was on October 2. The World Series began three days later and was over within a week.

This was still the era of day baseball and Sunday doubleheaders and train travel. When there was no franchise beyond Missouri, there wasn't much need for airplanes. The train rides to Boston, Philadelphia, and Washington weren't more than a few hours. And a western swing in those days meant Cleveland, Detroit, Chicago, St. Louis.

After a day game at the Stadium, we'd leave Grand Central Station around seven o'clock for a road trip. A couple of Pullman cars would be reserved for the team, plus a dining car. The sportswriters and players would hang out together, drinking and playing cards and shooting the breeze. Everybody was closer in those days, partly because it was unavoidable. The trip to St. Louis took eighteen hours. What else were you going to do but socialize?

You could get a Ph.D. in baseball just by sitting in the club car for a season. Everybody talked baseball—discussing other clubs, that year's rookies, arguing about strategies ("Now, this is how you pitch to Williams"). There was an informal mental "book" on every guy in the league, and it was updated every spring.

There were only four hundred players in the majors then and they were traded frequently. No matter which club you were facing, somebody on your team had played for them recently and could give you a rundown on every man on the roster.

The baseball talk didn't end on the train. It continued in the hotel lobbies after breakfast, before players took cabs to the ballpark, and after games while players were waiting to go out to dinner.

The clubs stayed at the big city hotels, most of them long gone now—the Del Prado in Chicago, the Book-Cadillac in Detroit, the Warwick in Philadelphia, the Shoreham in Washington, the Chase in St. Louis, the Cleveland in Cleveland. The players' favorite was the Kenmore in Boston, because you could walk to Fenway Park and because they had great seafood there.

St. Louis was an easy three games—the Browns were strictly second division—but a tough three days during summer, when the weather there was hot and muggy. Sitting through a doubleheader in a flannel uniform at Sportsman's Park was like sweating in a sauna. So the Browns used to put big tubs of ice at either end of the dugout and mount fans above them to cool off the players.

The ballparks themselves were more intimate then. All of them were either downtown or in residential neighborhoods, which meant that they were crammed between city blocks. That made for weird angles and walls topped by screens.

Every park in the league had its own personality. Briggs Stadium in Detroit was a double-decked square with a covered grandstand that ran all the way around. In Boston, Fenway Park had its green left-field wall which turned routine fly balls into home runs. Shibe Park in Philadelphia looked like a French Renaissance palace on the outside, but was a cockpit on the inside. Sportsman's Park had that inviting pavilion out in right field. Griffith Stadium in Washington, with no fence closer than three hundred and twenty feet, was the pitcher's friend.

Mel Allen and I would sketch the dimensions, describe the quirks, and let the listeners fill in the rest from their imaginations. In 1949, nobody televised games from the road, and the Yankees did very few from the Stadium.

Television wasn't an economic force then—it was still more of a marvel. The idea that you could bring the game into your living room was amazing. That's why the owners were leery of television. There wasn't enough money from it to justify what they were afraid they'd lose at the gate. Which is why the Yankees wouldn't allow a center-field camera that first year. They thought people would have such a great view of every pitch that there'd be even less reason to come to a game.

The Yankees were more sensitive to television because New York was the center of American TV in those days. All of the programs originated from there. There were only three hundred twenty-five thousand television sets in the country in 1948, but half of them were in New York.

So we did only about fifteen televised games that year and none at all from the road. Mel and I did half of the games and Dizzy Dean, the old Cardinals pitcher, did the other half.

Diz would get there just before game time because he'd have been out playing golf with Dan Topping. Dean was a great hustler. If you shot a seventy-four, he'd shoot seventy-three. If you shot eighty-six, he'd shoot eighty-five. Once, when we were taking a cab downtown, Diz opened his wallet and three or four Yankee checks fell out.

"Gee, Diz, don't you ever cash them?" I asked him.

"Naw, I live off my golf earnings," he told me.

Diz would go out in the morning and play with Topping and

other wealthy guys and win ten thousand dollars. Then he'd get to the Stadium at one-thirty for a two o'clock game. He never prepared much. In those days, you could get away with it.

The telecasts were still a novelty—and pretty primitive. There were three cameras—behind first, third, and the plate. No replays, no isolation shots, no slo-mos. And all in black and white. The stations didn't spend much money because there wasn't that much to be made. Not yet, anyway. The rights fee for the 1947 World Series went for only sixty-five thousand dollars.

Mel and I did the telecasts in simulcast, using the same audio as we did for radio. So they didn't pay us anything extra. The problem was that you can't really do baseball in simulcast because TV leaves nothing to the imagination.

Baseball was still a radio game in 1949 and the Yankees did more radio than anybody. While most clubs were doing only home games, we did all one hundred and fifty-four. The owners felt it was a good way to keep the fans interested. Even when the Stadium was dark, you could be at the game.

And as the pennant race wore on, you couldn't go anywhere in New York without hearing Mel's and my voices. People had portable radios on the stoops, inside barrooms, in offices.

The pennant races in both leagues were sizzling. Both of them went down to the final out of the final game. The Dodgers and Cardinals went back and forth in the National League. And the Red Sox, who'd been in fifth place on July Fourth, had come alive in August, winning twenty-four of thirty-two games. So the whole season came down to the final weekend at the Stadium, with Boston leading by one game with two to play.

There's never been a regional rivalry to match the Red Sox and Yankees, and it had been going on for a good thirty years by 1949. The resentment ran deep, especially on the Boston side. It was the Yankees who'd ruined the Red Sox franchise in the twenties, buying Babe Ruth and a bunch of other stars when Boston owner Harry Frazee ran out of money.

As the Yankees won pennant after pennant, the Red Sox had slipped into oblivion. After the war, when Ted Williams and great pitchers like Mel Parnell and Ellis Kinder made them contenders again, here were the Yankees, still in the way.

Now, all the Sox needed do was win one of those last two games in the Stadium to clinch the pennant. I can still remember the drama and the noise that final weekend, with the fans roaring on every pitch.

Stengel, who usually didn't get nervous before ball games, couldn't sleep the night before the first one. He kept writing down lineups, tossing them away, and conjuring up new ones. DiMaggio had been weakened by viral pneumonia. Yogi Berra had fractured a thumb.

It had been that way all season for the Yankees, as one player after another went down. The club counted up seventy-one injuries in all. Henrich, Berra, and DiMaggio were in the lineup together only fifteen times.

Stengel wrote them in at two-three-four now, but after the Red Sox chased Allie Reynolds and went up 4–0 on Saturday, it looked as though the season might be over. But Joe Page settled Boston down and Johnny Lindell, a .242 hitter who hadn't hit a homer since July, put one into the left-field stands in the eighth to win it. "I think we've got 'em," Stengel said. "I can feel it in my bones."

I took the El up to the Stadium early on Sunday and talked to the Yankee players before the game. They were confident. They had their twenty-game winner, Vic Raschi, on the mound and they were playing at home. If it came down to the bottom of the ninth, the Yankees believed they'd win it.

Things broke their way immediately. Phil Rizzuto ripped a drive down the left-field line. The ball hit the railing, caromed by Williams into left center, and Rizzuto had a triple. He came home on an infield out by Henrich and that's how it stood until the eighth.

Then McCarthy, who was managing the Sox now, made the decision that old-timers are still arguing about in the Hub. He took Kinder, who'd only let four Yankees reach base, out of the game for a pinch hitter.

McCarthy's reasoning was that there was one out, nobody on base, and the Sox had to score. And Kinder was a lousy hitter. Turned out that Tom Wright, the pinch hitter, walked. But Dom DiMaggio hit into a double play.

Now the Sox were in a pickle. McCarthy brought in Parnell, who'd pitched the day before, and watched him give up a homer to

Henrich and a single to Berra. Tex Hughson, who had a sore arm, came in and loaded the bases. Then Jerry Coleman blooped a ball to the opposite field that Williams still sees in his nightmares.

It was a looping, slicing ball. "Get in, get in," I was saying to myself behind the mike. Al Zarilla, the Sox right fielder, dove for it, but the ball bounced away and cleared the bases. Kinder went to his grave regretting what McCarthy had done. "If the old man had left me in," he said, "we would have won the pennant."

After that, the World Series with the Dodgers was almost an anticlimax—at least from the Yankees' perspective. They'd never lost a fall classic to Brooklyn, and I don't think they considered it a possibility. But that's not how the Dodgers saw it.

They'd lost the 1947 Series to New York in the seventh game, and the Dodgers believed they'd had the better team. This time they felt sure that their moment had finally come. MOIDER DA YANKS, the signs said, from Flatbush to Bay Ridge.

The Yankees took the Series in five games played in five days— you didn't need a travel day to go across a bridge. The final game was a rout and the Yankees, managed by a "clown," were back on top of the world.

"I am the same kind of manager I always was," mused Stengel over champagne. "But nowadays I seem to get a little more assistance from my help."

5

Something Rotten in the Garden

When I look back, it's hard to believe how naive we all were. Missouri's basketball team shutting down City College and their coach thinking it was merely great defense. Clair Bee betting everything he owned that his Long Island University team was clean. Adolph Rupp bragging that gamblers couldn't reach his Kentucky boys with a ten-foot pole. College kids fixing games? The best players from the best teams, coached by the best men in the sport?

Most people didn't believe it until they saw the photos on page one of the *New York Times*, players like Ed Warner and Sherman White led by detectives into the Elizabeth Street police station for booking. The scandals of 1951 ended the era of innocence in college sports and they nearly killed basketball in New York City.

Not until then did it dawn on us how big the college game had become in America, how much money was involved, and how great were the temptations for twenty-one-year-old players to grab a piece of it. Even in the fifties.

Bee talked about it in a story he wrote a year later for the *Saturday Evening Post* called "I Know Why They Sold Out to the Gamblers":

"I'm bringing in all these people and playing my heart out for them," the boys must have said to themselves. "Clair Bee is getting all the credit and Ned Irish and the college are getting all the gravy. Where do I come in?"

The irony was, the players' piece of the action was laughably small—a thousand dollars a game in most cases. And the reasons why star players took cash for shaving points was sadly adolescent. "Why did I do it?" said Fats Roth, one of the City College players who went to jail for his part in the scandal. "Because I wanted to be grown up. Sounds funny, doesn't it? I was sick and tired of asking my father for money all the time."

By the time the district attorneys were done, they'd found evidence of eighty-six fixed games in twenty-three cities in seventeen states by thirty-two players from seven colleges, four of the colleges in metropolitan New York. And there might have been more.

It wasn't the first scandal in college basketball. Phog Allen, the legendary coach at Kansas, had predicted in 1944 that there'd be one "that would stink to high heaven." A year later, five Brooklyn College players were caught trying to fix a game with Akron.

There'd also been some early-warning signals in 1948, when the Minneapolis outfit that established the point spread for college basketball stopped putting out the line for games involving New York teams. They thought something fishy was going on.

The problem was that the college game had gotten too big, too lucrative, and too focused on one place—Madison Square Garden. From the time Irish, the legendary "boy promoter," dreamed up his fabulous doubleheaders during the Depression, the Garden had been the cathedral of college basketball. The NCAA championships were held there seven times between 1943 and 1950. And the National Invitational Tournament, which was actually bigger than the NCAA in those days, was at the Garden every year.

This was the old building, on Eighth Avenue and Fiftieth Street, the big brick cockpit with two balconies that held nearly nineteen thousand people. Every cabbie could find it blindfolded and all three subway lines—the IRT, IND, and BMT—stopped there. The Garden was filled every night from early October to late May with everything from the hockey games to the circus to ski jumping.

In 1950, Don Dunphy and I did a weekly television show from there called *Saturday Night at the Garden*, broadcasting whatever was happening inside. It might be a basketball game, a boxing match, a dog show, the rodeo, or the Millrose Games track meet. If it was happening in New York, it was at the Garden.

By the time of the scandals, college basketball had been a fixture at the Garden for seventeen years, ever since Irish held his first doubleheader there.

Irish was just a twenty-nine-year-old kid in 1934, covering basketball for the old New York *World-Telegram* for forty-eight dollars and sixty cents a week. But after he ripped his pants one night crawling through a window to get into the jammed Manhattan College gym, Irish realized that the audience for college games was much bigger than the local bandboxes could hold.

Only Columbia and Fordham had gyms with more than twelve hundred seats, and Irish figured that more than ten times that many people would watch a big marquee game downtown. It wasn't that outlandish an estimate. Three years earlier, the Garden had sold out for a charity game matching six New York–area teams. Twice during the next two winters, huge crowds came out to watch triple- and quadruple-headers featuring local varsities.

Clearly, the city was crazy about college basketball. But Irish was the guy who figured out that there could be a lucrative career as a matchmaker. So he quit his job at the *World-Telegram* and cut a deal with the Garden management that allowed him to rent the building and put on whatever games he could arrange. Then Irish brought in Notre Dame to play NYU, sold sixteen thousand tickets, and turned a profit.

Nobody had thought that was possible. Colleges had always assumed that basketball lost money. NYU had been undefeated the year before, played to packed houses everywhere they went, and still lost three thousand dollars. Now Irish could guarantee them that much for one night's work. And for his trouble, Irish got to keep at least ten percent of the gate.

No longer did the New York teams have to settle for playing rivals within driving distance to keep expenses down. Irish would bring the cream of the country to the Garden, pay their expenses, and give them ten percent of the receipts to take home.

If a team was hot, Irish found a way to get them to Fiftieth Street. That first year, he drove twenty-eight thousand miles and saw a hundred and twenty-five games, looking for potential imports. During the winter of 1934–35, Irish put on eight doubleheaders at the Garden. The next year, he staged ten. Before long, the Garden became the temple, the showcase of basketball.

Those doubleheaders were blockbusters. City College, LIU, and NYU were all eastern powerhouses in those days, and teams from everywhere were vying for an invitation to play them before eighteen thousand people. Oklahoma A&M, Kentucky, Utah, DePaul—they all came to the Garden. And Irish got a cut of everything.

Since nobody had seen the potential profits in college basketball, Irish had been able literally to get the rights to stage games for a song. The Garden was dark many nights during the Depression, so management was happy to let anybody stage an event inside, as long as the Garden wouldn't lose money. All Irish had to do was make four thousand dollars—the cost of opening the building—and he could write his own ticket.

After the war, Irish was making more than a hundred thousand dollars a year just staging games in the Garden. He wasn't the most popular guy in Manhattan—people who knew him well said they'd never seen him laugh out loud—but that didn't bother Irish. "I don't care what they say about me," he once said. "As long as they buy my tickets."

Irish drove a hard bargain. If you didn't want to play on his terms, you didn't get in his building. And in those days, if you weren't in the Garden, you were nowhere. That's why the NCAAs moved there from Kansas City during the war. The NIT, which Irish and the New York sportswriters dreamed up in 1938, had become much more glamorous. If the NCAAs wanted to make money, they had to come to the Garden.

The college games always outdrew the Knicks there and received much more ink in the New York newspapers. The National Basketball Association was still a bush league in 1951, playing in places like Syracuse and Rochester and Fort Wayne. Six clubs had just gone out of business and even the stronger ones weren't drawing that well. In 1951, the Knicks drew only ten thousand fans for a playoff game with the Nats. City College was packing in eighteen thousand.

College basketball had changed dramatically since I was playing for Wyoming. I was a high school senior in 1937 when the center jump was abolished. Big men like Bob Kurland and George Mikan had come into the game and the scores were much higher.

Yet by today's standards, the pace was still relatively leisurely. Not much breakneck speed. There was a lot of halfcourt offense, with the playmakers walking the ball down and setting up.

Princeton plays that way now and City College did it then—springing a guy free with a give-and-go or a pick-and-roll, set up by plenty of passing. That was Nat Holman's style. The Old Master, they called him. Mr. Basketball. Holman was the shortest member of the Original Celtics (the New York version, not Boston), a professional team that was so good that the American Basketball League broke them up in 1928.

That was back when the game literally was played inside a chicken-wire cage and ball possession was everything. Holman was the best dribbler and ball handler in the game. He was the nerve center of the Celtics, directing the game as though it were chess on hardwood. His City College teams played the same way.

They were all New York kids, taken right from the boroughs. Ed Roman came from the Bronx, Fats Roth from Brooklyn, Ed Warner from the Upper West Side. None of them were on scholarships—Harry Wright, the school president, made a point of stressing that.

That probably should have been a warning signal. Everybody was making money off the City College kids except the kids themselves. They were teenagers who went to school on the subway. City College was located on Amsterdam Avenue up around 140th Street. To get to the Garden from the campus, you took the Number 1 train.

Maybe that was the team's secret edge in 1950. They didn't see themselves as playing in the cathedral, the way Bradley and Kentucky did. The City College kids were playing in their neighborhood gym, surrounded by classmates from the same street corners.

The City College fans had the most famous cheer in the country—the Allagaroo. It was just a bunch of nonsense words:

> Allagaroo-garoo-garoo
> Allagaroo-garoo-garoo
> Eee-yah, eee-yah
> Sis boom bah
> TEAM! TEAM! TEAM!

But when you got ten thousand people doing it at once in a brick barn with rafters, it was unbelievably intimidating. When City College won the double slam in 1950—the NIT and NCAA titles in the same year—New York went crazy. No team has ever managed that before or since, and City College hadn't been expected to.

They had only one starter—Irwin Dambrot—returning from a team that had gone only 17–8 the year before. Four of the City College regulars—Roth, Warner, Roman, and Floyd Lane—were sophomores. None of them were All-Americans and none of them was what you'd call a big man.

They'd had a decent enough season—17-5—but City College wasn't ranked and hadn't figured to do much in the NIT. Their draw was brutal—defending champion San Francisco in the first round, and defending NCAA champion Kentucky in the second. But Holman's boys ran the tournament like a pool table, beating top-ranked Bradley in the final. Then they came back ten days later and did it again.

Back then, the NCAAs weren't the sixty-four-team grind they are now. Only eight teams qualified—one win put you in the Final Four—and the whole tournament took only six days from start to finish. City College simply knocked off Ohio State and North Carolina State, then waited for Bradley to come east again from Peoria for a rematch.

That game still ranks as one of the greatest of all NCAA finals. With fifteen seconds left, City College led by a point but Bradley had possession. And in those days, the rules were tilted heavily in favor of the team with the ball. There was no shot clock in 1950. And in the final two minutes of the game, a fouled team not only got the free throws, but kept the ball.

Yet somehow Dambrot, playing with five stitches in his head from a pregame collision, stripped the ball from Squeaky Melchiorre, Bradley's great All-American. He arched a long pass to Norm Mager in the clear for an easy basket that clinched it, 71–68 and City College had its double slam. The Beavers had beaten the number two, three, five, six, and twelve teams in the country, and the number one team twice.

Well, they went crazy up on 140th Street. After celebrating all night, nearly seven thousand students staged a huge rally on campus the next day, forming snake dances and conga lines. The tower bell atop the main building, rung only on special occasions, pealed for five minutes.

Of course, everybody was expecting City College to repeat in 1951. Four of the starters—everyone but Dambrot—were back. But on December 9, Missouri came into the Garden and stuffed them by seventeen points. I broadcast that game, saw it dumped right in front of me, and never suspected a thing. And I knew basketball.

The Missouri coach, Sparky Stalcup, was a friend of mine. So when Mizzou arrived in town, I'd called Sparky and asked if he could fill me in on his squad. Sparky ended up inviting me to sit in on a team meeting while he diagrammed Xs and Os on a blackboard.

"'They may be the defending champs," Stalcup told his players, "but if we defense them properly, we can upset them."

After the players left, Sparky sat down with me alone.

"What do you think of my defense?"

"If your guys play well," I told him, "they'll give City College a good ball game."

Missouri did a lot more than that. Sparky's guys held City College without a point for eight minutes, scored seventeen straight points, and took a 31–14 lead at the half. City College seemed cold to me. They threw up clunkers, balls that slammed off the backboard. Or their guards would come down on the fast break and throw the ball just out of reach of the wing man.

I remember saying on the air that this was the worst I'd ever seen City College play, but that Missouri was also playing great defense, making City College take wild shots. "There is little question that City did much to damage its own cause," the *New York*

Times reported the next morning. "Its shooting was decidedly off all the way and such sure-fire tossers as Roman, Floyd Lane and Al Roth missed repeatedly."

City College missed forty-eight of their sixty shots from the floor. Roman was held to seven points, and he scored five of them near the end of the game before fouling out. You couldn't have done a better job of dumping a basketball game, yet nobody suspected a thing.

I certainly didn't. Neither did Mike Strauss from the *Times.* "Maybe it just wasn't in the cards for City College to notch its thirteenth straight victory last night," he wrote.

A hundred times since then, I've asked myself why I didn't recognize what was going on. I guess I wasn't looking for it, so I wasn't suspicious. I just never dreamed that college kids would fix games. After it was over and Missouri had won 54–37, I went down to the Missouri dressing room. Sparky was all smiles.

"What did you think of that defense?" he crowed. "My boys did just what I wanted them to do."

Well, that wasn't the last time City College was upset that winter. Arizona came in a couple of weeks later and beat them by three points. Then Boston College won by four. Each time, City College had been favored to win by anywhere from eight to twelve points.

And yet, nobody was saying anything about a fix. By late February, City College had lost seven of seventeen games but people seemed to be shrugging it off as one of those things that happen in college sports. Everything clicks for you one season and doesn't the next.

There were half a dozen good explanations for why City College was having an off year, but until February nobody settled on the obvious one. Its key players were dumping games.

The worst thing that can happen in any sport is a fix. The fans have to believe that it's an honest contest between two teams that are trying their best to win. Because once that belief is undermined, any upset is viewed as a fix.

That's why Kenesaw Mountain Landis, the baseball commissioner in 1919, kicked the Black Sox out of the game for life, even though they were never convicted of fixing the World Series. He felt he had to restore public confidence in the game.

It was funny how the whole thing broke. City College had gone down to Philadelphia on a Saturday night and had blown out Temple by twenty-four points. What neither Holman nor his players knew was that there were a couple of detectives from the New York district attorney's office sitting in the stands watching. And they already had the goods on Roth, Warner, and Roman.

When the team boarded the train back to Penn Station, the detectives joined them. By the time they had reached New Brunswick, they'd taken Holman aside.

"Nat, I'm sorry, but we're going to pick up some of your boys," one of the detectives told him.

Holman was mystified. "What for?"

"Well, there's a question of some fixed games."

Now, a Manhattan College player named Junius Kellogg had told the police in January that a gambler had approached him about shaving points. But nobody thought it might be widespread, or that anybody from City College might be involved. Roman was an A student. Warner had been a choirboy. They were clean-cut college kids. Holman was shaken, but he was convinced his players were clean.

"When they speak to you, boys, tell the truth," Holman told them. "If your conscience is clear, you have nothing to fear."

When the train reached New York, the three players were escorted off and questioned well into Sunday morning. By Monday, the world knew that a forty-five-year-old jewelry manufacturer named Salvatore Sollazzo, an ex-convict who had a penthouse suite on Central Park West, had paid the City College players that winter to shave points in three games—Missouri, Arizona, and Boston College.

By the time the district attorney's office was through, seven City College players had been arrested. "I fervently wish that any person who might be so tempted could have seen these stupid and dishonest young men as they admitted their guilt," said Frank Hogan, the D.A. "Tears, remorse, self-reproach and scalding thoughts of the perpetual heartache and disgrace—all of this was too late."

Well, I got on the phone to Sparky Stalcup back in Missouri. "Greatest defense I ever saw," I kidded him. But Sparky wasn't laughing.

"I'm sick about this," he told me. "I'm afraid it's really going to hurt college basketball."

Stalcup knew it would be more than just a case of one gambler trying to buy off a couple of guys on one team. But a lot of his colleagues didn't.

The next day I was having lunch with Clair Bee, the longtime LIU coach, at Leone's Restaurant.

"Isn't it terrible about Nat's team?" I said.

Clair reached into his back pocket, pulled out his wallet, and slapped it down on the table. "I'll bet my wallet, my house, my wife . . . everything I have that my boys aren't involved in this."

What Bee didn't know was that at that very moment his own star, Sherman White, and two other players had been taken in for questioning. They were held overnight at the Tombs, where prisoners await trial in Manhattan, and their faces were on the front page of the next day's *Times*, too. White, captain Al Bigos, and Le Roy Smith, a high-scoring forward, had begun fixing games the season before.

Sollazzo had gotten to Ed Gard, who'd been LIU's captain then, at a summer resort up in the Catskills. Lots of top college players used to get jobs as waiters and bellboys and lifeguards in the hotels there and they'd play the borscht circuit all summer, just as the comedians did. Technically, they were playing for free, so the players kept their amateur standing. The colleges all knew about the arrangement. In fact, they encouraged it.

Problem was, the resorts were a perfect place for big-city gamblers to find kids who could use a few bucks for "harmlessly" shaving points and who were already used to beating the system. That was the angle that Sollazzo used to convince them. He wasn't asking them to dump games, he said, but just to make them closer than the point spread. If City College was favored by eight, Sollazzo wanted them to win by six. "It's not like you're throwing your college," Sollazzo assured them.

It was a terrific investment for Sollazzo. He paid the players a total of thirty thousand dollars in bribes, bonuses, and walking-around money to fix ten games. He collected ten times that much in winnings. And the beauty of basketball was that you only needed to get to a couple of starters—the playmaker and the shooting forward—to make your scheme work. You didn't need all five men.

So Gard, Bigos, and Smith agreed to fix three games during the 1949–50 season—North Carolina State, Cincinnati, and the opener of the NIT tournament with Syracuse. Well, after the first one, which LIU actually lost, White guessed something was up and accused Bigos and Gard of laying down, of not feeding him the ball, of playing in a phony manner. So Gard met White in a Brooklyn candy store and got him in on the deal, too.

But shaving points is an inexact science. You can't control a basketball game with a thermostat. Turned out that LIU lost all three games that season. The next year, they fixed four—Kansas State, Denver, Idaho, and Bowling Green. By then, the LIU kids had learned the fine art of shaving. This time, they won all of the fixed games.

The players even had a phone code worked out to spread the word about which games would be fixed.

"Are you going to meet the girl today?"

"What girl?"

"Sally." (Sollazzo)

"Yes."

After the fourth game, the players decided to quit while the quitting was good. They'd made more than eighteen thousand dollars, and people were starting to get suspicious. Someone had written a letter to the school, complaining about LIU's erratic play. And the players themselves were having pangs of conscience. "I found myself sick of starting something I had never done before," Smith said. "I couldn't eat."

So the players told Sollazzo they were through, but he didn't believe them. He bet that LIU wouldn't cover the spread against Duquesne—and lost his shirt. White, Smith, and Bigos ran wild, scoring sixty-four points in LIU's 84–52 victory.

When news of the point shaving broke, it hit LIU like a thunderbolt. The school not only canceled the rest of the basketball season, it dropped all intercollegiate sports for six years. And Bee himself was devastated. He wept when he read the headlines. "I never dreamed a boy who played for me could be crooked," he wrote. "I was a naive chump."

Bee prided himself on being an honorable man. A few years

later, he was a coach and an investor in the original Baltimore Bullets, an NBA team which went under. Bee lost his shirt and he could have declared bankruptcy. But he worked and saved and made a point of paying back every dime he owed. Bee simply assumed that everybody did the right thing in life.

Bee had literally written the book on how to coach basketball. Not only had he produced several instructional books on his own, but Bee probably wrote a dozen more for other coaches which were published under their names. They'd give their ideas and notes to Bee, and he'd put them into prose.

When James Naismith, inventor of the game, needed an introduction for his volume *Basketball, Its Origin and Development*, he'd called Bee.

It was Bee who invented the 1-3-1 zone and proposed the three-second rule to keep big men from clogging the lane. He'd been coaching at LIU since 1931, only five years after the school was founded, and had won an amazing eighty percent of his games. Over the years, Bee's teams had winning streaks of forty-three, thirty-eight, twenty-eight, twenty-six, and twenty games. The only way they could lose games was if they tried. And Bee never dreamed they would.

He'd written a series of sports fiction books for kids. The hero was Chip Hilton, the All-American boy who had the whole checklist of virtues. Chip Hilton played for a small high school in West Virginia and he was always winning games with unbelievable last-second heroics. Bobby Knight once told me he read all twenty-six of those books when he was a kid. Chip Hilton would have died before he would have shaved points. But Chip Hilton existed only in Clair Bee's imagination.

After he'd heard rumors of fixed games, Clair had spoken to each of his players individually, asking him if he was involved. "I pleaded with them to tell me the truth," Bee said. "Each boy looked me in the eye and denied complicity with gamblers."

Bee loved his players as if they were his own sons. Once, when LIU was playing at Marshall, a local restaurant wouldn't let Dolly King, one of Bee's black players, eat in its dining room. Now, Marshall is in West Virginia, Bee's home state, and this was years before anyone had ever heard of civil rights. Well, Clair went into the restaurant kitchen and ate his supper there with King. He wasn't trying to make a federal case out of it, but Bee felt he owed it to King to be there for him. So when his own players lied to his face, Bee was crushed.

It wasn't simply a New York scandal, even though all of the schools involved had played games in the Garden. Bradley, the top-ranked team in America the year before, had three players named, including Melchiorre and another starter named Bill Mann.

And Kentucky, which had won back-to-back NCAA titles in 1948 and 1949, had its two great stars from those teams implicated—Alex Groza and Ralph Beard—plus captain Dale Barnstable. That came as a jolt to the entire state, which idolized its Wildcats and never dreamed that any of Adolph Rupp's players could be tainted.

They were such a dominant team that they were part of the United States squad in the 1948 Olympics in London, where they swept unbeaten through the draw and won the gold medal. Kentucky won a hundred and thirty games between 1946 and 1949, but the one that would be remembered was their first-rounder with Loyola in the 1949 NIT tournament. Loyola won it 67–56 and nobody gave the game a second look—until 1951.

Beard and Groza were playing in the NBA for the Indianapolis Olympians by then. They were sitting in Chicago Stadium, watching Rupp's College All-Stars play the Rochester Royals, when they were arrested.

When the City College and LIU scandals broke, Rupp had bragged that gamblers couldn't touch his players with a ten-foot pole. Well, when Groza and Beard were nabbed, some New York sportswriters got a twelve-foot pole, wrapped it up, and sent it to Rupp in the mail.

Beard, Groza, and Barnstable got three-year suspended sentences and were banned from playing.

And the NCAA forced Kentucky, which had won the 1951 title, to drop varsity basketball for the 1952–53 season after it came out that some of their players had taken payoffs from boosters.

City College was wiped out, too. Warner and Roth were sentenced to six-month terms in the workhouse and three of their teammates were given suspended sentences. Then a second scandal broke.

It came out that more than a dozen City College basketball players had been admitted on forged transcripts since the war, and that they had stayed in school by taking snap courses like oil painting and rhythm and dance. That was the final blow to Nat Holman, who'd been coaching at City College for thirty-four years. He took a year's sabbatical and went to Europe. While Holman was gone, the state Board of Education suspended him for "conduct unbecoming a teacher and neglect of duty."

Nat denied everything, but he was in a no-win situation. If he knew about the fixed games and the forgeries, then he was breaking the law. If he didn't, then he was naive and out of touch. Arthur Daley of the *Times* wrote what amounted to Holman's professional obituary. The headline was: CAESAR WAS AMBITIOUS.

Nat came back and coached on and off for four more seasons, but that was the end of City College as a basketball power. They still have a team up on 140th Street and they still wear the lavender and black, but the program has been scaled back dramatically. Instead of Kentucky and Missouri, City College plays Yeshiva and Medgar Evers these days. And they've never been back to the NCAAs.

LIU took a hammering, too. White was sentenced to a year in the workhouse and Bigos and three other players got suspended sentences. The program literally vanished until 1957. And Clair Bee, who *was* LIU basketball, never coached another college game. Something inside him had died, he said.

"A losing team is better than no team at all," Bee had realized. "Anything is infinitely better than waiting beside a telephone at four o'clock in the morning while kids in a police station downtown are signing confessions that will brand them as long as they live."

One New York school that was untouched by the point shaving was St. John's. I think Joe Lapchick, their former coach, had a lot to do with that. Joe had been Nat Holman's best man and his teammate on the original Celtics and he'd won three NIT titles himself. The main reason why St. John's probably wasn't sucked into the scandals was because Lapchick had always expected so much of the players. "Walk with the kings," he always told them.

He was the son of a Czech immigrant and he never went to high school, but Lapchick was a coaching genius. After he left St. John's in 1947, he directed the New York Knicks for eight years and took them to the NBA finals three times.

Years later, when Bobby Knight would bring his college teams to Madison Square Garden, he'd pass by Lapchick's seat and see Joe sticking his thumb under his chin and pushing it up. *Keep your head high*, the message was. *Walk with the kings.*

Every year, when he talked to his players before the season, Lapchick gave them the same instructions: "*We expect you to conduct yourselves in a way that brings credit to the team, the university, and yourself. If you don't, I will handle it however I see fit.*"

Lapchick's players respected him because he demanded it. When he first took the job at St. John's, he'd gone to Clair Bee for advice. "Your players are never to call you Joe," Bee told him. "They call you Coach or Mr. Lapchick. But never Joe."

That's why I think St. John's never got itself tangled up in the point-shaving mess. Even though Lapchick wasn't there by then, his code still was. The players simply respected Joe and themselves too much to do business with the Sollazzos.

The scandals ended the glory era of college basketball in New York. There was a big push around the country to get games out of the big arenas and back on campus, where the crowds would be smaller and gamblers easier to spot. The NCAA began treating the Garden like a radioactive site and hasn't staged the Final Four there since.

You don't hear much about the 1951 scandals these days, but all the same excesses and temptations that produced them are still around. There was another point-shaving scandal in 1961, and one in 1981 that involved Boston College. It only takes people a few years to forget. That's why, when Lapchick came back from the Knicks in 1957 to coach St. John's again, he assembled a huge scrapbook of newspaper clippings about the 1951 scandals. And every autumn when he began practice, Lapchick brought his squad together in middle of the locker room and laid the scrapbook on the table.

"I want you boys to see something and remember it," he'd tell them, turning the pages whose pictures showed twenty-one-year-old kids hiding their faces from the cameras. "It happened once. It can happen again."

6

The Prince and the Jester

They were the crown prince and the court jester of the greatest dynasty baseball has ever known. Joe DiMaggio was tall, regal, dignified. His pin-striped uniform looked as though it had been tailored by Savile Row. Casey Stengel had a face like Popeye's and a voice like a runaway gravel truck. He looked ridiculous in pinstripes.

Stengel said that DiMaggio was the greatest player he ever managed. DiMaggio said almost nothing about Stengel. But for three years they were champions together.

DiMaggio was already a Yankee immortal by the time I arrived in New York in 1949. Stengel, who'd just taken the job, was viewed as an outsider—if not an intruder. I first met him in the men's room at a team party during spring training in St. Petersburg.

"Hey, kid," he said. "I've got a good friend out on the coast who announced our games in Oakland. I'd sure like to see him get a shot at the major leagues."

I was puzzled. Who did Casey think I was?

"What can I do about it?" I asked him.

"I want you to get him a job."

"Hell, Mr. Stengel, I'm going to be lucky to hold on to my own job," I told him. "I just came up here myself. I'm a rookie."

"Oh, yeah? Then we're both rookies together," Stengel said. And from then on he called me a rookie.

He may have been a rookie, but Casey was no maiden. He'd been around the game for forty years, had played in three World Series, and had spent thousands of nights in Pullman sleepers. "You think I was *born* old?" he once rasped at Mickey Mantle.

Beneath his clowning and his Stengelese, the double-talk that passed for conversation, Casey was a baseball genius, the Old Professor. And all he wanted to do was live and talk the game.

"I don't play cards," Stengel used to say. "I don't play golf and I don't go to the picture show. All that's left is baseball."

When he first joined the club, a number of the Yankee veterans thought Stengel was just an old fool. Particularly DiMaggio.

"What do you think of our new manager?" he asked *New York Times* columnist Arthur Daley one day during spring training.

"I never saw such a bewildered guy in all my life," Daley told him. "He looks like he has no idea what it's all about."

"That's the impression I have," DiMaggio said. "And the rest of the fellows feel the same."

Yet as the season wore on and the Yankees kept winning despite an injured list that reached to the floor, it was DiMaggio who was bewildered. He'd look at this gnarled little old man, pacing the dugout and jabbering nonstop, and shake his head. "How does this guy win?" DiMaggio wondered.

Stengel hadn't won with the Dodgers and Braves because he hadn't had the players. "Sometimes I thought I was managing a golf course," he'd say. "You know, one pro to a club."

Now Stengel had a clubhouse filled with Hall of Famers. "Gowdy, this is the first time I've had any talent," he told me. "I just sit here in the dugout and marvel at it. Sometimes I'm speechless, looking at guys like Henrich and DiMaggio."

And it wasn't just Henrich and DiMaggio. Stengel had the best pitching rotation in baseball in Raschi, Reynolds, and Lopat, the best reliever in Joe Page, and the best bench in the game. Most of them could have started for any club in either league.

That's why Stengel was such a believer in platooning—because he could. "We're paying twenty-five men," Casey would say. "We might as well let them earn their money. Why wouldn't ya?"

Once he even tried DiMaggio at first base. The experiment lasted for one game and it was agony for DiMaggio, who was terrified of looking bad in front of his teammates and the fans.

He might have been near the end of his career, but DiMaggio was still a fiercely proud man. You've probably heard his explanation of why he played so hard in late September, after the Yankees had already clinched the pennant: "Maybe there's someone out there who's never seen me play before."

That was how DiMaggio led the Yankees—by his own uncompromising example. He never said much to his teammates because he didn't have to. A ballplayer who might be thinking of taking the day off against a last-place club would look at DiMaggio suiting up despite an aching heel or a sore shoulder and think twice about sitting it out.

Once, after he dragged himself off the diamond after a draining doubleheader during a heat wave, DiMaggio spotted Yogi Berra, who'd sat out the second game. "Goddamn rookie," DiMaggio said, scowling. "Can't even play two."

The rule with the Yankees was that DiMaggio was in the lineup unless he said otherwise. And no manager ever took him out of a game. That was DiMaggio's prerogative, and he exercised it in one of the biggest games of his career.

It was the final day of the 1949 season and the Yankees were playing the Red Sox in the Stadium for the pennant. The Yankees were in control of the game, leading 5–0 with one out in the ninth. DiMaggio was playing center—and quietly suffering. He was still recovering from pneumonitis and it had left him weak and aching.

When Bobby Doerr hit a triple over his head to score two runs, DiMaggio called time and I noticed him jogging to the dugout. "I didn't want to hurt the club by falling on my face," he said. It would have killed DiMaggio to blow a pennant, so he took himself out.

That's what Lou Gehrig had done in 1939 after two thousand one hundred and thirty straight games, when he knew his body had betrayed him. That was the Yankee way.

So there were shock waves when Stengel put DiMaggio at first base, even for a day. And when Stengel dropped him to fifth in the order, it made headlines. When I walked into Toots Shor's that night, Shor jumped all over me. He idolized DiMaggio.

"I hope you guys are satisfied now," he told me.

"What do you mean, 'you guys'?" I said. "I don't manage the team."

"You know what I mean," Shor said. "That guy of yours is humiliating one of the greatest players of all time."

DiMaggio never said a word about it. And he said nothing later in the season when Stengel benched him for six games. That was Joe's style. I'm always amazed now, seeing DiMaggio doing television ads. Back then he used to say about three words during the season.

There was that famous story about DiMaggio, Tony Lazzeri, and Frank Crosetti—who all lived in San Francisco—driving to Florida for spring training when DiMaggio was a rookie. None of them was much for conversation. When they got in the car, they said hello. When they got out of the car, they said good-bye. Nothing in between. It wasn't until they got to Alabama that Lazzeri and Crosetti found out that DiMaggio didn't know how to drive.

It took me a while to meet DiMaggio. You didn't approach him. You waited for him to come up to you. He finally did one day around the batting cage. He introduced himself, I told him who I was, and we shook hands. "Good luck," Joe said. "Hope you enjoy it up here."

He was never much for small talk, especially with people he didn't know. He had to feel comfortable with you. DiMaggio didn't trust a lot of people, and I think his early years with the Yankees had something to do with that. He had a nasty salary dispute in 1938 and I think it embittered him.

Joe had had a great year in 1937. He batted .346, hit forty-six homers, and drove in a hundred and sixty-seven runs. So he thought he deserved a raise. DiMaggio was making fifteen thousand dollars but wanted forty thousand, which would have made him the highest-paid player in baseball. Well, the Yankee front office treated DiMaggio like an impudent kid.

They were offering him twenty-five thousand, which was what Franklin Roosevelt made that year. DiMaggio refused it and held out. "DiMaggio is an ungrateful young man," owner Jacob Ruppert said. The press took the Yankees' side and most of the public did, too. So DiMaggio finally gave in—a player had no leverage in those days—and the Yankees ended up docking him eighteen hundred dollars for the games he missed while he got himself into shape.

I don't think Joe ever got over that. He realized that he couldn't count on people being with him even when he was convinced he was right, so he kept to himself. Very few people could say they knew him well—even his own teammates. Ed Lopat said that DiMaggio was the loneliest man he ever knew. "He leads the league in room service," Lopat said.

I don't think DiMaggio would have had any alternative. He could go to Shor's, where Toots made sure Joe had a seat at Table One and kept people from bothering him. But I think DiMaggio would have been pestered most other places—especially if he'd gone alone.

He was always the last guy out of the clubhouse after a game at the Stadium because he knew he'd be mobbed for autographs. "Gee, Joe, aren't you going home tonight?" I'd ask him after a couple of hours had passed.

"Yeah, after the last one's gone out there," he said.

DiMaggio didn't like the rush around him, all the pushing and shoving. Sometimes we'd share a cab back downtown. In all the years he played in New York, DiMaggio never took the subway.

He wasn't a recluse, but whenever Joe went anywhere he had a companion, partly to ward off strangers. Sometimes it would be a trusted writer like Jimmy Cannon, sometimes a blonde showgirl. Most often it was George Solotaire, a ticket broker and man-about-Broadway. Solotaire was DiMaggio's all-purpose sidekick, buffer, and gofer. He'd bring Joe sandwiches, even get his suits pressed for him.

DiMaggio wasn't one for hanging around the rich and famous. When he went out with a teammate, it was usually a rookie or the twenty-fifth guy on the team. Billy Martin was one of his favorites. And DiMaggio would always pick up the tab. "When you eat with the Dago," his rule was, "the Dago pays."

Even though DiMaggio kept his distance in the clubhouse, his teammates considered him their leader and admired him. There was no envy, no jealousy. Before Stengel was hired, there was talk that DiMaggio would be named player-manager, as Joe Cronin had been with the Red Sox and Lou Boudreau with the Indians, but DiMaggio dismissed it. "You fellows know me," he said. "I'm just a ballplayer."

So DiMaggio did whatever the manager told him to and kept his feelings to himself. He and Stengel had a strange relationship—it was strictly a one-way admiration society.

"You know, this guy talks about you incessantly," I told DiMaggio. But he never told me what he thought about Casey. I guess his opinion never changed from that first spring training.

Joe rarely spoke to Stengel, but that never bothered Casey. "DiMaggio doesn't get paid to talk to me," he said. "And I don't, either."

Stengel talked enough for the both of them. That's why he was great copy for the press. You'd go to the ballpark an hour and a half before the game, you'd see a big cluster of reporters, and you knew right away who was in the middle.

Most of the time, Casey spoke in code known only to him. "Butcher boy, butcher boy," he'd shout through cupped hands from the dugout. That meant chop at the ball, get wood on it. "Run, sheep, run" meant steal. A "road apple" was someone worthless. There were no road apples on the Yankees, and that delighted Stengel. He loved managing that ball club.

"What's this big crowd in town tonight?" he said one time when we were in a jammed hotel elevator in Cleveland.

"Don't you know?" someone told him. "The Indians and Yankees were playing."

"Oh, yeah? Who won?"

"Aww, those damned Yankees."

"Who's managin' them now?" Stengel said.

"Ahh, that crazy Stengel."

"Well, I hear he's smart as hell," Casey said. Then he got off the elevator, laughing.

He loved tweaking the Indians and especially their manager, Al Lopez, whom Stengel called the "Mexican." Before the 1954 season, Lopez said he thought this would finally be the year his ball club caught the Yankees.

"Tell the señor unless my team gets hit by a truck and my brain rots, he ain't gonna win," Stengel said. "Because the Yankees are."

Well, Cleveland had a season for the books, winning an incredible one hundred and eleven games, and took the pennant. "We had a splendeed season," Stengel said. "But the señor beat me and you could look it up."

You could look it up, but Casey never did. He remembered everything and everyone. Once we were in Chattanooga, barnstorming our way back north, and this old fellow came down and leaned against the fence.

"Hey, kid, is Stengel around?" he asked.

"Yeah, end of the dugout."

"Tell him so-and-so is here."

"Yeah, I played against him in the minor leagues," Stengel said, and went over to chat.

"Yessir, yessir," he said, shaking hands. "I remember, bases loaded, the count was two-and-two and I overshifted, figuring you'd pull the ball, and you hit it into left center and you cleaned the bases, and you could look it up."

Casey was a walking baseball computer with total recall. These days, managers have printouts and charts to help them make decisions during games. Stengel had nothing but his head. But he always seemed to remember who hit better against what pitcher or which pitcher was more effective against what batter. And he was never better than he was in the seventh game of the 1952 Series against the Dodgers at Ebbets Field.

The Yankees were leading 4–2 in the seventh, but Brooklyn had loaded the bases with one out. Now they had Duke Snider up, with Jackie Robinson on deck. Stengel had already used his aces—Lopat, Reynolds, and Raschi. So he signaled for Bob Kuzava, a lefty who was only 8-8 that year.

Now, the left-field fence at Ebbets was only ten feet high. Most people would have thought it was suicide to bring in a southpaw in that situation. But Stengel knew something. Kuzava got Snider to pop up on a full count. Then, with another full count to Robinson, Kuzava curved him. Here is how Stengel described what followed to Maury Allen of the *New York Post*:

> We had this lefthander Gazzara and they had that brilliant Mister Rob-a-son at the plate and all of a sudden, whoops, here comes a slow ball when you expect a fastball, and why wouldn't ya tap it into right-field if you was righthanded, but Mister Rob-a-son tried to hit the ball

over the building and instead he hit a ball up the chute, excuse me, as hard as Ned in the third reader and Mister Collins which was my first baseman was counting his money so he never seen it and Mister Berra my catcher is standing with his hands on his hips yelling for Mister Collins and Mister Gazzara did the pitchin' and he ain't about to do the catchin' so that leaves the second baseman, and you know who that is, to come in, lose his cap and get it before it hits the grass, which if he did would be kicked because he was runnin' so fast and almost tripped over the mound which was a mountain in Brooklyn to help them sinkerball pitchers, Mister Erskine and them and McGraw used to do that too, and why wouldn't ya if you had spitters in the staff, but my rooster caught it and it didn't hit off his schnozz like a lot of them would have. Get it?

What happened was that Robinson had popped up, the ball looked as though it might drop in the infield, and Billy Martin had gloved it two feet before it hit the ground, saving the pennant.

That was Stengelese for you. Casey was like a driver who took you from New York to Philadelphia by way of Chicago, but he got you there. Eventually.

After the Yankees won the Series in 1949, I took my father to the team celebration and he ended up having a couple of beers with Casey.

"How'd you like him?" I asked my father afterward.

"Mr. Stengel is very friendly," he said. "But I'll be damned if I knew what he was talking about."

Everything that was going through Stengel's brain tended to come out of his mouth in a torrent. He talked about baseball as though he'd just discovered it that morning and had to tell you everything he knew by nightfall.

"Give me a little inside baseball, Casey," I'd ask him, when we'd be up in his hotel suite on road trips.

"What do ya want to know?"

"How about your bunt plays?"

Well, Stengel would rearrange the chairs to designate the bases, then shift them around to show how he moved the infield in or back.

If you had a bottle of bourbon with you, Casey would go on until four in the morning. When he had a few beers with you, it was usually a few a minute. Once, in Detroit, we each ordered a glass of

Army's Doc Blanchard (Mr. Inside) and Glenn Davis (Mr. Outside): To people like me, sitting at home in Cheyenne and listening on the radio, they were very nearly gods. (*Acme*)

Columbia's Lou Little: "Oh my, my, my, my, my," he would say in distaste, whenever a player missed an assignment. (*Acme*)

Notre Dame's Frank Leahy: "I ask you, in the sacred name of Our Lady, to go onto that field and shake down the thunder. Go and persevere. Our Lady demands it." (*Associated Press*)

Oklahoma's Bud Wilkinson: His players nicknamed him "The Great White Father," as though Wilkinson were some sort of blond god. (*Associated Press*)

George Mikan and Harlem Globetrotters owner Abe Saperstein: "I was a freak," Mikan said. "I was like the fat lady in the circus or the tattooed man." (*Boston Globe*)

Kentucky's Adolph Rupp and Curt Gowdy: The Baron was a complete dictator. He could charm you, scare you, threaten you. (*Curt Gowdy*)

Kentucky's Adolph Rupp, enjoying a thirty-point lead: "I'd rather be the most hated winning coach in the country than the most popular losing one." (*Associated Press*)

Casey Stengel: "Some people my age are dead at the present time." (*Acme*)

DODG
CLUB

KEEP

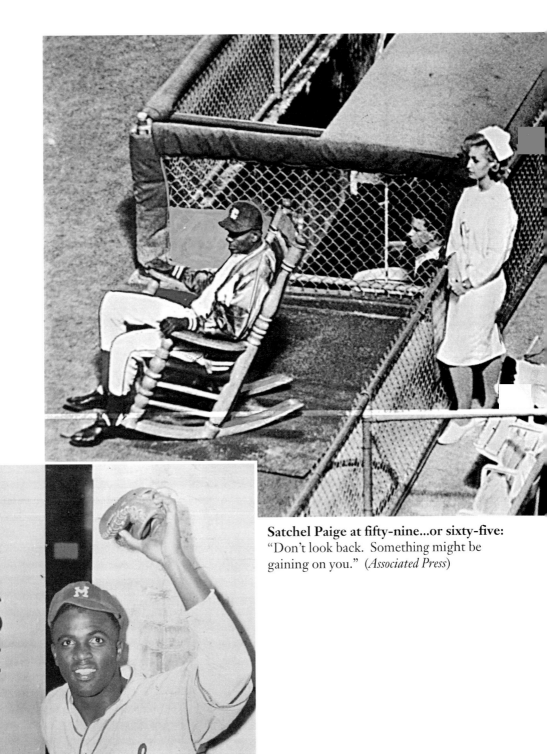

Satchel Paige at fifty-nine...or sixty-five:
"Don't look back. Something might be
gaining on you." (*Associated Press*)

Jackie Robinson: "You know why
they didn't like him?" said Carl
Furillo, the Dodger rightfielder.
"Because he could beat them."
(*Associated Press*)

City College's Nat Holman: The Old Master, they called him. Mr. Basketball. (*United Press International*)

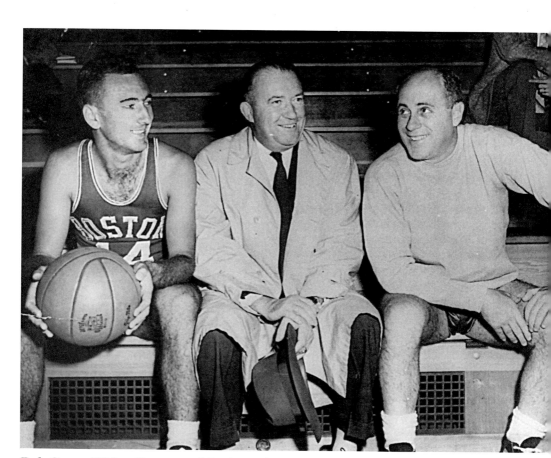

Bob Cousy, Walter Brown, and Red Auerbach: The only green the Celtics had in those days were their jerseys. (*Boston Globe*)

Bill Russell: He was angular, with long spidery arms and huge hands. An eagle with a beard. (*Boston Globe*)

The DiMaggios — Vince, Joe, and Dom: They weren't even the best players in the family. Their oldest brother Tommy was. (*Associated Press*)

Jimmy Piersall: He played like a man possessed. I've never seen a man with so much pent-up energy. He never stopped talking, never stopped moving. (*Boston Globe*)

Yankee owner Dan Topping with wife Sonja Henie: He was a handsome man who traveled in society—a jet-setter before there were jets. (*Boston Globe*)

(*Opposite*) **Bill Veeck:** If you had an idea for a trade, you didn't have to write him a letter. You just had to lean over the popcorn and tell him. (*Associated Press*)

Eddie Gaedel: "I've got a man up in the stands with a high-powered rifle," Bill Veeck warned the midget. "And if you swing at any pitch, he'll fire." (*Associated Press*)

Ted Williams and Tom Yawkey: If the league didn't require it, they probably wouldn't have bothered with a contract at all. (*United Press International*)

Curt Gowdy: Radio was the theater of the mind. It supplied the words, you created the pictures. The only limits were your imagination. (*Boston Globe*)

draft beer. Well, as I was taking my first sip or two, Casey just gulped his right down and then ordered another one.

"Casey," I said, "I've never seen anyone drink beer as fast as you do."

"Well," he said, "it's always been that way since my accident."

"What accident?"

"Somebody knocked my glass over."

No matter how much Stengel drank or how late he stayed up, he'd still be at the ballpark early in the morning, because he didn't want to miss a minute of his baseball life. He savored it like some rookie just up from the bushes.

Stengel loved the young guys like Jerry Coleman and Mickey Mantle. But his favorite was Martin. "The fresh little bastard," Stengel would say. "How I love him."

As far as Casey was concerned, he and Martin were contemporaries, both at the start of their Yankee careers. It was DiMaggio's career which was winding down. When I came to the club, his black hair was flecked with gray and he was coming off that heel injury.

He still had the same grace and dignity and pride he'd always had and there were a couple of fine seasons left in him. But Joe knew that his time was ending.

"Have you ever felt that you know you could have done things better, but you can't do them now?" he asked me once. "It's really frustrating." DiMaggio shook his head. "It's hell to get old."

But it was worse to be pitied, and that's how DiMaggio felt in 1951. He was making a hundred thousand dollars a year by then, yet he'd never played worse. He was thirty-six and his body was shot, from his throwing shoulder to his heels. "It was agony for him just getting in and out of a taxicab," Phil Rizzuto noticed.

After bad days at the plate, DiMaggio would wave aside writers who wanted to commiserate with him. "I'm not looking for sympathy," he told them. "I don't want sympathy. I don't deserve sympathy."

Once, after he'd beaten the seventh-place Senators with a triple and a homer and writers crowded around his locker, DiMaggio felt patronized. That hurt him more than anything. "I don't want your pity," he told them. "I have not asked anything from anybody."

He'd told friends that 1951 would be his last season, "because I don't want them to remember me struggling." The Dodgers' scouting report on him, which ended up in *Life* magazine after the Yankees beat the Giants in the World Series, made certain of it.

"He can't stop quickly or throw hard," the report said. "You can take the extra base on him. He can't run and won't bunt. His reflexes are very slow and he can't pull a good fastball."

It might as well have been a coroner's report for DiMaggio, and he announced his retirement. "I just gave the Big Guy's glove away to the Hall of Fame," Stengel said. "Where the Big Guy will be going himself."

But Stengel still had plenty of baseball left in him—seven more pennants and four more Series championships. "Some people my age are dead at the present time," he observed. Even after the Yankees dismissed him in 1960—"I'll never make the mistake of being seventy again," Stengel declared—there was a job for him in New York.

The Mets hired him to manage their collection of kids and castoffs. They played in the Polo Grounds, where Casey used to play the sun field back in the twenties, and they lost their opener by seven runs. "When you're losin', everyone commences playin' stupid," Stengel said.

While the Mets were losing a hundred and nineteen more games, Stengel pronounced them "amazin'." Baseball people insisted they'd be the death of him, but Casey lived another thirteen years, long enough to see them win the World Series. When he died, at eighty-five, his family put a few of Stengel's own words on his gravestone: THERE COMES A TIME IN EVERY MAN'S LIFE AND I'VE HAD PLENTY OF THEM.

7

Celtic Green

I still have the contract somewhere. It's just a letter, really, that I typed up and Walter Brown signed, agreeing that I'd broadcast the Boston Celtics during the winter of 1951 and that he'd pay me a few thousand bucks. I never did get the money. "I don't have it," Walter told me, flat out, when the season ended. "I'd love to pay you, but I can't pay you what I don't have."

The only green the Celtics had in those days were their jerseys. They had no stockholders, no waiting list for tickets, no championship flags. When I got there, they didn't even have a broadcaster. That's why Red Auerbach called me one day during the summer when I was doing the Red Sox and asked me to lunch.

"This isn't a basketball town," he told me. "This is a hockey town. The Bruins are a fourth-place club, yet they're packing the Garden every night. We're averaging about six thousand fans a night, and we're lucky doing that. Believe me, we're really struggling."

"What can I do about it?" I asked him.

"Well, I'd like to get somebody to announce who knows the game and can maybe teach it to the fans and get them interested in it. Nobody knows anything about pro basketball here. The sportswriters don't, and if you lecture to them about it, they get

mad. Now, you played in college and broadcast the games in Oklahoma and at Madison Square Garden. You'd be ideal for us."

Basketball had always been my first love, so I was eager to sign
on. I met Brown, the genial Irishman who owned the Celtics, and I
agreed to do the games.

"Okay," I told Brown. "Let's talk about some kind of a contract."

"Red and I don't have contracts," Walter told me. "We just
shake hands."

"Well, that'd be all right with me," I said. "But I'd like to have a
contract that will spell out what I'm supposed to do and how much
I'll be paid."

"Okay," Brown agreed. "You write it up. Write a letter and you
sign it and I'll sign it and that'll be our contract."

I didn't use a lawyer. I was my own lawyer. I wrote a very simple
letter, throwing in the possibility of doing TV games. And if we
made the playoffs, that would be extra. Brown just glanced at it, said
fine, and signed it.

Well, I guess I knew in my heart that I'd never see the money.
Brown was broke. The franchise had almost gone under the year
before I got there and it was getting by on a shoestring.

One year, Brown couldn't pay the players for a while, but they
trusted him and agreed to wait for the money until after the season.
These days, the league would have stepped in and taken care of the
players. But back then, the league was living from week to week, just
as Walter was.

They called it the National Basketball Association, but it was
anything but national. There was no franchise west of Minneapolis
or south of Indianapolis. Three of the teams were in the state of
New York. One of them, the Rochester Royals, was in the Western
Division and that was geographically accurate. Rochester was still
farther west than the teams in the Eastern Division.

The NBA had progressed from the days when pro basketball
was called a "dance-hall sport"—but not by much. Franchises came
and went with the wind. In 1950, there were seventeen NBA teams.
The next year, there were eleven. By the time I began broadcasting
the Celtics, only three of the cities in the league—Boston, New
York, and Philadelphia—had been there since the NBA began in

1946. And half of the cities that were in the league in 1951 don't have teams now.

To tell the truth, the NBA didn't have the most marketable product in the world back in the early fifties. Pro basketball was still in the Middle Ages because nothing forced the team with the ball to shoot. So if one team was ahead late in the game, they would stall, dribbling and passing and dribbling again. A guy like Bob Cousy, who was a master ball handler, could eat up five minutes all by himself.

That was the difference between the college and professional games. College kids weren't skilled enough to hold on to the ball for five minutes. The pros were. So it got to be a horror show to watch an NBA game as the clock was winding down. It would take half an hour to play the last three minutes.

Games turned into wrestling matches. The team that was ahead would hold the ball. The team that was behind would deliberately foul. And they wouldn't just slap guys, they'd wrestle them down to the court. So a lot of free-for-alls broke out.

"They can't go on like this," I once told Joe Costanza, my statistician, as we were broadcasting yet another stall-and-foul derby. "Nobody is going to watch this stuff. It'll be the end of the league."

Well, a few years later Danny Biasone, who owned the Syracuse Nats, came up with the twenty-four-second clock and it revolutionized the game. If you didn't shoot within twenty-four seconds, the other team got the ball. Now you had to get the ball upcourt, make a play, and take a shot. In a forty-eight-minute game, that meant at least a hundred and twenty shots. That meant more action, more scoring, more interest.

But the shot clock was still several years away when I was in Boston—and so was solvency. By and large, the NBA owners didn't have deep pockets—at least not deep enough to withstand a couple of seasons worth of empty seats. Some of them were basketball men who were in it because they loved the game. Walter Brown wasn't one of them.

He was a hockey guy in a hockey town and he owned a building—the Boston Garden—which had been built for hockey. So it was ironic that Brown ended up with the greatest basketball team in the world. Walter knew almost nothing about basketball, and until Auerbach arrived, what he didn't know had almost ruined him.

In four years, Brown had lost half a million dollars on the Celtics. He'd mortgaged his house and sold most of his Ice Capades stock to keep the club afloat. But the Celtics were still in last place, drawing only a few thousand diehards a night.

It might sound crazy now, but the Celtics lived from week to week then, like some little storefront business during the Depression. They operated out of a tiny office in the Garden mezzanine, which was up above the Boston & Maine Railroad Station on Causeway Street. You could only find it if you weren't looking for it. There was an old metal-and-glass door, covered by some green drapes. Above the handle was a painted leprechaun spinning a basketball—the team logo.

The Celtics probably could have done without an office entirely because Auerbach did most everything himself. He wasn't just the coach. He was general manager, road secretary, head scout, promotions director. He handled everything from contracts to meal money, which was five dollars a day back then.

He watched every dime—if you overtipped a cabbie, you heard about it from Auerbach. One time, Brown gave Auerbach hell for taking two men on the road and not playing them. "What am I paying ten men for," Brown said, "if you're going to lose with eight?"

Keeping the franchise alive was just one challenge. The other one was getting anybody in Boston to care. Crazy as it sounds now, before Auerbach arrived, people there thought that the Celtics couldn't beat Holy Cross, which was the best local college team.

Holy Cross was a small Catholic school on a hill in Worcester, about fifty miles west of Boston, but they'd won the NCAA title in 1947. Their star was Cousy, who was a wizard with a basketball. The sportswriters dubbed them the Fancy Pants A.C., and some of them were convinced they could beat the Celtics.

Auerbach thought the very idea was insane, but he finally concluded that the only way to show people was to actually put his pros on the floor against those college varsities. Of course, the Celtics ran them off the court. Seeing was believing.

So Auerbach barnstormed with his club whenever he could.

They played exhibitions all over New England, doing one-night stands. They went by car, and everybody tried to duck out of riding with Auerbach because he was a wild man. He'd drive eighty or ninety miles an hour around curves. Cousy actually had it written into his contract that he didn't have to ride with Auerbach in an automobile. I don't think there's ever been a clause quite like it in NBA history.

Red was always on the move, giving clinics, speaking—anything to give the game exposure. One reason why the Celtics have always been terrific about doing all sorts of civic and charitable stuff is because they'd had to do it to survive.

Any publicity was good. That's why Auerbach wanted to do the home games by radio, even though the Celtics were playing in front of ten thousand empty seats at the Garden. We even did some road games, even though Brown didn't have an extra nickel to send along a broadcaster. We just re-created them with a Western Union ticker.

Now, I'd done baseball that way, but baseball is different. You've got natural breaks between every pitch and you can fill in with anec-dotes and stats and trivia. You can't do that in basketball.

In baseball, the pace is leisurely enough that the telegrapher could tap out every pitch—S1, B1. You couldn't tap out every pass in a basketball game. Things move too quickly. Our telegrapher tried to do it for a while, but it got crazy.

"Tell him just to give me the scoring," I told the Western Union people. "*Jones hook shot. Brown set shot. Smith rebound.* I'll make up all the rest."

Now, I also had a picture of the basketball court in front of me to help me frame the action. And we put some crowd noise in. I did a real bullshit job on it. It had to be terrible to listen to, but if you were a rabid Celtics fan, you at least had some semblance of a game.

Looking back, it seems ludicrous to do basketball games that way, but I was anxious to do anything to get basketball on the air. Getting the games on television, though, would be even better. So I went to Channel Seven, which was the flagship of the Yankee Net-work in New England, and their general manager agreed to do eight home games.

Then Auerbach and I sat down with Brown and tried to talk him into it. It was a hard sell. Walter was very dubious about television, just like the baseball owners had been in the late forties.

"We're not drawing anything now," he told us. "If people can see the games for free on TV, they won't want to come at all."

"I disagree," I told Brown. "What this game needs is exposure. If fans can see it, it will stir up interest and you'll actually sell more tickets, not fewer. And I can help educate the fans at halftime. I can diagram simple plays on the blackboard, show how the fast break works. I can show them what a good team is trying to do out there. The more the fans know about the game, the more they'll want to watch one."

Auerbach was sitting there, nodding his head. "That's right, Walter. We've got to educate these people."

Brown was far from sold, but he finally agreed. "All right, you two guys," he said. "You're gonna kill me, though."

Turned out our first televised game was on a Sunday afternoon against the New York Knickerbockers, probably the Celtics' biggest rivals. And there weren't more than three thousand people in the stands.

At halftime, I suddenly felt an arm go around my neck. It was Walter, and he was choking me.

"You're ruining me," he shouted. "You're ruining me. Look at this crowd here today."

"Walter," I pleaded with him. "We're on the air here."

"I'm going to kill you when this thing is over," he vowed. "You cost me my ball club. I never should have listened to you and Auerbach. I'm gonna go broke."

I couldn't believe it. *This guy is a madman*, I thought.

We finally got him outside the booth, but Walter was beside himself. "I'll see you after the game, Gowdy," he shouted. "You're fired. I never want to see you again around a basketball."

It ended up being a fabulous game. Cousy went crazy, Bill Sharman couldn't miss, and Ed Macauley was deadly from the outside. It was a great showcase for the Celtics and for the pro game. Afterward, I found Walter downstairs and pulled him aside.

"Can I talk a little sense to you?" I wanted to know. "Have you cooled down?"

"Yeah," Brown said. "I'm sorry I grabbed you in the booth. I shouldn't have done that and I apologize."

"Walter, believe me, this is what we need," I told him. "Besides the three thousand people here today, thousands more saw this game around New England on the Yankee Network. They had to be impressed by what they saw. I'll bet you next Sunday there'll be a much bigger crowd."

"Well, there better be," Brown grumbled. "Or it's going to be your fault and you'll be out of here."

The next Sunday, the Celtics nearly sold out the Garden. Almost twelve thousand people showed up and Walter couldn't believe it.

He came up to the booth again and put his arms—both of them this time—around me. "This is great," he said. "You were right."

One thing about Walter, he'd always admit when he was wrong. He was an emotional guy who did and said everything from his heart. When the Celtics were playing badly, Brown would be in the corridor afterward, cussing them out, calling them chokers and saying that he shouldn't be paying them anything. Then, before the next game, he'd come in to apologize.

Auerbach understood how Walter was, and he realized that Brown's whole life—not to mention his nest egg—was tied up in these guys. But Red made it clear to Brown that Walter couldn't be getting in his way, that he couldn't be undermining Auerbach's authority.

"Walter, you don't know anything about basketball," Red would tell him. "Let me run this thing."

"Yeah, you're right," Brown would admit.

Red had demanded complete authority when he took the job and Brown had agreed. Even if Walter hadn't, he couldn't have afforded to hire separate people for those positions, anyway. Auerbach had to do them all. So whether or not his players respected him as a basketball man, they had to respect the control Red had over them. Because it was total. The players knew that it all stopped with Auerbach.

If you were a Celtic, Auerbach controlled your playing time. He negotiated your salary. He could trade you or cut you. And he wasn't impressed by statistics. Your importance to the club was defined by one man—and he smoked a cigar.

Auerbach always appreciated stars, but he knew that championships were won by the role players, the overlooked guys who did the mundane things that won ball games, the defensive guards and power forwards whose contributions didn't show up on a stat sheet.

Red wanted guys who didn't care who got the glory, who'd work and sweat alongside each other, then go out for a beer later. That's what his Celtics were about. When they were on the road, they went to the same restaurant. When they went to a movie, they went as a group. Black men and white men together.

The Celtics were years ahead of the rest of the NBA in how they dealt with race. Basically, they ignored it—from the day in 1950 that Brown brought the first black player into the league, Chuck Cooper of Duquesne.

"Do you realize Mr. Cooper is a colored boy?" one of the owners asked Brown after Boston had taken him.

"I don't care if he's plaid," Brown replied. "All I know is, this kid can play basketball."

The Celtics were the first team to start five black players and the first to hire a black coach. They never issued press releases about it. That's just the way it was. Where other people saw black and white, Auerbach and the organization saw Celtic green.

That's one reason the club had such great esprit de corps, even in the years when they didn't have two dimes to rub together. Because they respected each other not just as players, but as men. The way the Celtics saw it, you didn't need to draw up a club policy on race. You just roomed a black player with a white player. That was a policy that spoke for itself.

Auerbach never thought things had to be complicated—especially on the court. During all those years they were winning championships, the Celtics had only half a dozen basic plays, with options off each. Everybody in the league knew what they were, but it didn't matter. Auerbach had the players, and the players could execute.

The more involved you made the game, the more things could go wrong. So Auerbach was always working to keep basketball simple. When the State Department wanted somebody to go overseas and explain America's game to people who didn't know whether the ball was blown up or stuffed, they sent Auerbach. He didn't need to know your language to teach you the basics.

Nobody stressed basics more than Red did, starting with conditioning. His teams were always in fantastic shape because Auerbach drove them hard from the first day of training camp. All the players knew they were going to run until their legs buckled. Auerbach made no secret of that. So he assumed you'd show up ready to go. "If you puke," he'd say, "it's your fault."

Then he drilled the plays into them, until the Celtics could run them in their sleep. Any high school kid could understand them. The secret was in the execution.

But when it came to gamesmanship, Auerbach was as complex as a chess master. He was terrific at psychology, whether it came to his own players, the opposition—or the refs. Nobody baited them better than Red did. He figured it might get him one or two calls that he wouldn't get otherwise. He knew just how to beef and bitch and when to get himself tossed out of games.

Red was always looking for the edge, and he'd take it anywhere he could find it. He had every angle figured out. When he wrote his book on basketball, he had a whole section on strategic moves.

> Grabbing or pulling the pants or shirt of the opponent can be very aggravating. I do not condone this at all. Merely mention it as it might occur.
> Jockeying from the bench can be very annoying.
> When your opponent makes a good play don't congratulate him, merely mention that he was lucky.
> Use a complicated scoreboard and time clock.
> The location and condition of dressing rooms can affect a team's play.
> Wait until the other team has started warming up and then request their basket. This request must be honored away from home.

It was amazing how quickly Auerbach turned the Celtics around—at least on the court. They went from last place to the playoffs in one season. Of course, that guy named Cousy didn't hurt.

Funny thing was, Auerbach hadn't wanted him. Cousy had been an incredible ball handler at Holy Cross, but Auerbach hadn't been impressed. The man he wanted was Charlie Share, a seven-footer from Bowling Green. The Celtics needed a big man more than they needed a guard. Cousy himself told me later that he didn't mind the Celtics passing him over. If he was Auerbach, he said, he would have done the same thing.

But the Boston sportswriters, who thought Cousy was a god, had demanded an explanation from Auerbach as soon as he arrived in town.

"Walter, am I supposed to win?" Auerbach asked Brown, his new boss. "Or am I supposed to worry about some local yokel and please these guys?"

"Just win, Red," Brown said.

Turned out that the Celtics got Cousy later that year, completely by accident. The Chicago Stags, who'd gotten him in a trade with Tri-Cities, went out of business. When three of the clubs disagreed about who should inherit Chicago's best players, the league dumped their names in a hat. When Boston's turn came, the only one left was Cousy's. He became the greatest playmaker the NBA ever saw.

It was complete serendipity, the way Cousy ended up a Celtic. He hadn't wanted to play for Tri-Cities—"Where's Tri-Cities?" Cousy asked when he was drafted by them. And he hadn't wanted to play for the sixty-five hundred dollars that was being offered. He didn't think the NBA was that big a thing to begin with, and he was right.

Cousy figured he could have made five thousand a year just barnstorming with his own team. In fact, he did play half a dozen games with the Harlem Globetrotters. And Cousy also had some business opportunities in Worcester, where he was a household name. So he'd held out for ten thousand. But he settled for ninety-five hundred—just to play in Boston.

Well, Auerbach realized right away that this was no local yokel. Cousy was an absolute magician with a basketball. I covered him for fun in practice a few times, and he had the best peripheral vision of anyone I've ever seen. The man had eyes on the side of his head.

"I can sit in a chair, look straight ahead, and see most of the wall behind me," Cousy admitted. "Not with full clarity, perhaps, but well enough so that I can tell what color it is. And that's all you have to catch on a basketball floor—the color of the jersey."

There wasn't a better middle man in basketball on the fast break than Cousy. If you were open, you'd get the ball, right where you wanted it.

Cousy led the league in alertness—even when he wasn't awake.

Frank Ramsey, who used to room with Cousy on the road, told me how he once came out of a sound sleep to see Cousy sitting on the edge of his bed with a mean look, staring at him. Ramsey was scared, but Cousy suddenly sank back down and went to sleep again.

"Gee, I was a little frightened last night when you woke up," Ramsey told Cousy the next morning.

Cousy was puzzled. "I never woke up," he said. "What are you talking about?"

"Yes, you did," Ramsey told him. "You were staring at me."

The next year, Auerbach came up with Sharman, who was to shooting what Cousy was to passing. This time it wasn't luck, it was shrewdness. Sharman was a minor-league baseball player in the Brooklyn system. In fact, as a late-season call-up, he'd been in the Dodger dugout when Bobby Thomson hit the home run to win the 1951 pennant playoff.

He'd played for the Washington Caps, and the Pistons held his rights. But Sharman clearly preferred baseball. So Auerbach got him as a "player-to-be-named-later" from a previous trade—then convinced him to give up baseball.

Sharman could have played for the Dodgers, but he was a Hall of Famer for the Celtics. There wasn't a surer two points in the league than Sharman's jumper. His teammates would set picks for him fifteen or twenty feet out and Sharman would shoot a beautiful one-hander with soft backspin on the ball. "When Bill let the ball go, we'd all turn around and head back upcourt," Ramsey once told me. "Because we knew it was good."

All of a sudden, the Celtics had the best backcourt in the league. They also had a great shooting forward in Macauley, whom they'd gotten in a lottery when a couple of NBA clubs went under. But they still couldn't get over the hump. They still couldn't survive more than a round or two in the playoffs. They needed the great rebounder, the guy who could get the ball off the boards and set things in motion. They finally got one in Bill Russell.

Russell was a tall, skinny kid from San Francisco who did something no center ever had—controlled a game on defense. And the way the Celtics got him was typical Auerbach—a little inside information, a little shrewdness, a little bluff, a little luck.

Russell led the University of San Francisco to a record fifty-five victories in a row and back-to-back NCAA championships in 1955 and 1956. But Auerbach had already heard about him when Russell was a sophomore. Bill Reinhart, Red's old coach at George Washington, had tipped him off.

So Auerbach checked Russell out with a few of his old friends and former players—he wanted to know about character and toughness—and decided he wanted him. The only question was getting him.

Boston was only drafting third in 1956, behind Rochester and St. Louis. So the Celtics had to find a way to swap places with one club and hope that the other one didn't grab Russell.

Now, Macauley came from St. Louis and was eager to get back there because his year-old son had gotten spinal meningitis. So Auerbach arranged a deal with the Hawks, throwing in Cliff Hagan, whose rights Boston held and who was just coming out of the service.

The Hawks were delighted. They got two quality players, and they probably wouldn't have taken Russell anyway. It wasn't really a time for black athletes to be comfortable in St. Louis, which was still something of a Jim Crow town then.

So the Celtics moved up a place in the draft order. Then Rochester decided against taking Russell, and Auerbach was home free. The Royals were the worst team in the league and hurting for money. Word was that the Harlem Globetrotters were offering Russell twenty-five thousand dollars to play for them, and Rochester couldn't afford to match that.

Besides, Russell would be playing for the U.S. team in the Olympics, which that year were held in December because they were in Australia. The Royals couldn't wait that long for their top draft choice to report. So they passed on Russell and took Sihugo Green instead.

Well, the first time Auerbach saw Russell play, in an exhibition game with a college all-star team before the Olympics, Russell looked awful. "God, I've traded Ed Macauley and Cliff Hagan for this guy," Auerbach moaned, holding his head in his hands.

Turned out that Russell was well worth waiting for. I broadcast the first game he ever played for the Celtics on the NBA Game of the Week and I could tell by halftime that he was something special.

"This guy is going to make the Celtics the world champs," I told Costanza. I may not have called all that many right in my time, but I nailed that one right on the head.

Russell wasn't an intimidating physical specimen the way Wilt Chamberlain was. He was angular, with long spidery arms and huge hands. An eagle with a beard, one opponent called him. But Russell showed how a big, agile, determined man could turn defensive skills into an offensive weapon.

He'd intimidate guys he wasn't even covering, because you never knew when Russell would appear out of nowhere and get that big hand between the ball and the basket. And he wouldn't block shots out of bounds—he'd block them *to* somebody, keeping the ball in the court so his teammates could recover it.

Russell was a superb rebounder, too, a master of timing and touch. He'd get the fast break moving in a split second and the Celtics would be off downcourt before anybody was back. He was the missing piece Auerbach needed, the complementary gear to Cousy and Sharman.

Well, the Celtics beat the Hawks that year for their first title and won ten of the next twelve. And Russell was the thread that ran through all of them. If the Hawks had gotten Russell, they would have won all those championships. But that's how Auerbach did it—by finding ways to get the right guy before other people did.

He got Jo Jo White in 1969 because White was military draft bait and other clubs were afraid to touch him. Auerbach drafted White instead—and got him into a Marine reserve unit.

Red took Larry Bird as a junior in 1978. He was willing to wait a year for his payoff; other teams weren't. Two years later, Auerbach fixed the Celtics for another decade just by swapping draft choices with the Golden State Warriors. The Warriors ended up with Joe Barry Carroll. The Celtics got Robert Parish and Kevin McHale to go along with Bird up front. They won the title the very next season—then won a couple more.

Auerbach was remarkable at salvaging other teams' castoffs. He picked up Don Nelson after the Lakers had cut him loose. Nelson ended up beating the Lakers for the title with a jump shot and played eleven years in Boston. Auerbach was terrific at getting guys from obscure schools, too. Sam Jones went to tiny North Carolina

College. He played twelve years in Boston and won ten championship rings.

Yet Auerbach had no paid scouts. He relied on his former players, college coaches he knew well, and friends whose basketball judgment he trusted. Before I left for the NCAA Final Four at Louisville in 1962, Auerbach called me.

"Take a look and let me know if there's anybody you like," he said. Well, after the tournament was done, I called Auerbach with a hot tip.

"This guy Havlicek from Ohio State," I told him. "Red, it's like he's got a motor up his ass. He's always moving."

"Ahh, c'mon," Auerbach said. "We *know* about him. Gimme a sleeper."

Turned out that the Celtics got Havlicek in the last pick of the first round. He was a Hall of Famer, yet eight clubs passed him by. That's what Auerbach had to do, because in those days, as champions the Celtics were always picking last in the draft. They never had a chance at the Oscar Robertsons or the Kareem Abdul-Jabbars or the Wilt Chamberlains. They got the sleepers, the guys from winning programs who were overlooked—and made them into champions.

Auerbach managed to pull off the toughest thing in sports—he kept a dynasty rolling. Continuity, keeping the core of the squad together, was a big part of it. That's why Auerbach never believed in trading stars. If he gave up a Macauley, he got a Russell. So the heart of the Celtics' championship teams stayed together—but Auerbach was always grooming replacements on the bench.

Once, after a game in Detroit, Auerbach asked me to go to a Chinese restaurant with him for chicken wings. Before the food came, he was just sitting there, rubbing his head and moaning.

"What's the matter with you?" I asked him. "You're going to win this division by ten games."

"Ahh, these Jones boys. They're driving me crazy. They want more playing time."

"You know, I feel really sorry for you," I told him. "Cousy and Sharman are one of the greatest backcourt pairs of all time, and you've got two guys sitting on your bench who could probably step in and be the next to the best. You've got the four best guards in the NBA on one team and you're sitting here groaning?"

"You're right," Red grunted. "Let's eat."

After a while, getting the players wasn't the challenge anymore. Motivating them was. And I don't think anyone was ever better at figuring out what makes human beings tick than Auerbach was.

He wasn't a trained psychologist, but Red had a knack for knowing where a player's button was and how to push it. He was at his best with Russell.

One day during Russell's rookie year, when the Celtics were playing a big game at St. Louis, I walked into the coffee shop of the Chase Hotel. Auerbach and Bob Cousy were having breakfast and they invited me to sit with them.

"Listen, you're the captain," Auerbach was telling Cousy. "I want you to get on this guy. I'm getting sick of this stuff. We have a shot at the title this year—but this guy has got to get out there and play."

"Okay, I'll get on him," Cousy agreed. "But I don't know whether it'll do any good or not."

"What's the problem?" I asked Auerbach.

"Ahh, that Russell, f'crissake. Every time I look up, he's got a muscle pull. He's always moaning about injuries. I'm getting tired of it."

I was stunned to hear Auerbach talking that way about the guy who was his ticket to the championship.

"Do you know what you *have* here?" I asked him.

"Sure I know," Auerbach said. "But that doesn't mean he can get away with not playing with injuries."

Russell was funny that way when he first started playing. Maybe he'd never been hurt much in college, but relatively minor injuries seemed to bother him more than you'd expect.

Once, he had a tooth knocked out in a game. Now, most of the guys on the Celtics had lost a few teeth, especially under the boards. But Russell came over to the bench like a little kid with his tooth in his fist and held it out.

"Aww, you lost your baby tooth, Bill," said Jack Nichols, who'd been going to dental school on the side.

If Russell had been looking for sympathy, he never got it. Not from those guys, and certainly not from Auerbach.

When we got to Kiel Auditorium, Auerbach went to the back of the Boston dressing room, where Russell was lying on the training table. He took off his coat, jammed a cigar in his mouth, and turned around.

"Now what the hell's the matter with you?"

Russell said something about a tight hamstring.

Well, Auerbach tore into him and gave him one of the worst lacings I've ever heard a coach give a player. He crawled all over Russell, really raked him.

"Get off that table and get suited up and get out there and play," Auerbach ordered. "We're paying you damn good money and we're expecting you to perform."

I thought Russell would get up and slug Auerbach, but he didn't say a word. He just took it. Then he went out and had a great game.

"Hey, you took a big chance," I told Auerbach. He shook his head.

"If the other players know I let someone get away with something, they'll completely lose their respect for me," he told me. "They may not like me, but I know one thing. They have respect for me."

Russell was a proud man, so Auerbach aimed at his pride. Cousy was a perfectionist. Tom Heinsohn was brash, Tom Sanders quiet. Auerbach tailored his approach to the man.

He was at his best with Russell. Now, Russell might have been a bit of a hypochondriac, but nobody in the game gave more of himself than Russell did when he was on the floor. So when he loafed in practice occasionally, Auerbach let it slide. He wasn't worried about having one set of rules for Russell and another for the rest of the team. Because Auerbach knew that without Russell, there would be no championship. Russell was playing at least forty-five minutes a night, going all out. It didn't make sense for him to wear himself out on the practice floor.

Before the big games—especially the hand-to-hand battles with Chamberlain—Russell would literally psych himself sick. He'd go into the bathroom before the Celts came out for warmups and vomit into the toilet. That was a good sign, his teammates came to realize. It meant that Russell was ready.

So nobody minded that Russell might sit out the last half of practice. The other guys wanted him to conserve himself for games, because they needed his defense so badly. So Russell would referee the team scrimmages, the big-man team against the little-man team. The little men usually tore the big men up. They'd sprint up the court for layups, then put on a full-court press.

Russell did his best to even things up, though. He never called anything on the big-man team. "No foul, no foul," he'd cackle. "Big men don't foul." Russell had his own rules, and that was fine by Auerbach—as long as he gave his all when it counted.

Auerbach had a natural sense about when he should climb all over the Celtics and when he should back off. Red being Red, he usually went against the grain. When the Celtics lost, he usually left them alone. His best tirades came after victories, when he sensed his players might be taking things for granted.

The fans might assume that championship rings arrived every spring, but Auerbach never did. If you were a Celtic, the next season started as soon as you washed the victory champagne out of your hair. Auerbach made sure of that.

He knew that if he let his players get fat and happy over the summer, they'd be ripe for a fall. In those days, when there were only nine teams in the league, everybody had good talent. Almost every year, the Celtics were going seven games with somebody in the playoffs.

And the longer they stayed on top, the more people hungered to knock them off. People may admire dynasties, but they root against them. So the Celtics were anything but popular in those days—and Auerbach had a lot to do with that. He might not have been a gracious loser, but he was an infuriating winner.

Every night, when the clock was ticking down and the Celtics had piled up an insurmountable lead, Auerbach would reach into his jacket pocket, pull out a huge cigar, and light it. Then he'd sit back, like a man who'd just won a million dollars in the lottery, and blow smoke. I mean, he really savored that cigar.

There wasn't a rival coach, player, or fan who wouldn't have

loved to see that cigar explode in Auerbach's face. Red knew that—
and he wanted to make sure his players knew it, too. Nobody loved
the champions outside of their own city.

Auerbach's biggest fear was that his players would forget how
hard it was to hold on to a championship after you'd won it. So as
soon as training camp started, Auerbach told the Celtics what he
told them every year: "I'm not married to any of you guys."

A Celtic had to win his job all over again every season. There
were no guaranteed contracts. If you came back out of shape, some
rookie would grab your position. Auerbach was always preaching
that nothing was written in stone, but if you look back at those old
Celtic rosters, you'll see amazing consistency and longevity. The
fringe players might change from year to year, but the best six
almost never did.

Auerbach might run them ragged and ream them out if they
weren't playing well, but he was incredibly loyal to his veterans. If
you gave everything you had to the franchise, you got your number
retired and hung from those grimy Garden rafters. You might not
ever make the Hall of Fame, but that didn't count with Auerbach.
The only yardstick was whether you had done what was asked
of you.

After a while, Red didn't have to ask—not specifically, anyway.
His players walked out onto that old parquet floor in the Garden,
looked up at all of the white championship banners and the retired
numbers hanging from the rafters, and knew what was expected. It
was a matter of Celtic pride. You could not let down the guys who'd
played before you—or the guys you were playing with now.

When Frank Ramsey was playing, he'd get up in front of the
blackboard every year just before the playoffs and calculate the winning share right down to the penny. "Gentlemen," Ramsey would
inform his teammates, "you're playing with *my* money now."

That's what kept the Celtics winning all those years—and why
they always rose quickly out of the ashes whenever they hit bottom
for a year or two. It was pride—and the knowledge that Boston still
wasn't a basketball town. When Bobby Orr arrived in the sixties and
the big bad Bruins won a couple of Stanley Cups, hockey fever took
over.

Even when Auerbach's teams were beating the Lakers all those years for the title, the Garden was still only half filled most nights. It wasn't until Larry Bird arrived that the guaranteed sellouts happened. "You know, I never thought I'd say this about a player," Auerbach told me after Bird signed for two million dollars a year. "But he's worth every penny."

And the Celtics now are worth probably five hundred times what they were when I was doing their road games by Western Union ticker. They're listed on the stock exchange now, right along with IBM and Ford. I laugh whenever I think about that.

Once, during his week-to-week years, Walter Brown approached me about buying a piece of the club. I didn't have the money then, but I should have scraped it together. That piece would be worth twenty million or so now, I guess.

I've still got that contract, though. For years I kept it in a safe-deposit box at the bank. Every now and then, I look at it and smile—remembering the Celtics in those days.

8

The Olde Towne Team

I never thought baseball was a provincial religion until I broadcast it in Boston. It took me exactly two days—and two losses to the Yankees in New York—to learn that.

When I got back to Fenway Park, there were telegrams and letters and postcards stacked up on my desk. "You Yankee lover," most of them said. "I don't know why the Red Sox ever hired you."

I was stunned. I was a guy from Wyoming and I'd always gone out of my way to be impartial. Then Helen Robinson, the woman who's run the Fenway switchboard for generations, told me that the owner wanted to see me.

Oh-oh, I thought. *I must have butchered those first two games.*

Well, I walked into Tom Yawkey's office expecting the worst. This chunky fellow with a crewcut stood up. He was wearing an old pair of khaki pants and a sports shirt and he looked as though he didn't have a dime.

"Curt, I hope I haven't bothered you," he apologized, extending his hand. "I just wanted to welcome you to the Red Sox. I've listened to you a lot, and we're thrilled to have you up here with us."

I told him I wasn't sure that the listening audience felt the same way. Not from the mail I'd gotten.

"Don't pay any attention to that," Yawkey advised me. "These are real fans up here. They're going to give you hell for a while, but eventually you'll be accepted. There's no town in America that knows big-league baseball better than Boston does. We've had it here since 1876."

Boston wasn't anywhere near the size of New York, Chicago, St. Louis, or Philadelphia, but it had had two major-league clubs since 1901. The Braves, one of the charter members of the National League, played in a concrete ballpark wedged between Commonwealth Avenue and the Charles River. The Red Sox were across town at the edge of the Fens, the city's swampy district. And both of them drew well.

In 1948, when the Sox were one game away from playing the Braves in a subway Series, their combined attendance topped three million. Not bad, for a city of seven hundred seventy thousand.

Of course, Bostonians never doubted that they deserved two clubs. They called their city the Hub of the Universe with an absolutely straight face. "Why should I go anywhere?" a proper Boston dowager is supposed to have replied when asked why she never traveled. "I'm already here."

There are more than a dozen universities in Boston, world-class museums, a famous symphony orchestra, and a professional team in every major sport. It's a cosmopolitan town—but it's parochial, too. I found that out after I mangled a few place names over the air. I'd called Worcester *Wor-chester* instead of *Wistah*, Gloucester *Glow-chester* instead of *Glostah*, and Haverhill *Hav-er-hill* instead of *Hayvril*.

So I got another barrage of mail, ripping my pronunciation. "How can you broadcast the Red Sox," the letters said, "if you can't even pronounce the names of the towns?"

I don't know how the guy before me ever did it. Jim Britt had broadcast both the Red Sox and Braves games. The owners—Yawkey and Lou Perini—had worked out a deal that neither team would broadcast its road games because it would hurt the other's attendance. So Britt did a hundred fifty-four games a year, saw all sixteen clubs, and never left town. How he managed to convince the fans he was neutral mystified me.

Well, that arrangement went by the boards as soon as Yawkey

realized he could boost his own gate by broadcasting the road games. That's what the Yankees had found out. There was a certain mystique to bringing the games back from Chicago and St. Louis. It made your own club larger than life and fueled interest. So Yawkey told Perini that he wanted to broadcast the Sox both home and away on WHDH.

Perini was very unhappy, of course, and accused Yawkey of breaking a gentleman's agreement. They'd never signed a contract, though, so Yawkey was free to do as he pleased.

By the time I got there in 1951, the Sox were clearly the team of the future. The Braves had sunk to fourth in the standings, and attendance had dropped by more than half a million. The Sox had drawn more than a million three hundred thousand fans in 1950 and finished only four games behind the Yankees. They had a nicer ballpark than the Braves did and a well-heeled owner who didn't mind spending cash. And they had fans who knew good baseball from bad.

"You're not going to kid them," Yawkey warned me. "So don't make any pop flies into line drives. And don't make excuses for the ballplayers. Just give 'em the ball game."

That had been Yawkey's credo ever since he'd bought the Sox in 1933, when they were at rock bottom. The glory days of 1915 through 1918 had vanished after Harry Frazee sold Babe Ruth and practically everybody else to the Yankees for cash. By the time Yawkey stepped in, the Sox had been last for nine of the previous eleven years, attendance had dropped to a hundred and eighty-two thousand, and owner Bob Quinn was three hundred and fifty thousand dollars in debt.

Yawkey had changed all that. He was the adopted son of Bill Yawkey, who'd once owned the Tigers, and had spent his life around ballparks. When he reached thirty and his inheritance kicked in, Yawkey decided to spend it on his fantasy.

He shelled out nearly three million dollars buying the club and renovating Fenway Park and another half million stocking his ball club with expensive stars like Lefty Grove, Jimmie Foxx, and Joe Cronin. Cynics began calling his club the Gold Sox and said that Yawkey should rename them the Millionaires.

But the Red Sox were contenders now and attendance quickly tripled. Their farm system began producing players like Ted

Williams and Bobby Doerr, plus pennant-level pitching. By the time World War II was over, they were just good enough to break your heart.

The Sox made it to the World Series in 1946 for the first time in twenty-eight years—and lost to the Cardinals by one run in the seventh game. They lost the 1948 pennant to the Indians in a playoff. Then they lost the 1949 pennant to the Yankees on the final day.

Red Sox fans can recite a lengthy litany for you by now. Three more World Series—1967, 1975, and 1986—lost in the seventh game. The 1978 playoff game dropped at home to the Yankees. They blame it on everything from Calvinist predestination to what Boston *Globe* columnist Dan Shaughnessy calls the Curse of the Bambino.

Fenway Park opened in 1912—the same week the Titanic went down. Maybe that was an omen. It was a brick playground on the edge of the Fens, just beyond Kenmore Square. From the outside the ballpark looked like one of those old New England shoe factories, but it was folksy and charming inside.

John Updike, who used to attend games during his days at Harvard, called Fenway a "lyric little bandbox." I always thought of it as an intimate nightclub. You were right next to the entertainer, part of the show. You felt as though you could reach out and touch the guy in the on-deck circle.

The ballpark had only thirty-four thousand seats, and many of them had been sold when there was still snow on the ground. Fenway had only one deck to it and the grandstands were pressed right up against the diamond. There wasn't a better place in America to watch a ball game—or a tougher place to play.

If the wind was blowing out, scores ended up 11–9. If it was blowing in, they'd be 2–1. That's why the first thing I did every day when I got to the ballpark was pop out of the dugout and see how the wind was. As the summer wore on, in July and August, it would usually be blowing out. *Oh, boy*, I'd think. *We're going to have some fun today.*

Joe Cronin, who'd played eleven seasons with the Red Sox at Fenway and seven more as a visitor, called it a "pissy" ballpark. He used to complain about it all the time. "Trying to build a club here is almost impossible," he told me. "You build it for here, you lose on the road. You build it for the road, you lose here."

You talk about Jekyll and Hyde. The difference between the Sox at Fenway and the Sox anywhere else was astounding. In 1949, the year they lost the pennant at New York on the final day of the season, Boston was 61-16 at home, 35-42 on the road. The second year I was there, they were 50-27 at Fenway, 26-51 on the road.

The Wall—up in Boston, it's referred to with a capital letter— was the whole reason. It's thirty-seven feet high, topped by a screen that goes up another twenty-three feet. It runs from the left-field foul pole to dead center and it's got a scoreboard at the bottom of it. And it's not as close—three hundred and fifteen feet from the plate—as people think. It's even closer—roughly three hundred and ten feet.

Rising line drives that would go out of most ballparks end up smacking the top of the Wall for doubles—or even singles. Lots of guys who think they can go into second standing up find themselves thrown out.

And fly balls that would be routine outs at most places end up homers at Fenway. Anybody in Boston will swear to you that the Sox would have won the 1978 pennant if the playoff had been at Yankee Stadium instead. The ball that Bucky Dent dumped into the screen would have ended up in Carl Yastrzemski's glove.

That's why Joe McCarthy second-guessed himself in 1948 and ended up losing another pennant in a playoff. Everybody thought he'd start Mel Parnell against the Indians. But Parnell was a southpaw and McCarthy was afraid that with the wind blowing out, the Indians would pound him.

"Sorry, kid, it's not a day for left-handers," McCarthy told Parnell, and gave the ball to Denny Galehouse, a journeyman righty. But the Indians started a lefty named Gene Bearden, jumped all over Galehouse, won 8-3, and took the pennant.

Back then, nobody in Boston was talking about curses or jinxes. Sox fans just thought it was a run of lousy breaks. Casey Stengel agreed. "That man up there had had luck," he told me. "That man" meant Yawkey. Casey never was much for names. "If he had those three pitchers, he'd be winning this thing instead of us."

Those three pitchers were Boo Ferriss, Tex Hughson, and Mickey Harris. When the Sox won the 1946 pennant, Ferris won twenty-five games, Hughson twenty, and Harris seventeen. The next year, they all had sore arms, won only twenty-nine games among them, and were never the same again. Ferriss only pitched one more full season after 1947. Harris never won more than seven games in a season after that, and Hughson won only seven more in his career.

The Red Sox' flaw was always pitching. They never had quite enough of it—and they still don't. They always seemed to be one starter shy, and their bullpen never had quite enough depth to it. That's why the Yankees always beat them. New York had that terrific rotation of Allie Reynolds, Ed Lopat, and Vic Raschi, with Joe Page coming out of the bullpen.

Boston had two great pitchers—Parnell and Ellis Kinder. Now, Parnell was a walking contradiction of that theory that Fenway was a graveyard for left-handers. He actually had a better record at Fenway than he did on the road and pitched a no-hitter there. After ten years of pitching to righties with that Wall behind him, Parnell won a hundred and twenty-three games. In 1949, when the Sox lost the pennant on the last day of the season, he won twenty-five. In 1953, when Boston finished fourth, Parnell still won twenty-one games.

He had a great sinking fastball and a screwball that broke away from righties. They'd try to pull it and they'd hit it to the right side of the infield. When Parnell was on the mound, you knew the infield was going to be busy. He and Bob Lemon of the Indians had the best sinkerballs in the league. It was hard to get the ball up in the air off him. That's why he survived at Fenway, because he was able to make guys hit the ball on the ground.

Mel knew he didn't have much margin for error, though, and if the umpire wasn't giving him the close ones, he'd get upset. Parnell would hold his arms out to the umpire, like he was pleading. So one of the Boston columnists nicknamed him Mel the Pleader.

Now, Kinder was a character. You could scratch a match on him, he was in such great shape. He was a pretty good drinker, too, but it never seemed to affect him on the mound. The Sox had picked up Kinder from the St. Louis Browns and he won twenty-three games in 1949. By the time I got there, he was a reliever—as good as anybody who ever lived.

He still had a good fastball, great control, and a nasty change-up. But Kinder had the guts and street smarts of a reliever, too. He'd come in with the bases loaded or a man on third and nobody out, and nobody would score. In 1951, he was 11-2 out of the bullpen, with fourteen saves.

We were on a train out of Chicago one night, headed for Cleveland and a doubleheader the next day. I was with Kinder and some of the other guys in the club car, sitting around talking and playing cards. Kinder was really putting the booze away.

"Ellie, c'mon, you better get to bed," Lou Boudreau, the manager, told him.

"Nahh, the hell with it," Kinder replied. "I'm gonna stay here."

They tell me he sat up and drank until about three in the morning, until he got run out of there.

The next morning, I saw Kinder being taken off the train in a wheelchair. His head looked like a rubber doll's head. It was just weaving around, completely out of control. I don't even think he was conscious.

"Well, we won't be seeing him today," I told Bob Murphy, who was doing the broadcasts with me. "We may not see him again for another week."

The heat that day was brutal. We were overwhelmed by it as soon as we stepped onto the station platform in Cleveland. "It's going to be a hundred degrees today," I told Murphy. "We're really going to suffer out there."

That afternoon, when the Indians start rallying, we saw somebody warming up in the Boston bullpen. I almost dropped my teeth when I realized it was Kinder coming in.

"This is incredible," I said to Murphy. "I wouldn't give you a dime that he can even walk to the mound, let alone pitch."

Well, Kinder pitched three or four innings of relief, didn't allow a run, and the Red Sox hung on to win.

"This is the miracle of all miracles," I told Murphy in between games. "You'll never see anything like this again."

Then Kinder came in and saved the second game, too. He was

like Babe Ruth that way—drink all night, take a shower, and still get it done.

If they'd had one more pitcher like Kinder or Parnell, the Red Sox would have won three or four pennants during those years. Still, they were far from a bad ball club. From 1946 through 1950 they won four hundred and seventy-three games, more than anybody else in baseball. If they'd been in the National League, they would have won three pennants in those years. It was just a matter of bad timing. The Yankees happened to be having their renaissance in the late forties and early fifties.

Even though the Yankees had just swept the Phillies in the World Series, Sox fans still thought they had a chance at the pennant in 1951. The core of the lineup was back—Bobby Doerr, Junior Stephens, and Johnny Pesky in the infield, Williams and Dom DiMaggio in the outfield, and Parnell and Kinder on the mound. The Sox had stayed in the race until the last week of September and finished only four games out.

The fans didn't know it yet, but the club's best days had already passed. DiMaggio, Doerr, and Stephens were near the end of their careers and the pitching was thin. And Williams was coming off a nightmarish injury from the 1950 All-Star Game at Comiskey Park.

He'd chased down a long drive by Ralph Kiner and crashed into the wall at full speed, breaking his elbow in seven places. Williams came back in September and ended up hitting .317. But he was never quite the same player again.

"Did you see me play in 1949?" Williams asked me once.

"Yeah, when I was broadcasting the Yankees."

"Good," he said. "Then you saw me when I was great."

By any standard, Williams was still great in 1951—great enough for the Yankees to be interested in trading for him. Every year, there were stories in the magazines—WHY I'D TRADE TED WILLIAMS. In 1947, Yawkey had a tempting offer from the Yankees. They were offering Joe DiMaggio for Williams, straight up. But the Yankees backed off when the Sox also asked for a rookie named Berra.

Well, one night I thought Yawkey might do it. He'd invited a bunch of us to his Ritz suite for a party after a game.

"Curt, I want to talk to you a minute," Yawkey told me after we'd had a couple of drinks.

We went into the bathroom and closed the door.

"What would you think of this trade?" Yawkey asked me. "Dan Topping's called me a couple of times this week about it. Williams and another guy to New York for DiMaggio, Bauer, Coleman, and a pitcher. What do you think?"

"I imagine DiMaggio would love it," I said. "Playing seventy-seven games with that wall in left field? And Williams ought to like it, with that short right-field stand in the Stadium."

"Would you make the deal?"

"No, I wouldn't," I said. "Williams is four years younger than DiMaggio. DiMaggio had that heel injury, and he's had a shoulder problem. He's a funny guy, T.A. If he doesn't think he's going to be an effective player, he'll get out of the game. He's got too much pride to sit on the bench."

It turned out that 1951 was DiMaggio's last year. His body was giving out on him and he couldn't play to his own exacting standard anymore. So he quit after the Series. But Williams played another nine years. At age thirty-eight, Williams was still hitting .388 and hitting thirty-eight homers. He was an automatic All-Star until the day he retired. Yet he was still at war with the Boston sportswriters, whom he bitterly called the "knights of the keyboard."

The city still had half a dozen newspapers then—the *Globe*, *Post*, *Herald*, *Traveler*, *Record*, and *American*. Each one sent writers on the road with the Red Sox and all of them were scrambling for a scoop. If five of them said that Williams was a great hitter, the sixth would say that he was lousy. Just to be different.

Usually, that sixth man was Dave Egan, a columnist for the *Record*. Now, the *Record* was a paper you read on the subway—and left there. It was a crime-sex-and-sports tabloid, the paper of the people. And Egan was one of the big reasons you read it.

He could make you laugh, he could make you cry, or he could make you so damned mad you'd throw the paper against the wall. But Egan was never boring.

His nickname was the Colonel and the photo next to his column showed him wearing a Confederate hat, a mustache, and sideburns. Nobody ever explained why. But Egan was anything but gentlemanly. He was a well-educated guy—he'd gone to Harvard—but he had a drinking problem. Many of his columns were pure vitriol—especially the ones about Williams.

He'd been ripping Williams for a dozen years when I got there, most of the time unfairly. To hear Egan tell it, Williams was a prima donna who never delivered in the clutch and who was jealous of his teammates. "Defeat with him starring is preferable to victory when he must stand in the shadow of another," the Colonel wrote.

Egan was so brutal to Williams that the *Record*'s lawyers warned the publisher that Williams might have grounds for a libel suit. But Williams never bothered. "I wouldn't give the bastards the satisfaction," he said. Some writers *were* very unfair to him. Williams lost the 1947 Most Valuable Player award to DiMaggio by one vote because a Boston writer named Mel Webb left him off his ballot completely.

Williams would cuss out writers he thought had been rough on him, but he did have guys he respected, like Joe Cashman of the *Record*, Arthur Sampson of the *Herald*, and Arthur Daley of the *New York Times*. He'd go hunting and fishing with Bud Leavitt, who was sports editor of the Bangor *Daily News* up in Maine. And he was very accommodating to guys from small-town papers or kids from little radio stations.

"Where you from?" Williams might growl.

"Biddeford, Maine," the kid might say.

"Oh, yeah? How big's Biddeford? Pretty town? Well, what do you need?"

That's the way Ted was. He liked the little guy, the common man. He hated big shots and he hated politicians. Thought they were phonies. His people were firemen, cab drivers, bartenders. And he was great to the people who worked in the Red Sox clubhouse. After they won the 1946 pennant, Williams wrote out a check to Johnny Orlando, the clubhouse boy, that equaled the players' Series share.

The Fenway fans might boo him from time to time, but most of them stuck with Williams because he had one thing they admired. He was his own man. The papers would rip him, and he'd tell them all to go screw themselves. The fans liked that. They even liked him after he spit at them.

The Great Expectoration happened in 1956. The Sox were playing the Yankees in extra innings in the rain and Mickey Mantle hit this towering pop-up to shallow left which Williams dropped among the raindrops. Well, the fans hooted him, Williams got so mad he couldn't see straight, and he spat toward the grandstand, which in Fenway is right up against the foul line.

Oh-oh, I thought up in the radio booth. *What do I do now? It's going to be in the papers. I've got to report it.*

"Ladies and gentlemen, Ted Williams has just spit at the stands on the way to the dugout," I said over the air. "Who he was spitting at I don't know, but it's a nasty sight."

Yawkey, who'd always treated Williams like a son, chastised him—"We can't have that"—and fined him five thousand dollars, which was the equivalent of a hundred thousand in today's salaries. Yawkey never did collect it, though.

Now, the next game was Family Night at Fenway, and Williams figured that the fans would crucify him. But the first time Williams came to the plate, they gave him one of the biggest ovations of his career. That's when Williams realized that no matter what the knights of the keyboard wrote about him, the fans were with him.

There was no question they were with Williams in 1951—and they were still with the Sox, even though they probably knew that the Yankees were gradually slipping out of reach.

Even though I'd been broadcasting the Yankees and saw the Red Sox twenty-two times a season, I had no idea how passionate the folks in New England were about them. After I read my first batch of mail following the opening series of 1951, I realized that Cronin had been right. "You're going to be a pretty big man in this town," he had told me when I took the job. "The Red Sox announcer always is."

The Sox had a network that covered most of New England. Everybody from South Boston longshoremen to Vermont dairy farmers to Maine lobstermen tuned in. Everybody knew when the Sox were playing. Even when the Sox were rained out, it was news. The weather tower atop the John Hancock Building, the tallest structure in the city, had a special signal for Fenway postponements—flashing red.

Compared to today, our broadcasts were uncluttered. We had only two sponsors—the Atlantic Refining Company and Narragansett lager beer. "Hi, neighbor," I'd say. "Have a 'Gansett."

If I wanted anything more than batting averages and pitching records, I had to dig them up myself. I had a card on every pitcher, listing the date of every outing, the appearance number, the opponent, innings pitched, runs, hits, walks, strikeouts—the whole thing. So when they brought in a guy from the bullpen, I had everything at my fingertips.

Every morning, I'd get the newspaper and cut out the box scores from every American League game and paste them onto a page in a special notebook. I'd also list where the Red Sox were in the standings—May 17, second place, 22-12, two games out. That way I could trace their progress over a whole month or more.

Boston fans hungered for that kind of information—especially because of the roller-coaster rides the Sox usually treated them to. The Sox might lose eighteen of thirty during one month, drop three places in the standings, then win eighteen of thirty the next month and climb back up.

That's the kind of season it was in 1951. The Red Sox started slowly, then Williams went on a tear, batting .537 at one stretch and the club heated up. In early July, they swept New York at Fenway and moved ahead of them in the standings.

As the Yankees filed silently through the Boston clubhouse on the way to the parking lot, Orlando began razzing Joe DiMaggio.

"Hey, looks like we'll be in the World Series *this* year, baby."

"Long ways to go, John," DiMaggio told him solemnly. "Don't count your money. Long ways to go."

By now, pennant fever was gripping the Hub. And the man of the moment wasn't Williams, but Clyde Vollmer, a journeyman outfielder who'd only hit twenty-three homers in six previous seasons.

Well, in July alone he rapped thirteen, drove in forty runs, and put together a sixteen-game hitting streak. Nobody in club history had ever had a month like that. Vollmer was Dutch the Clutch now, and the Sox were riding high with him.

At the All-Star break, the Sox trailed the White Sox by only a game and were heading for Chicago for a showdown for first place. Well, they swept a doubleheader the first day, with the second game going seventeen innings, the longest night game in league history. We didn't get back to the hotel until three in the morning.

It seemed everybody in New England lost sleep listening to that doubleheader. Edison reported that its customers used the highest number of kilowatt hours in history for that time of the morning. And a Northeast Airlines pilot, flying down from Maine, thought that war had been declared. When he looked down from his cockpit at one o'clock in the morning, he saw a blanket of white lights for miles. Somebody in almost every house was awake, listening.

That was the high point of the season. The Sox lost in nineteen innings the next day, eventually dropped to third and never got back in the race. And Dutch the Clutch returned to earth. Three years later, he was out of baseball.

DiMaggio ended up being right. The Yankees won their third straight pennant and took the Series from the Giants. The Sox finished third, eleven games out. And it was the Yankees who thrust in the final dagger, as Allie Reynolds no-hit Boston on the last day of the season, with Williams fouling out to Yogi Berra to end it.

The next year, Williams was gone. The Korean War had heated up, the Americans needed experienced jet pilots, so the Marines called him up in April. Williams got only six games in, and missed all but thirty-seven games of the 1953 season, too.

As it turned out, he almost ended his career for good. While he was flying a recon mission over North Korea, Williams's plane caught fire after being hit and he ended up having to bring it in without landing gear.

Williams had gone willingly, but he was privately furious. He was thirty-three and he'd served for three years in World War II. There was no reason to call him up. Even though he still had the hand-eye coordination and the reflexes, Williams was flying jets that kids in their twenties should have been flying. He thought he'd been taken strictly for political reasons, to help recruiting.

Williams didn't want to plead his own case; it would have made him look unpatriotic. But he felt somebody else should have.

They gave Williams a special going-away ceremony at Fenway before his last game. Nobody knew how long the war would last or whether Ted would ever play again. The mayor and governor showed up, and Williams was given a memory book signed by four hundred thousand fans. As a dramatic farewell, he belted a homer off Dizzy Trout to beat the Tigers. But the next morning, the Colonel ripped him.

"It seems disgraceful to me that a person such as Williams now is to be given the keys to the city," Egan wrote. "We talk about juvenile delinquency and fight against it, and then officially honor a man whom we should officially horsewhip for the vicious influence that he has had on the childhood of America."

Once Williams left, the team fell apart. They ended up in sixth place, nineteen games out. Even after he returned, the Sox didn't finish above fourth place for another four years.

The heart of their great clubs of the late forties—Bobby Doerr, Vern Stephens, Johnny Pesky, Birdie Tebbetts—was gone by 1953. And Dom DiMaggio, who'd been a starting outfielder since before the war, was thirty-six and in his final season.

Dom was the most underrated ballplayer I ever saw. He didn't have the power that his brother Joe did, but he was still a fine hitter and a great fielder with a strong arm. But from the day Dom arrived in the big leagues, people underestimated him.

Maybe it's because he wore glasses before most other people in baseball did. Dom got the nickname "The Little Professor" when he was in the minors and it stuck with him. He did take a scholarly approach to the game. Before games, you'd see Dom in the dugout with Williams, studying the other team's hitters. DiMaggio dressed next to Williams in the Sox clubhouse, too, so he got to hear Ted's thousand-and-one theories about hitting.

"You think I'm full of crap, don't you, Dommie, when I talk about hitting?" Williams asked him one day.

"No," DiMaggio assured him. "You make a lot of sense."

Real baseball people appreciated DiMaggio. Lots of them felt that the Sox would have won that 1946 Series if DiMaggio had been able to finish the seventh game.

He'd just tied it in the eighth with a double off the right-field wall when he pulled a muscle and had to come out. A few minutes later, Harry "The Hat" Walker hit the ball into left center that scored Enos Slaughter from first and won the championship for the Cardinals. Up in Boston, they still stay that if DiMaggio had been able to stay in the game, he would have handled the ball better than Leon Culberson did and Pesky's relay would have nailed Slaughter at the plate.

One day, after DiMaggio had gone three-for-four and made a couple of marvelous catches, Joe McCarthy broke his usual club rule and invited Dom to have a drink with him on the plane. The only problem was, they weren't sitting together. McCarthy was up in the front row, and DiMaggio was back with the players. So Johnny Orlando, the clubhouse boy, brought a paper cup back to DiMaggio.

"How about a drink, Dom?" Orlando offered.

"We're not allowed to take a drink," DiMaggio reminded him.

"Well, the old man's got a bottle of scotch up there," Orlando said, "and he wants to show his appreciation for the great day you had."

So DiMaggio took the cup. Fifteen minutes later, Orlando came back down the aisle.

"The skipper wants you to have another drink with him."

DiMaggio didn't get along nearly as well with Lou Boudreau, who'd taken over as manager in 1952. Dom had developed a spot on his eye and wasn't playing as well as he had, so Boudreau put Tommy Umphlett in center field. That made up DiMaggio's mind for him. "After all the good years I've had," he told me, "I'm not going to be sitting on the bench."

So he retired. That was how the DiMaggios were. They were proud men, and they got out of the game when they sensed themselves starting to go physically. They were baseball's first family. Three of them played in the majors—Vince was an outfielder for ten years for five clubs in the National League. And both Joe and Dom told me that they weren't even the best players in the family. Their oldest brother Tommy was.

Dom told me that when he was a kid growing up in San Francisco, people would point to a spot way, way out on some sandlot field and say, there's where Tom hit one. But he hurt his arm, then he had to help their father make a living fishing, so he never got a shot. Dom was the last of the DiMaggios to wear a uniform. When he retired, Williams was the only guy left from the Sox pre-war teams.

When things were going badly during those seasons, Yawkey would send Cronin on the road trips. "You better go out there and straighten your club out," he'd tell him. "It's not doing so well." That's what Cronin always told me: "When we win, it's his team. When we lose, it's my team."

It was Cronin's team a lot in the mid-fifties. Once, the Sox were having a horrible time, losing eight or nine in a row, and Cronin showed up in Detroit. "It's my team again," he told me. "We're lousy."

One day when we were in Detroit, Cronin phoned my hotel room.

"Curty, come on up. There's someone here I want you to meet."

I walked into his suite and there was an intense-looking old man sitting in a chair. "Curty, I'd like you to meet Ty Cobb."

Cobb was a living legend, of course. He'd played twenty-two years for the Tigers and made the Hall of Fame. He was considered the greatest hitter and the most feared base stealer who ever lived. Now he'd come back for an old-timer's game.

"Mr. Cobb, it's an honor to meet you," I said as we shook hands.

"Ty, show Curty here your hook slide," Cronin told him.

I couldn't believe that Cobb would actually do it. I mean, he was in his sixties and hadn't played since before the Depression. But Cobb set a chair at one end of the room to use as a base, then came running and hit the bare floor with a crash that shook the room.

"Now show him your fadeaway," Cronin urged Cobb.

Here came the old man again, tearing across the room and hitting the floor with a thud.

"See how he fades away, Curty?" Cronin said. "You can't tag him. Ty knew how to use those spikes, too. If you got in his way, he'd rip your shins wide open."

"Naww," Cobb said.

"The hell you wouldn't," Cronin told him.

Now, Cobb had a reputation among ballplayers as the meanest bastard who ever lived. Even his own teammates hated him. Once, when he and some other ballplayers were hunting in Georgia during the off-season, Cobb refused to share a cabin with Babe Ruth because he thought Ruth had black ancestry.

"I've never bedded down with a nigger," Cobb said. "And I'm not going to start now." He was always abusive to Ruth, and nobody knew just why. Cobb would call him "an egg on stilts" and "a beer keg on two straws."

Cobb wasn't an educated man, but he was unbelievably shrewd. He began buying stock in General Motors and Coca-Cola back in the twenties, and by the time I met him he was already a millionaire. But it hadn't done much to mellow him.

Cobb had a violent temper that erupted for no reason at all. You could be having a normal conversation with him, say something you thought was entirely innocent, and he'd explode. Some people said he'd been an angry man ever since a bizarre incident that happened when Cobb was a teenager.

His father, who suspected that Cobb's mother was having an affair, snuck up onto the porch roof outside their bedroom to check on her. Cobb's mother, thinking it was a prowler, shot him dead. Or at least that was her story.

Anyway, Cobb attacked both baseball and life with this incredible fury after that. He made the Hall of Fame—but he made life-long enemies, too.

That night in Detroit, at the old-timer's banquet, Cobb was asked to speak. But he'd no sooner stood up than Doc Cramer, one of the old Tigers, was shouting at him.

"Sit down, you selfish son of a bitch," Cramer yelled. "Nobody wants to hear you."

I was astonished. "Gee, Doc, aren't you being kind of rough on him?"

"Ahh, he's the nastiest son of a bitch who ever played the game," Cramer said.

Well, as soon as Cobb opened his mouth again, somebody else shouted at him. "Sit down, you bastard."

What was Cobb going to do? He sat down.

Old as Cobb was by then, I think the Red Sox could have used him in the mid-fifties. The way they were losing, they could have used anybody who could steal a base.

I'll tell you, it got depressing. The toughest job in broadcasting is doing a losing baseball team, because you're with them every day for six months and because you think your future is tied up with the success of the team.

When the Sox lost, it would kill me. I'd go home and open the door and my wife would look at me and know right away. "The Red Sox got beat today, didn't they?"

The funny thing was, the biggest criticism I got during my fifteen years in Boston was that I didn't root enough for the Sox. Some folks thought they'd win more if I rooted for them, but I always thought people would resent it if I did.

But the fans themselves never stopped rooting. Even when it was clear the team had no chance of catching the Yankees, attendance was still over a million. Of course, after 1952 the Red Sox were the only game in town. I'd just finished broadcasting an exhibition game between the Braves and Sox in Sarasota that spring when I got the word.

"The Braves just announced they're moving to Milwaukee," Cronin told me. "That's great news. We have it to ourselves now."

The news caught everybody by surprise. The club had already printed tickets for home games at Braves Field. But it wasn't really a shock. Attendance had dropped from well over a million in 1947 to two hundred and eighty thousand. Perini, who was not a rich man, couldn't hold on any longer.

I've often wondered, though, what would have happened if he could have kept the team in Boston for another couple of years. What I'd seen of the Braves in that exhibition game had impressed me.

They still had Warren Spahn, the greatest left-hander in baseball history, on the mound. They had a couple of promising players named Eddie Mathews and Lew Burdette and a nineteen-year-old farmhand with the quickest wrists I'd ever seen.

This kid hit a line drive four hundred feet over the center-field wall in Sarasota which was out of there like a rocket. His name was Henry Aaron and he was a second baseman.

The Braves had two more guys who came up in 1953 named Del Crandall and Bill Bruton. I could see that the Sox were going to have some troubles because the Braves were coming on. Five years later, they won the World Series. Mathews ended up in the Hall of Fame and Aaron broke Babe Ruth's career home run record.

If the Braves had done all that in Boston while the Red Sox were slowly sliding toward last place, the Braves might have become the dominant team. And maybe the Red Sox would have ended up moving instead.

Once the Braves left, though, the Sox owned the city by default. Some people thought that was part of their problem. They had a monopoly—and the most generous owner in the game.

Some people ripped Yawkey for running a country club instead of a ball club. The truth was, he admired his players, felt close to them, and paid them well—much better than most other owners would have. And as long as you were loyal to him and Yawkey thought you were doing your best, you'd have a job.

Cronin was general manager of the Sox for twelve years. They never won a pennant, but Yawkey never fired him. He believed that Cronin knew the game and he was grateful for all those years that Cronin had played and managed for him and for the one pennant he had brought him.

Cronin had a tougher time with his wife, Millie, who was the niece of Clark Griffith, the Senators' owner. She knew baseball inside and out and Cronin couldn't con her. I was there one day when he tried.

It was the day before Christmas the first year I was there and we were at the ballpark. "Let's have a little Christmas drink, Curty," Cronin said.

Well, we had three or four and before long it was four o'clock.

"Geez, I should have been home three or four hours ago," Cronin told me. "Why don't you stop by my house and maybe grease the skids for me a little bit? Tell my wife we had a meeting."

Now, Millie had known Cronin since he was a rookie. When we walked in, she was down in the basement, folding laundry.

"Where've you been?" she asked him.

"Oh, Curt and I had to go over some broadcast materials," he said.

"This is December," Millie informed him.

"Well, we're planning for next season."

Millie just shook her head. "Cronin, it's a good thing you could hit. Because you can't do anything else."

Cronin made the Hall of Fame, had his number retired, and eventually became the president of the American League. One time, though, I was sure Yawkey was going to fire him.

One day when I was at the ballpark, I could hear them arguing inside Yawkey's office. I walked in and there they were, wrestling on the floor. "I think Cronin's going to lose his job," I told my wife when I got home. But the next day, Yawkey and Cronin were back together. No problem.

The Red Sox weren't as much a ball club as they were a family. That's how Yawkey was. He wanted people he felt comfortable with, from All-Star outfielders to the kids who worked around the clubhouse. Yawkey wasn't one of those owners who sat behind a big desk and never ventured downstairs. So his employees weren't in awe of him.

In fact, Johnny Orlando used to portray himself as Yawkey's official emissary on the road. At least in taverns.

"I'm here representing Mr. Thomas Austin Yawkey of the Boston Red Sox," Orlando would announce, placing a twenty-dollar bill on the bar. "He wanted me to say hello to you."

Orlando would act as though he were running the club, deciding who'd stay and who'd be farmed out. He'd go down the line of lockers before we broke camp in Sarasota every spring.

"Out—Louisville," Orlando would declare, ripping a player's name down. "Out—Double A. Yeah, this guy will make it."

Some owners would have fired Orlando for impertinence, but Yawkey liked him. He'd come down to the clubhouse when Orlando was puttering around just to listen to him.

"Aw, hell, T.A.," Orlando would say, mentioning some washed-up veteran. "We've got to get rid of this guy."

But Yawkey rarely did. That was part of his charm and one of his flaws—if you were on his payroll, you were usually on it for life.

Even when they were losing, though, the Sox had individual stars and colorful players. "You guys had the kookiest outfield that ever played the game," I told Williams once. "You, Piersall, and Jensen."

Now, Jimmy Piersall was a fabulous center fielder in a ballpark that was tough to play well. At Fenway, the wall ran well into center, which meant you had to learn how to play caroms. Right where the wall met the bleachers in dead center there was a sharp angle, complicated by a flagpole. And in right center, the bullpens jutted out.

So playing center in Boston was like playing in the middle of a billiards table.

But Piersall had a terrific jump, great range, and a gun for an arm. He played very shallow, defying you to hit the ball over his head. The batter would swing, Piersall would hear that *thok*, and he'd be off. He knew right where the ball was hit and he'd go to it.

Of the five greatest catches I saw in nearly thirty years of broadcasting, Piersall made three of them. The best of them came at Fenway against the Yankees. Mantle was up, batting right-handed with the bases loaded and two out in the ninth.

Well, he drove that ball on a line into the deep crevice where the bullpen meets the bleachers in right center. And Piersall caught the ball over his head and crashed into the wall to end the game. "I've been around the big leagues all my life," Casey Stengel said. "That's the greatest catch I've ever seen."

Piersall played like a man possessed. I've never seen a man with so much pent-up energy. He never stopped talking, never stopped moving. It took people months to realize that he was mentally ill.

Piersall was a competitive guy with an overbearing father and he was obsessed with making it in the big leagues. But once he got there, the pressure busted him apart.

Piersall was used as a shortstop when he first came up, and I remember one day when Lou Boudreau had penciled in somebody else's name. Piersall spat on the lineup card in the dugout and burst into tears.

"I knew Boudreau didn't like me," he told me. "He doesn't want me on the ball club."

"Don't be ridiculous, Jim," I told him. "He has nothing against you."

"Aw, don't give me that. He hates me. They all hate me around here."

Nowadays, Piersall would have been diagnosed early on as a manic-depressive and treated. Back then, people just thought he was a flake.

I'll never forget the night against the Browns in 1952 when Piersall rattled Satchel Paige into giving Boston a victory on a grand-slam homer. The Sox were behind 9–5 when Piersall led off the ninth with a warning to Paige.

"Satchmo, I'm going to bunt on you," Piersall shouted. "And then watch out."

Piersall did bunt, and beat it out when Paige covered too late. Then he began hopping around like an ape, trying to distract Paige.

"Oink, oink, oink," Piersall kept shouting, waving his arms and clapping his hands. Paige would throw over to first, Piersall would scoot back to the bag, then start all over again.

"Oink, oink, oink."

Paige gave up an infield single to Hoot Evers. Now Piersall was on second, cupping his hands and turning up the volume so Paige could hear him.

"Oink, oink, oink," Piersall shouted, mocking Paige's slow and easy windup.

By this time, I'm ashamed to say, I could hardly broadcast I was laughing so hard. Everybody was. Nobody had ever seen antics like this at a ballpark. Certainly Paige hadn't.

Satch was forty-five that year and had seen almost everything. It took a lot to distract him. And while Paige insisted afterward that he hadn't heard a thing, he wasn't the same pitcher after Piersall began oinking him.

He'd come into the game with a string of twenty-six straight scoreless innings. Now he walked George Kell and Piersall was on third. Every time the right-handed Paige wound up, he was looking right at Piersall.

"Oink, oink, oink," Piersall yelled. "You sure look funny on that mound."

Paige walked Billy Goodman to force in Piersall. Ted Lepcio nicked him for a single. Then Sammy White cleared the bases with a shot just inside the left-field foul pole. Red Sox 11, Browns 9.

Piersall's teammates thought it was hilarious. "I've never seen a show like tonight's anywhere," Kell said. "Not even in a circus."

Problem was, it wasn't a show. "Want to know something? I believe that man is plumb crazy," Clint Courtney, the Browns' catcher, said later. A few weeks earlier, Piersall had gotten into a fistfight with Billy Martin, the Yankees' fiery second baseman, before the game had even started.

"Ahh, you stink," Piersall had shouted while Martin was taking infield.

"You better shut up," Martin warned him. But Piersall kept it up.

"Yeah, you stink."

In those days, the visiting team had to go through the Boston dugout to get to their clubhouse. When Martin came in, he and Piersall came to blows in the runway. A few minutes later, Piersall brawled with Maury McDermott, one of his own teammates.

After the oinking incident, the Red Sox realized they had a problem with Piersall, so they sent him down to their Birmingham farm club. One night, when I was with Yawkey and Cronin up in Yawkey's lounge after a game, the phone rang. It was Eddie Glennon, Birmingham's general manager. Yawkey handed the phone to Cronin.

"Yeah," Cronin said. "He did what? All right, Eddie. Okay."

Piersall had cracked up in Alabama. He'd been hanging numbers on the scoreboard while he was in the outfield and had squirted home plate with a water pistol.

"This is a sick boy here," Glennon told Cronin. So the Sox flew him back to Boston and put him in a sanatorium, where he had shock treatments. When Piersall was released, he didn't remember a thing. He was back the next season and was starting in right.

Then a year later, Piersall blew out his right shoulder in a throwing contest with Willie Mays prior to a charity game with the Giants before a sellout crowd at Fenway. Gunning the ball to the plate from right field, Piersall felt a sharp pain in his upper back, just below the shoulder. The next morning, he couldn't move his arm. He played thirteen more seasons, but the arm was never the same.

Jackie Jensen never had the career people hoped he would, either. He was one of the finest athletes in the country. He'd been California's fullback in the Rose Bowl and he could have played in the National Football League. Pappy Waldorf, his old coach at Cal, swore Jensen would have been a star in the pros.

But he'd signed with minor-league Oakland Oaks instead and they'd sold both him and Martin to the Yankees in 1950. The Yankees had plenty of outfielders then—Joe DiMaggio, Mantle, Hank Bauer, Gene Woodling—so they dealt him to Washington.

Well, one day when the Red Sox were playing the Senators, Cronin got up from the table where he, myself, and Yawkey were having lunch before the game. "I'm going to watch the Jensen kid take batting practice."

I went down with him and we watched Jensen whack the ball around the park.

"What a player he'd be here at Fenway," I told Cronin.

"Yeah, but he's not hitting for too high an average," Cronin said.

"But he'd knock this wall down," I said.

All those four-hundred-foot drives that Jensen was hitting were wasted at Griffith Stadium, where it was three hundred and fifty feet down the line in left and four hundred and eight to dead center. At Fenway, they'd be homers.

So Cronin made the trade before the 1954 season, dealing off McDermott and Umphlett. He got razzed for it in Boston. McDermott had won eighteen games the year before and Umphlett had hit .283. But it turned out to be a great trade. Jensen ended up hitting twenty-five homers and knocking in a hundred and seventeen runs that year. He went on to lead the league three times in runs batted in and was Most Valuable Player in 1958.

I've never seen a ballplayer who looked as good as Jackie Jensen did. With his blond hair, blue eyes, and tan, he looked like a California beach boy. He was married to an Olympic diver and drove around in a gold Cadillac convertible. And he had the body of a Greek god. "Look at that sonovabitch," Ted Williams told me years later at the Red Sox' first old-timers game, pointing to Jensen. "He could go out there and play football right now."

His football training had given Jensen great body control and Jack Fadden, the Sox trainer, said he was one of the best there was at playing hurt. Jackie just had one problem. He was afraid to fly. I mean literally terrified. He couldn't sleep for days before we'd go on a road trip. Getting on a plane at all took every ounce of will he had. And the flight itself was agony.

Any time he could drive to the next city, Jensen would. We'd get on the bus to go to Logan Airport and he'd jump into his car and drive all night and the next morning.

There was no way you could do that for seventy-seven games

every year, so Jensen quit after the 1959 season. The National League had already expanded to the West Coast and he knew that the American League soon would, too. Even a gold Cadillac couldn't cover three thousand miles overnight.

Finally, Jensen found this hypnotist out in Lake Tahoe who seemed to be able to help him and he came back to the club for the 1961 season. As long as the hypnotist was with him, Jensen could fly. Then the charm wore off and Jensen was back on the ground—with the hypnotist in the passenger's seat.

Here's how crazy it got. After an afternoon game at Fenway, Jensen dashed out to his car, which the hypnotist already had running. Then they tore off at ninety miles an hour for Albany to catch up with a train which had already left Boston and was headed for Detroit.

Another time, Jensen drove all night, getting to Briggs Stadium just before game time. That's how it went for half the season, until Jensen couldn't stand it anymore. He went back to see his hypnotist, flew from Los Angeles back to Boston, and decided to call it quits.

It wasn't Yawkey's fault. He tried as hard as or harder than other owners and spent more money than anybody. But things kept going wrong for him. A pitcher named Frank Baumann was better than Herb Score in the minors. A real fireballer. The Sox gave him a hundred-thousand-dollar bonus. Then Baumann went into the service, worked out in a cold armory one day, and came up with a bum arm. In six years with the Red Sox, he won a total of thirteen games. When they let him go to the White Sox, he won thirteen the first season he was there.

There was always talk of some hot new pitching prospect coming up through the system. "Wait till this kid gets up here, Joe," guys would tell Cronin. "He's gonna be great."

"Yeah, let him come up here and strike out Mantle with the bases loaded," Cronin would crack. He'd been burned often enough to be cautious.

The Red Sox spent more money on bonus babies than anybody else in baseball—and got the worst results. One year, they signed a terrific prospect named Billy Consolo, who ended up playing in their infield at age nineteen. "I'd trade my whole ball club for that

Consolo," Bucky Harris told me when he was managing the Senators. Well, Consolo ended up as a utility player for five clubs in ten years—including the Senators—and batted .221 lifetime.

Was it all bad scouting? The other clubs had wanted those guys, too. Was it a jinx? Nobody thought so back then. Some people thought that Yawkey spoiled the players. There's no question that players loved to be traded to Boston because Yawkey treated them so well. He really admired big-league ballplayers and he was incredibly loyal.

But Stengel was right—the man had bad luck—and so did some of his best players. The most tragic of them all was Harry Agganis, the kid they called the Golden Greek.

He was the son of immigrants and he'd grown up in Lynn, a working-class city on the North Shore. Agganis was a fabulous athlete. His high school football games were televised for one reason—because Agganis was playing.

He'd been a star quarterback for Boston University when BU still had a big-time program. The Cleveland Browns drafted him in the first round when he was still a junior, envisioning him as Otto Graham's successor. The St. Louis Browns offered Agganis fifty thousand dollars but he signed with the Red Sox for ten thousand less, just to play in Boston.

After only one year in Triple A, Agganis took over as the Sox' first baseman and hit eleven homers—eight of them at Fenway. Except for Williams, no left-handed hitter had done that in twenty-five years. In one home stand alone, Agganis knocked four balls into the right-field bleachers.

"You know, Gehrig would come in here and never hit a home run," Cronin told me. "This kid hits three or four."

Without a doubt, Agganis would have been the All-Star first baseman in the American League for the next ten years. Then, suddenly, he got sick.

"Kid's got a bronchial infection," Fadden told me. Well, after Agganis was released from the hospital, I went over to the ballpark on an off day and saw Agganis coming off the diamond, drenched in sweat.

"What are you doing?" I asked him, stunned.

"Working out."

"Are you crazy?" I said. "You should be taking it easy. You're nuts, Harry."

"No, no," Agganis told me. "I've got to get back in the game."

Well, a few days later I was sitting in the hotel lobby in Kansas City when Fadden came downstairs with Agganis, who was carrying his suitcase.

"We're sending Harry back home," Fadden told me. "He's taken a turn for the worse."

The bronchial infection had developed into pneumonia and then into a severe pulmonary problem, complicated by phlebitis. Then a large blood clot broke loose and killed him. Agganis was only twenty-six. Yawkey was hit hard by that.

It seemed that one disappointment followed another for him. After Williams retired, the Sox had some terrible teams. Seventh, eight, ninth place. They dropped a hundred games in 1965. But Yawkey never lost his enthusiasm. He still turned up at the ballpark every morning, waiting for the pennant that was just around the corner.

9

T.A.

He was worth forty million dollars back when a million was more than a man could spend in a lifetime. But Thomas Austin Yawkey dressed like a pauper, drank bourbon straight out of a tumbler, and hated to be referred to as Mister. "Call me Tom," he told me, the first time we met. But that sounded too familiar to me, so I addressed him as T.A.

He was the last of baseball's "sportsman" owners, wealthy men like Phil Wrigley and Walter Briggs who bought a ballpark and a club and ran both themselves. During the fall and winter, Yawkey lived on his private island off the coast of South Carolina, spending his days hunting and fishing. But when spring came, he lived at Fenway Park, savoring the game he'd played as a boy. Baseball was the passion of his life.

No owner knew more about the game between the white lines than Yawkey did and that's all he cared about. He left the whole business of contracts and television and radio to his general manager. Yawkey never cared much about marketing, either. He hated the gimmicks that guys like Bill Veeck would use to get people into the ballpark.

"I get criticized for not promoting," he'd tell me. "I don't put on shows. I don't have exploding scoreboards. Well, the best promotion you can have is eight skilled players on the field and some good pitchers. Win. Just win. That's the best promotion."

It's a simple game, Yawkey always said. That's how he lived, too. He might have owned thirty-two thousand acres in South Carolina, but Yawkey left them pretty much as God made them. He was an environmentalist before the word was invented. To reach Yawkey's island, you had to cross a drawbridge. I thought that was strange, but Yawkey didn't.

"Curty, the public will ruin anything," he told me. "If I didn't have the drawbridge, they'd come over and trample my fields and shoot my birds and wreck my property. The public doesn't have respect for anything."

Yawkey could have built himself a lavish antebellum mansion on that island, but he lived in a simple lodge. After it burned down, he and his wife, Jean, lived in a trailer. Yawkey just didn't need more than that.

He bummed around his plantation in old clothes, drove a pickup truck, and worked the fields with his hired hands. He'd always talk about how good he felt coming home after a day of hard physical work.

Most people remember Yawkey the way he was in the seventies, a frail man with a crewcut and a deeply lined face, but that was after he'd given up drinking and lost forty or fifty pounds. The man I met in 1951 was sturdy and robust. He'd go off on big-game trips with his cronies, hunting grizzlies in Wyoming and bighorn sheep in Alaska. But as he got older and less fit, Yawkey gave that up.

"Don't wait until you retire to do things," he advised me. "Do it now, while your health is good. If I went hunting in Wyoming now, they'd have to take me off the mountain in a sled. When I was young and vigorous, I could do all that. But I can't do it now. So I won't."

But Yawkey still loved to hunt quail on his plantation—he was a superb wing shot—and enjoyed fishing. That was my entrée with him; we were both outdoorsmen. He'd pack a beautiful big box of quail and send it to my house. And I'd bring him back trout from those cold, clear streams near where I'd grown up in Wyoming.

During the winter, he'd ship me a few bass plugs he'd discovered or some new flies. Once, I was doing the world trout-fishing championships from Argentina for *Wide World of Sports* without a landing net. I'd forgotten to bring one. Well, Yawkey watched the show on television and sent me a telegram—7500 MILES AND NO LANDING NET. WHAT HAPPENED? T.A.Y. He thought that was hilarious.

Yawkey would stay on his island every year until May. He had sinus problems, so he wouldn't come north until the weather had warmed up. But once he reached Boston, he was there until at least September. By there, I mean Fenway.

T.A. could have afforded the finest brownstone mansion on Commonwealth Avenue or a spread in an expensive horse suburb like Dover or Hamilton. But he and his wife lived in a suite at the Ritz-Carlton Hotel across from the Public Gardens. Every day, whether the Red Sox were at home or away, Yawkey came to the ballpark.

Fenway was more than an office for him. It was his social club, his playground, his sanctum. He'd arrive there around ten in the morning and talk with Joe Cronin, his general manager. Then he'd roam around the offices, make calls to the other owners, and have lunch. Nothing fancy, just good old American food. T.A. wasn't much of a gourmet.

If the club was on the road, Yawkey would go down to the field wearing these khaki pants and an old moth-eaten team jacket and take batting practice with the clubhouse boys and some of the kids who hung around the ballpark.

There were a couple of unwritten rules whenever T.A. took bat in hand. No photographers were allowed. And every pitch to Yawkey had to be grooved. He loved banging brand-new balls off that left-field wall, and he'd keep count. "Hey, Curty," he'd tell me, when we talked by phone. "I hit the wall eight times today."

On game days, Yawkey would sit with Cronin in a private box above home plate, next to the broadcast booth. His wife was in the adjacent box, separated by a glass partition. T.A. didn't want to be distracted while he was watching the ball game.

He wouldn't keep score on a card, but Yawkey didn't miss anything that happened on the field. He really knew scientific baseball. I always thought he could have been an owner-manager, the way Connie Mack was in Philadelphia.

Yawkey had never been much as a player—he didn't make the varsity at Yale—but he studied the game like a scholar. He knew infield play well because he'd sat all those years with Cronin and Eddie Collins, both Hall of Famers. He was always talking about outfield placement and pitching strategies. When we were on the road, Yawkey would call me in my room from his office and pepper me with questions.

"What kind of pitch did Williams hit for that home run?" he'd say.

"A fastball," I'd tell him.

"Why didn't you tell us about it?"

Yawkey always wanted to know about the wind, too. It was a big factor at Fenway, since the wall faced the Charles River, and Yawkey always wanted to get a picture in his mind of the day's conditions. He wanted to hear about the wind right at the beginning of the game.

"Don't tell me it's blowing from east to west," Yawkey would tell me. "Tell me it's blowing from first to third or from center-field in."

Yawkey knew everybody in his farm system and every rival player in the league. He'd search his radio dial for other clubs' games and had his own private ticker which kept him up-to-the-minute on every game.

"Who do you think the best player on the Yankees is?" Yawkey would ask me.

"I'd have to say Mantle."

"Well, he's something," Yawkey would say. "But Kubek's the guy I like."

Yawkey had a guy like that on every team. He loved players who could beat you in a lot of ways. T.A. had favorites on his own club, too, like Williams, Bobby Doerr, and Johnny Pesky. He liked guys with a work ethic who tried to improve themselves. But men who took their talent for granted, like Maury McDermott did, drove Yawkey crazy.

"He's got a million-dollar arm," Yawkey said about McDermott. "And a ten-cent head."

And he was a little down on Dom DiMaggio at the end of his career. Dom was the player rep and he was pushing for player rights, which didn't sit too well with Yawkey. T.A. began calling DiMaggio "D.D."—for Dead Dog.

But generally Yawkey treated the Red Sox like surrogate sons. When you saw him in the clubhouse, he'd be talking to some pitcher who hadn't won in a while or a guy who hadn't had a hit in a couple of weeks. "You're doing fine," T.A. would be telling him. "We're all behind you."

Yawkey wasn't in the game for a profit. He didn't see his ballplayers as depreciable assets. If he had to sell off everything he owned, Yawkey once said, the Red Sox would be the last thing he'd part with. They were his heirloom.

After a home game, Yawkey would go back to his office, have a drink, and wait for the traffic to thin out. If an old baseball man like Casey Stengel was in town, T.A. might sit for hours in his lounge, drinking and talking baseball with him. He'd put a bar towel around him like an apron and pour himself a bourbon with a glass of water on the side. If he got excited or upset about something, he'd pound the table.

But only the people he was close to ever saw that Tom Yawkey. He guarded his privacy jealously that way. That's why he valued Johnny Pohlmeyer. Pohlmeyer was Yawkey's man—his chauffeur, bartender, jack-of-all-trades. What Yawkey liked about him was that he kept his mouth shut. "I can talk about the most intimate details of my life in front of Pohlmeyer," Yawkey would say. "And nobody will ever know about it."

Loyalty was extremely important to Yawkey. If you betrayed his loyalty, you were gone. Word got back to him once that his catcher, Birdie Tebbetts, had been criticizing a couple of the Red Sox pitchers on the banquet circuit. You didn't do that. So Yawkey sold Tebbetts to the Indians.

But if you were loyal to the ball club, Yawkey would keep you around forever. T.A. was never one for résumés. He thought he could read character in a guy's face. "He's got a good jaw," Yawkey would say. He liked people who'd look him in the eye, rugged guys who came through. T.A. had to have people around him that he felt comfortable with. If he didn't feel comfortable with you, you didn't last too long.

When I first went to Boston I had a three-year contract with the club, not with the radio station, because the Yankees had insisted on it as a condition of letting me go. But when the contract was up, nobody in the front office had talked to me about the future and I was getting nervous. After the season started, I went to Yawkey and asked him about it.

"Tom, I hate to bother you about this, but I'm working here without a contract," I said.

Yawkey looked puzzled. "What do you need a contract for? You've got a job here for life."

He stuck out his hand. "Here," Yawkey said.

"I know, but you could have a heart attack," I told him. "The club could be sold. . . ."

Yawkey seemed genuinely wounded. "You don't trust me?"

"If there's anybody I trust, it's you," I assured him.

"If you'll feel better, hell . . ."

So I got a contract, but I wouldn't have needed one. In 1957, while I was missing the whole season with back spasms, Yawkey came to the hospital one day to see me and we talked for about an hour. After he left, the doctor came in to see me.

"You know what Mr. Yawkey told me?" he said. "He said not to worry about a thing, even if you're out for the year. He said, 'Tell that boy his job will be waiting for him.'"

Yawkey's word was his bond. That's how he operated with everybody, including his fellow owners. He'd get on the phone with Dan Topping in New York or Briggs in Detroit, make a deal, and send the papers along later.

Yawkey had the most valuable player in baseball in Williams, but they never sat down together to negotiate a contract. Williams would sign it and send it back and let Yawkey fill in a figure. And if the league didn't require it, Williams and Yawkey probably wouldn't have bothered with a contract at all.

If you produced for him, as Williams always did, T.A. would take care of you handsomely. After the 1946 club made it to the

World Series for the first time since World War I, Yawkey called everybody from the leadoff hitter to the trainer into his office individually for a private talk. He thanked every man and gave him a bonus over and above the Series share.

Even if you didn't produce, Yawkey would keep you around as long as he liked and trusted you. That was the biggest problem with the Red Sox, as some people saw it. Yawkey didn't consider it a business.

He hated letting people go, even if they deserved it. "Ever fire anybody, Curt?" he asked me once. "It's the hardest thing in the world to do. Especially when he's a good man."

Yawkey wept when he fired Mike Higgins in 1959. He couldn't bring himself to do it face-to-face, so he sent Bucky Harris, his general manager, down to Baltimore to do it.

Harris ended up taking Higgins to a bar and trying to talk him into quitting. A couple of Boston sportswriters noticed them and paid a barmaid to eavesdrop.

"The little one [Harris] keeps saying 'You gotta quit, you gotta resign,'" she reported. "And the big one [Higgins] keeps telling the little one to go *bleep* himself."

That was how you ran a country club, not a business. But then, Yawkey never said he was running a business. He didn't treat the Red Sox the way he treated his lumber and mining interests. The bottom line wasn't the same for him.

Yawkey figured he spent $10 million on the ball club in the four decades he owned it. Now and then—and especially in the early sixties, when they were finishing in or near the cellar every year—there'd be speculation that he was going to sell the Sox and be done with it.

"They're always hinting around that somebody's going to buy this club," Yawkey would tell me. "Yawkey doesn't care anymore, the papers say. He's lost interest in the game."

But if he ever got offers, Yawkey never mentioned them and I never asked him. That was a no-no. You never talked about the ball club being up for sale.

The only time he ever talked to me about unloading the Red Sox was one night in 1960, when I saw T.A. at his lowest point. The club was mired in seventh place, going through its worst season since the war. Billy Jurges, who was going to be fired as manager before the summer was done, was trying everything he could think of to get something going.

One of his ideas was to take Bobby Thomson, who'd hit the "Shot Heard 'Round the World" in the 1951 playoff between the Giants and Dodgers, and change him from an outfielder into a first baseman.

Well, that night Thomson, still wearing his outfielder's glove, let four throws go through him at first. After the game, I was putting away my briefcase in my office when I heard Yawkey's voice.

"Curty, come on in."

When I entered his office, I could tell he'd been drinking.

"Want to buy a ball club?" he asked me. "I'll sell it for seven million. Seven million will take it."

"Come on, T.A.," I told him. "You'll never sell this."

"I can't believe what I saw here tonight," Yawkey said. "A guy playing first base in the major leagues with a finger glove on. A *finger* glove at first base. I'll sell this club. Take it off my hands."

Yawkey was shaking his head. "This is the major leagues?" he kept saying. "*This* is the major leagues?"

The major leagues Yawkey knew were changing fast. The Dodgers and Giants had already moved to the West Coast, and the Senators were packing for Minnesota. The American League was about to expand to ten teams, with Los Angeles and a new club in Washington. The National League was planning to add new franchises in New York and Houston.

The days of those leisurely train trips to St. Louis were gone. There were more night games, fewer doubleheaders. Yawkey had seen the changes coming, and he thought that most of them were for the better.

He was smart enough to know that baseball needed to expand to prosper and he thought that air travel was better for the players than trains. But the rise of corporate baseball drove him crazy. CBS owning the Yankees?

"Instant geniuses," Yawkey would snort. "They've never been to a ball game, but they know it all."

Yawkey had admired the sole owners like himself and had sympathy for them. Even though the Red Sox and Yankees were the most bitter of rivals, he had been close to Topping because he felt Topping always kept his word.

Topping was a sportsman, too, but his blood was considerably bluer than Yawkey's was. Both of his grandfathers were industrial tycoons—steel on one side, tin on the other—so Dan never needed to worry about where his next million was coming from. He'd lose thousands of dollars in an afternoon playing golf with hustlers like Dizzy Dean, then write out a check and never give it a thought. Topping had the luxury of indulging himself with expensive toys—yachts, planes, and sports teams. His mother bought him a pro football team, and he shared the Yankee ownership with Del Webb.

Topping was a handsome man who traveled in society and was a jet-setter before there were jets. Yet he was a regular guy, very much approachable and down-to-earth. The ballplayers and the press all liked him. Dan was extremely thoughtful and generous, especially to guys who were down on their luck. He'd quietly see to it that a white envelope filled with cash was delivered—anonymously. He wasn't a guy who made much of his charity.

When I was offered the job broadcasting the Red Sox, Dan called me in to see him. "Are you sure you're doing the right thing?" he asked me. "This is New York, not Podunk. You're doing well here. You've got a great future. This is the center of everything in your business."

"That's true," I told him. "But I'll be the second man here behind Mel Allen for a long time. I think I'm better off being the top man somewhere else."

"You're probably right," Topping conceded. "But I think you have to protect yourself. I wouldn't want to see you go up there and work for the radio station or a sponsor. The station could lose the rights or the sponsor could drop the club. Then where would you be? So I'll call Tom Yawkey and tell him that if we agree to let you go, the ball club has to hire you. You have to work for him."

Topping got on the phone and it was done. A gentleman's agreement. That's how Yawkey liked it. He never had much use for lawyers in baseball, and now there were more of them all the time. "I used to call Briggs on the phone," T.A. would tell me. "We'd make a deal, hang up, and that was it. We used to do it on a handshake. Now you need eight lawyers to dot all the *i*'s."

Yawkey was a true baseball capitalist. He spent his money the way he chose and if the club lost or attendance dropped, that was his concern and nobody else's. He was mad at Bill Veeck because Veeck wanted the clubs to share their income the way the National Football League does.

Veeck claimed that St. Louis and some of the smaller towns couldn't get the rights money that the bigger markets like New York and Boston got and that it was making them less competitive. So Veeck wanted to share the wealth. "Goddamn socialist," Yawkey would say about him.

Veeck wasn't a socialist, but he was the greatest promoter the game has ever known. Nobody was better at luring people to a ballpark—even if he had to give the tickets away. That was the cornerstone of his philosophy. "Don't worry about letting people in free," Veeck wrote in *The Hustler's Handbook*. "Seats you have aplenty."

Filling them was an art, and Veeck was always dreaming up new ways. When he owned the Cleveland Indians, he let ladies in for free on Saturdays and handed them orchids and silk stockings. When he owned the Chicago White Sox, Veeck installed a scoreboard that exploded in fireworks after home runs. And when he owned the St. Louis Browns, the worst team in baseball, Veeck put a midget in the batter's box.

His name was Eddie Gaedel and he stood three feet seven inches tall. Veeck found him doing a theatrical act in Chicago, signed him to a contract for a hundred dollars, and put him in a kid's uniform with the number 1/8 on the back. Then he sent him up to bat against the Tigers in 1951, on a day when the commissioner of baseball, Happy Chandler, was in the stands.

This was the stuff of fiction. In his book *You Could Look It Up*, James Thurber wrote about a midget named Pearl du Monville, who stepped into the box with the bases loaded under orders to walk in the winning run. Instead, du Monville swung at a pitch, tapped it weakly in front of the plate, and was thrown out. His manager, infuriated, had swung the midget by the ankles and launched him into center field.

Veeck wanted to make sure that didn't happen with Gaedel. "I've got a man up in the stands with a high-powered rifle," he warned the midget. "And if you swing at any pitch, he'll fire."

As you can imagine, all hell broke loose when Gaedel emerged from the dugout to pinch hit for the Browns' leadoff man. The Tigers howled, but umpire Ed Hurley deemed Gaedel's contract in order. "Play ball," he ordered.

So Gaedel stepped in, spread his feet wide and hunched over, and reduced the strike zone to about six inches. Well, the Tigers tried to figure out a way to get a strike past him. But the umpire wouldn't let Bob Cain pitch underhand and he wouldn't let the catcher sit on the ground. So Cain walked Gaedel on four pitches up high, and the Browns promptly sent in a pinch runner.

Needless to say, when Will Harridge, the American League's stuffed-shirt president heard about Gaedel, he went nuts. Harridge ordered his appearance struck from the record and banned all midgets from the game.

Veeck protested—and he was right. Nowhere in the rule book does it define how tall a midget is. "Make it five-feet-six," Veeck told Harridge. "Then we can get rid of Phil Rizzuto."

If anything, Veeck later knocked himself for being too conservative. If he'd only thought to use nine midgets, he said, the Browns would have won the pennant.

The important thing, as Veeck saw it, was that everyone in the ballpark—except maybe for the Tigers—had been entertained. That was the secret to being a promoter, he said. You want to make the rest of the world kick themselves for not being there.

One thing was certain. If you came to Veeck's ballpark, Veeck was there. Some owners all but lived in ivory towers. You couldn't get close to them. But anybody could get close to Veeck. You'd see him greeting fans at the turnstiles, chatting with them under the stands, or sitting with them in the bleachers. If you had an idea for a trade, you didn't have to write a letter to Veeck. You just had to lean over the popcorn and tell him.

The fans weren't just fans to Veeck. They were customers. So he was always doing market research—in person. Once, he declared Grandstand Managers Day, handed out YES and NO cards to the fans, and let them vote on what the Browns should do. Bunt? Steal? Bring in a reliever?

Veeck always found ingenious ways to involve the fans. When the Indians won the 1948 pennant, their first in twenty-eight years,

Veeck held a black-tie reception at the team offices. He invited the cream of Cleveland society, the top politicians, the leading citizens of the city. Then he put them to work mailing out World Series tickets. He made an event out of it.

And when the Indians were eliminated from the race by the Yankees the next season, Veeck made an event out of that, too. He staged a mock funeral procession, with a hearse and pallbearers dressed in top hats and white gloves and actually buried the pennant in centerfield. Tom Yawkey would have died before he held a funeral in his ballpark, but baseball wasn't life and death to Veeck. It was only a game, and the ballpark was his playground.

Veeck was easy to find there. He was the guy wearing a white short-sleeved sports shirt, even when it was only thirty degrees outside. Veeck would be smoking a cigarette and flicking the ashes into a receptacle he'd carved out of his wooden leg. When he'd had been with the Marines in Bougainville during the war, an antiaircraft gun had recoiled and smashed his right foot. Eventually the leg was amputated. Veeck later developed emphysema from all that smoking, so he was constantly coughing, and he was all but deaf in one ear, too. When he wrote his autobiography, he titled it *Veeck—As in Wreck*.

Yet Veeck had the energy of three men. He'd speak at a breakfast to promote his club, drop in on a civic luncheon, then go to the ballpark. After the game, Veeck would sit in the press room and we'd join him for drinks. Maybe he'd order in some Chinese food, and we'd eat and drink and talk baseball. Some nights, Veeck would be there until dawn.

When he was in Cleveland, Veeck would go to the Copacabana—in New York. He'd catch a flight to La Guardia after the game, get to the club in time for the late show, drink until the place closed, then fly back to Cleveland in the morning.

Veeck was always on the hustle. He had to be, because he never had enough money. He wasn't like Yawkey or Wrigley. He didn't have an inheritance or a chewing-gum company. Veeck had to struggle to scrape together enough money to buy a club, and he rarely had enough cash for a contender.

When he bought the Browns with fifteen other investors for

two million dollars in the middle of the 1951 season, they were in last place, twenty-three and a half games out. He bought the club in the morning and they were rained out that night. Veeck promptly announced that he was considering signing two pitchers—a guy from Japan and Satchel Paige, who by now had lost all his teeth and was somewhere between forty-three and fifty.

When Veeck purchased the White Sox in 1959, he had no idea what he was getting. "Let's go to Opening Day," Veeck told his new partners, "and see what we've bought." The light-hitting Sox—"We rely on bingles, bobbles, and bunts," Veeck cracked—ended up winning the pennant. But even if they'd finished in the second division, Veeck wouldn't have cared. To him, the fun was luring people inside his carnival tent and partying with them.

"Sometime, somewhere, there will be a club no one really wants," Veeck wrote in his autobiography. "And then Ole Will will come wandering along to laugh some more."

Yawkey never wanted any other club but the Red Sox. And he kept pouring money into the franchise, even as the team kept getting worse. And by the mid-sixties, the Sox were as bad as they'd ever been. They sunk from third in 1958 to ninth in 1965, when they lost a hundred games for the first time since before the Depression.

Boston finished forty games out that year and drew only six hundred and fifty thousand people at Fenway, the lowest total since the war. Then they ended up last the next season, too. T.A. was really down during those years. He never said a lot about it, but he was a competitor. He wanted to give the city a winner.

Well, in 1967 he did, and it was completely unexpected. The Sox were hundred-to-one shots to win the pennant, but a scrappy new manager—Dick Williams—prodded and drove them all summer.

The club was only a game over .500 on Memorial Day, but after they won ten straight games in July, people began believing. Attendance doubled overnight and as August turned into September and the Sox were still in the race, everyone began talking about the Impossible Dream and radio stations began playing the song from *Man of La Mancha*.

Yawkey was still watching quietly from his box behind the plate. He was superstitious, like a lot of baseball men are. He was always fearful that something was going to happen, that the dream would vanish. But you could see that Yawkey's spirits were buoyed. The pennant race produced quite a change in him.

T.A. wasn't talking about selling the ball club anymore, and you began seeing him around the clubhouse more often. He'd been staying away for the previous few years, mostly because of his health. He'd complained to Jack Fadden, the trainer, about having no pep, no stamina, and Fadden had convinced him to go to the Lahey Clinic for some tests.

They discovered that T.A. had serious diabetes, made worse by those years of drinking bourbon by the tumbler. Well, as soon as he stopped drinking, all that weight came off and Yawkey looked like a thin little old man. But the Impossible Dream energized him.

He loved that team because they were overachievers. The 1967 club had one great star in Carl Yastrzemski, but most of them were rookies and ordinary guys having career years. Jim Lonborg, who won twenty-two games, had never had a winning season in the majors.

On the final day, after the Sox beat the Twins at Fenway to clinch a tie for the pennant and the players carried Lonborg off the diamond in the twilight, Yawkey came down to the clubhouse and joined them around the radio, where everybody was listening to the Angels–Tigers game. When the final out was made and the Tigers had been beaten, everybody jumped up and shouted at the same instant. As the champagne was uncorked, Yawkey went around to each cubicle and hugged and congratulated every player.

That season turned baseball around for good in Boston and it added years to Yawkey's life. The last time I saw him, in 1975, was another pennant year. The Sox had a terrific club that season—Yaz, Luis Tiant, Carlton Fisk, Rick Burleson, Jim Rice, Dwight Evans, Fred Lynn. They demolished Oakland's world champions in the playoffs and went seven games with the Reds in the best Series ever played.

My most enduring memory of T.A. was right after Fisk hit the home run that won game six in the twelfth inning. Yawkey didn't jump up and down or clench his fist or cheer. No emotion whatever. He just sat there and stared at the left-field wall and shook his head. Then T.A. got up and walked out of his box. Nine months later, he was dead of leukemia. The greatest owner baseball ever had died with the pennant flying above his ballpark.

10

Teddy Ballgame

 I can still hear his voice booming through the Red Sox clubhouse: "Who's the best goddamn hitter you ever saw?"

Teddy Ballgame. Without a doubt.

Few mortals ever hit a baseball better than Theodore Samuel Williams. And nobody ever thought more and talked more about it. Hitting wasn't just an art to Williams, it was a science. And he was the Nobel laureate.

Williams never went to college, but he had a scholar's mind—inquisitive, disciplined, organized. As soon as I walked into his workshop at his home down in the Florida Keys, I knew everything I needed to know about him. Every item was sorted, labeled, and in its place. Even the screws were separated and marked by size.

One spring, when Ted had invited us to stay at his place, my wife noticed that his shelf paper had gotten a little ragged. So she got some new oil papers and put them down instead. It was a very small thing, but Ted noticed right away and made a point of thanking me.

No detail was too small to escape his attention and everything had to be flawless. His cap and uniform had to fit perfectly. He spent hours boning his bats and rubbing them with olive oil and resin. And he didn't wear a helmet until the league forced him to.

We were riding in a cab one day when I saw the headline in the Boston *Record*: HELMETS TO BE MANDATORY FOR PLAYERS. "Hell with that," Williams growled. "I'm not wearing any helmet. Don't want one." He thought they were awkward, that they threw him off balance. The most he wanted was a protective insert.

That's one thing that set Williams apart—things that the average guy didn't notice or shrugged off as unimportant were vital to him.

"You go out fishing with Ted?" Bobby Doerr asked me once. Now, Doerr, who'd known Williams since their minor-league days in San Diego, was a great outdoorsman himself.

"Yeah, bonefishing two or three times in the off-season," I told him.

"He's a pain in the ass, isn't he?"

I knew what he meant. If you were two minutes late, Ted would be prowling the dock, waiting for you. He was punctual for everything he did, so he expected everyone else to be.

"What a lousy cast," Williams would say, watching you on the water. "Can't you cast better than that?"

Doerr had warned me that Ted would be like that. "Look, he's going to give you hell all the time," he said. "Don't hesitate. Fire back at him. Criticize *him* on something."

"C'mon, c'mon, balance the goddamn boat," Williams would bark at me.

"How can I balance the boat with you overweight back there?" I'd shout back. Well, Williams would laugh like hell.

But fishing wasn't just a hobby to him. Nothing was. If Ted Williams did something, he set out to be the best who ever lived, whether it was hitting, fishing, or flying a jet. John Glenn, who was his squadron commander in Korea, said that Williams was as good a wingman as there was.

He was the most competent man I ever met in my life—and the most demanding. Everything had to be just perfect, or else he was complaining about it. The waves would lap against the boat and he'd curse the waves. Or the sun wasn't just right and he'd curse that, too.

But Ted was just as exacting about himself. He made all his own leaders and all his own lures. I don't think he trusted anyone else to do it. I'd watch him tie flies in his hotel room when the Red Sox were on the road—these big hands tying these little trout flies, the size twenties and twenty-twos. So tiny you could hardly see them.

"Aww, this is no good," he'd snap, and yank the fly out of the vise and start again.

When Sears hired him to promote their fishing and hunting equipment, Williams tested everything himself, from rods to tents to shotguns. And he was conscientious about it. He'd take a rod and break it if he didn't like it and send it back to Sears that way. He'd give them an honest appraisal.

Ted was scrupulous about what he endorsed. He turned down offers to do cigarette and beer ads because he didn't smoke or drink. Why should he mislead the public?

If you think he was particular about his fishing gear, you should have seen Williams with his bats. He'd go down to Louisville during the winter to pick out the wood personally and have them custom made. And when they arrived at Fenway, Williams treated his bats like Heifetz would his Stradivarius. He was a master craftsman, after all, and they were the tools of his trade.

Ted could tell you if a bat was an ounce off, just by the feel. That's why he told his teammates never to leave their bats on the grass during night games, because they'd pick up half an ounce or so of moisture. The same thing happened on airplanes, Williams insisted, when the bats were stashed in the cargo bay.

And if anybody argued with him, Ted would have a clubhouse boy weigh the bats on a special postal scale he kept there. And of course, he'd be right. They would have picked up an ounce or so. To Williams, it might as well have been a pound.

That's why Williams stopped fishing during the season. He used to go to the lakes outside of Boston where he knew there were bass. But once, the day after he'd fished for two or three hours with a fly rod and a popper, Ted sensed a subtle difference in his right wrist. Nothing major, but he didn't like it. So he quit fishing until October.

Now, Ted was no hypochondriac, but his body was his livelihood. If there was anything wrong with it, he wanted reassurance that the injury wouldn't wreck his career.

So whenever he was hurt, the club sent Williams to see James Poppen at the Lahey Clinic. Poppen was a neurosurgeon, but he'd also been a minor-league pitcher and he knew just how to deal with Williams.

"If I play on this heel, am I going to damage myself for life?" Williams would ask Poppen.

"Naww, go ahead and play," Poppen would reassure him. "It might hurt you a little, but you can get through it. It won't be any better if you rest it." And Williams would go back and play, his mind at ease.

Williams was concerned with every twinge, every ounce, every millimeter. Nobody ever had a better feel for the strike zone than he did. If Williams let a pitch go by, you knew it was a ball. The umpires did, too. If they'd called him out on strikes, they'd ask Ted about it the next time he came up.

"Do you think that third one was a strike?"

"Yes, I do," Williams would tell them. "Too close for me to take."

Yet he'd take the pitch with a clear conscience. Ted could have hit pitches that were an inch or two outside and probably have driven them into the bleachers. But he wouldn't swing at them.

Getting a good pitch to hit—that was Williams's credo. People criticized him for taking a close one with men on base. Why didn't he go for it?

"If I start going for that, pretty soon I'm reaching out farther," Williams reasoned. "And it'll destroy my hitting."

That was the difference between Williams and Joe DiMaggio. DiMaggio would swing at an marginal pitch if the game were on the line. Williams never would. It was the purist in him. It was also the optometrist in him. Ted could tell the difference between a pitch that was on the black and one that was a smidgen off.

When he got back in the game after two years in Korea, Williams complained to Joe Cronin, the general manager, that the plate at Fenway Park was out of line. Cronin thought Williams was crazy but he had it checked and Williams was right.

Williams had terrific eyesight—20/10. That's one reason why he was such a great fighter pilot. When he was being examined for the Marines, the doctors couldn't believe his vision. The optometrist who examined Williams called another one in. Pretty soon, all of the doctors came in to check him out. They told him that only six people in a hundred thousand had eyesight like his.

"They tell me that you can read the label of a forty-five rpm record," I told him once.

"Yeah, I can."

"No kidding," I said. "That's amazing."

"When it's standing still," Williams said. "Naww, where do they get all these myths going?"

By any standard, though, Ted's eyesight was exceptional. We were in a duck blind one time when Williams pointed to the sky.

"Three ducks coming at two o'clock," he announced.

"Where, where?" I said. "What, what?"

Now, I had good vision, too. I could broadcast football without glasses. But I didn't see anything in the sky that day. Well, about a minute later, I spotted the ducks. I don't know how he saw them.

Baseball people said the reason why Williams hit so well was because he could literally see the stitches on the ball as it was humming toward the plate, that he could tell a fastball from a curve from a slider almost as it left the pitcher's hand.

That wasn't true, either, Williams insisted. There were times, he told me, that everything simply clicked for him, that the ball looked as big as a grapefruit. But there were other reasons for that besides 20/10 eyesight.

No ballplayer studied every facet of hitting more than Ted Williams did. He was always the first guy at the ballpark and the last guy to leave. In the hours between, he soaked up as much knowledge as he could.

One reason why Dom DiMaggio and Johnny Pesky hated hitting before Williams was that Ted would grill them about the pitcher—"What's he throw?"—as soon as they returned to the dugout. When the opposing team was taking batting practice, Williams would be standing on the dugout steps, his chin in his hands, studying, while his teammates were having sandwiches in the clubhouse.

Williams never understood that. "Listen, the average time you're going to spend up here is five years—if you're lucky," he'd tell the younger guys. "I don't see any of you going to have big careers. Why don't you get the most out of it—or you'll look back and regret it."

Just watching Williams work at his craft was inspiring. He had so much natural talent that he could have been a drunk and still hit .300. But he'd go out there day after day and work on tiny things nobody else would have bothered with.

"If a guy like Williams will work that hard on something he's already an expert at," I told myself, "then I can do the same."

That's when I began learning as much as I could about every player on every team, studying box scores and statistics and keeping transcripts of interviews I'd done. The more I knew about the game and the men who played it, the better it would be for the listener.

"Ted, I want to thank you for making me a better broadcaster," I told him one day.

Williams was mystified. "What the hell are you talking about? I don't know anything about broadcasting."

"Your work ethic," I told him. "The way you approach the game."

"Well," he said, "I've always tried to give back $1.10 for every dollar they paid me."

With Ted it was always, what can I do to get better? Who can I learn something from? From the day he arrived in the majors, Williams had been a terrific brain-picker. He loved talking with the great old-time hitters, guys like Paul Waner and Rogers Hornsby and Jimmie Foxx, who was still playing with the Sox when Williams came up. And he always regretted that he never stopped in to see Shoeless Joe Jackson when the Sox came through his town on their way north from spring training.

Williams respected them all as master craftsmen and he could recite their records by heart. Only three ballplayers I ever met knew that much about the old-timers—Pete Rose, Reggie Jackson, and Williams.

Maybe it was his time in the service that did it, when Williams realized how short life really could be, how nothing was guaranteed. He was a different man when he came back in 1946. Williams was twenty-seven then, and he realized that he only had a few more years to make his mark. So baseball stopped being a game to him, and began being a craft.

When Williams came into the league, it was assumed that slug-
gers needed heavy bats, even up to thirty-eight ounces. But he'd
already figured out that was wrong when he was in the minors at
Minneapolis. The Millers were playing in Columbus on the hottest
day of the summer and a teammate named Stan Spence handed him
an incredibly light bat.

Well, Williams hit a grand slam with it. That's when he concluded that bat speed, not bat weight, was the key. So he settled on
thirty-three ounces, not much more than a high school kid would
use. And he worked religiously on building up his hands, wrists, and
forearms.

The whole secret, Williams believed, was from the fingertips to
the elbows. That's where a hitter's strength came from. So Williams
had a whole regimen of exercises he went through and he traveled
with a lead bat. Up in his hotel room, Williams would swing it two
hundred, three hundred, four hundred times a day in front of the
mirror.

He was always swinging a bat. In the minors, Williams would
take imaginary cuts while he was playing the outfield. "Hey, Bush,"
his manager shouted. "More this," he said, punching a make-believe
glove. "Less this," he said, mimicking a swing.

Once, when his roommate Broadway Charley Wagner was
sleeping, Williams was taking cuts in the hotel room. Suddenly the
bat smashed into the bedpost and everything came crashing to
the floor—including Wagner. "Damn," Williams marveled. "What
power."

If he wasn't swinging a bat, Williams was talking about swinging
a bat. And not just with his teammates. If guys from other teams,
like Al Kaline or Mickey Mantle, went to him for tips, Williams
would tell them anything they wanted to know. He didn't believe in
trade secrets.

"What the hell are you helping the opposition for?" Tom
Yawkey asked Williams one day.

"Look, T.A., I'm helping the game," Williams told him. "We've
got to have more hitting in baseball. You tell me—you're a block
away from a ballpark and you hear the crowd roar. What happened?
I'll tell you what happened. Somebody hit the baseball."

Every road trip with Williams was a traveling seminar. Baseball

Physics 101: The Theory and Practice of Hitting. If we were taking the train to Cleveland, say, Williams would be in the club car, in the middle of a long monologue about the Indian pitchers. He'd be talking about Bob Lemon and his sinker, how hard it was to knock out of the park. Or about Mike Garcia and how heavy his ball was.

Hitting was a lot more complicated than just bat striking ball. Williams took half a dozen factors into account—the wind, the weather, the pitcher, the score, the count, and what the pitcher had thrown in similar situations. He always remembered every pitch a pitcher ever threw to him.

Ted was always talking about the background, too, and how important it was. That's why he loved hitting in Fenway, where the white ball would come out of that big green Wall. And why he hated playing in Memorial Stadium in Baltimore.

There was a house up on a hill just beyond center field where the lights were on at night, and the pitch would come right out of those lights. Williams was always complaining about it. "What do you want us to do?" Cronin said with a shrug. "Have the people sit in their house in the dark?"

When Williams first came up, he never thought about any of that stuff. He'd always been able to hit a baseball. That's how the Sox noticed him. Eddie Collins, their general manager, had made a scouting trip to San Diego in 1936 to check out a shortstop. He ended up signing a smooth second baseman named Bobby Doerr. But he also noticed a tall, skinny teenager in the batting cage.

"Who's that?" Collins asked the team owner.

"Oh, that's the kid. Williams. He's seventeen and sort of squirrelly—but he can hit a baseball."

So the Sox took an option on him and eventually bought his rights for thirty-five thousand dollars and a couple of players. "We gotta get that camel-gaited kid with rubber wrists," Cronin, who was manager then, told owner Tom Yawkey.

But when Collins went back out to San Diego to sign Williams at his house, he was disappointed when Williams didn't get up from his easy chair when Collins entered. "Where are his manners?" Collins wondered.

What he didn't find out until later was the chair had a hole in it and Williams was ashamed to have Collins see it. He came from an unstable home where there wasn't much money. His mother was out of the house a lot, working for the Salvation Army, and his father wasn't around much.

Williams was a sensitive, complex kid with a lot of insecurities, but he was totally at home on a baseball diamond. Every day of the year, Williams would leave the house in the morning with a glove around his belt, run down to North Park a block and a half away, and play until after it got dark.

He was only seventeen when the San Diego Padres signed him to a minor-league contract for a hundred fifty dollars a month. In those days, when there were only sixteen major-league clubs, the Pacific Coast League was really strong. A lot of guys there had played in the majors. Most teenagers were overmatched there.

The first time Williams got up, he took three fastballs right down the middle. Then he ripped doubles his next two times up and never stopped.

Williams turned up for spring training with the Red Sox the next year with one pair of pants and said "Hiya, sport" to everyone he met. Cronin dubbed him "Meathead" and Doc Cramer, Joe Vosmik, and Ben Chapman—the outfielders who saw Williams as a threat to their jobs—rode him like you wouldn't believe.

Williams got farmed out to Minneapolis, but his brash confidence never wavered, even as he was boarding the bus out of Sarasota. "Tell them [Cramer, Vosmik, and Chapman] I'll be back," Williams told Johnny Orlando, the clubhouse man. "And tell them I'm going to wind up making more money in this game than all three of them put together."

Williams was back the next year and had an incredible rookie season—he hit .327 at cleanup, slugged thirty-one homers, and led the league in runs batted in. It was incredible, that is, to everyone but himself. His teammates got a taste of the unabashed cockiness of "the Kid"—his new nickname—opening day at Yankee Stadium after Red Ruffing had struck him out in his first two at-bats.

"What's the league look like to you now, Bush?" cracked Sox pitcher Jack Wilson.

"If he puts it there again," Williams said, "I'm riding it out."

Williams nearly did, whacking the ball four hundred and seven feet off the right-field fence, a foot from the top. Then, in Detroit a couple of weeks later, he did something nobody had ever done before. He cleared the right-field roof of Briggs Stadium. Yet when the season was done, Williams felt oddly let down. He'd thought everything would be tougher in the majors.

"I thought it would be more elaborate, more *everything* than it actually was," Williams told me. "Guys had told me about blinding fastballs and exploding curves. I never really saw them." Of course, what was blinding to most batters was routine to Williams.

For the first few games, he saw knockdown pitches from veterans trying to test the rookie's nerve. Williams had been hit in the head in the minors and spent a couple of days in the hospital. But when he came back, he'd dug in harder than ever.

"All I kept saying to myself was: This . . . is . . . not . . . going . . . to . . . stop . . . me," Williams told me. "Till the last day I played, I kept thinking: Hang in there."

It didn't take long for the pitchers to realize that beanballs merely infuriated Williams. After he put a few balls into the seats, the word got around. Just keep the ball low and away and pray that the Kid didn't pull it into the bleachers.

The Sox front office knew immediately that they had a home-run king in Williams, so that winter they built bullpens in front of the right-field bleachers—"Williamsburg," the writers dubbed it— to shorten the distance by twenty feet.

Of course, by the next season, the pitchers had wised up. They have a fraternity, you know, so they passed the word along. They weren't feeding Williams fastballs over the plate anymore. They were either pitching him low and away or up high.

Ted figured out what they were doing and became more of a hitter and less of a slugger. So he hit for a better average that year, but had fewer home runs. And the fans started to boo him—especially after he let a ball go through his legs in right field. That's when Williams vowed he'd never tip his hat to them again.

When the fans and the press started on him, Williams took umbrage and fought back the only way he could—with words and gestures. Then he got so far into it that he felt if he backed out, they'd think he didn't have any guts. Williams was a very stubborn man, with a lot of pride.

At one point he said he ought to quit and become a fireman like his uncle. Well, Jimmy Dykes, who managed the White Sox, was a hell of a bench jockey. The next time they played Boston, he'd out-fitted everybody with papier-mâché fireman's hats and rigged up a siren you could hear all over the ballpark. As soon as Williams stepped to the plate, the White Sox let him have it—"Fireman, save my child!"

Well, it didn't take him long to get into hot water with the Boston sportswriters, who then, as now, are among the toughest in the country. By the end of his second year, he was already at war with them.

After Williams complained in print about what a lousy town Boston was and how low his salary of twelve thousand five hundred dollars was, columnist Dave Egan ripped him. "Williams is the all-time, All-American adolescent," Egan wrote. "The prize heel ever to wear a Boston uniform."

"It was immaturity on my part," Williams told me years later. "I antagonized them. But a lot of that stuff the writers themselves knew was unfair. They knew it was wrong. If I did anything well, they didn't acknowledge it that much. If I failed, it was the end of the world. The front office should have stepped in and told us to get together."

Then Ted put together a season in 1941 that nobody could find fault with. No ballplayer in more than a decade had hit .400 and none has done it since. Williams did it when he was barely twenty-three, with everyone trying to pitch around him.

In a hundred and forty-three games, he drew a hundred and forty-five walks. He didn't achieve his .406 by tapping singles into right field. He hit thirty-seven homers and posted a slugging average of .735. And he did it with a fierce integrity.

He was batting .3995 going into the last day of the season, a doubleheader at Philadelphia. Cronin offered to scratch Williams from the lineup and let the league mathematician round him up to .400. But Williams refused.

"If I'm a .400 hitter, I'm a .400 hitter for a whole season, not part of one," he told Cronin. "If I'm not capable of holding the mark, I don't deserve the honor."

Now, the Athletics were the last-place team, but Connie Mack had warned his players that he'd run them out of baseball if they took it easy on Williams. He still played both games, went six-for-eight with a homer, and improved his mark by six points. "Ain't I the best goddamn hitter you ever saw?" Williams crowed in the clubhouse later.

That was the Kid speaking, and he never changed. If he believed something was true, he said it. Not a whole lot of his sentences included the word *maybe*. He admitted that Joe DiMaggio was the greatest all-around ballplayer in the game. But Williams insisted that he himself was the greatest hitter. In 1942, when he'd only been in the league for four years, he did a story for the *Saturday Evening Post*. The title was: I WANNA BE AN IMMORTAL.

No question, Ted was larger than life. He had the looks of a Hollywood movie star and this great speaking voice that really projected. You could hear him all over the clubhouse. There was never any doubt about what Williams was saying.

Some people might have thought he was a braggart, but they had to accept it as fact because Williams was producing the numbers to back his statements up. And his numbers probably would have been even better in the National League. The right-field foul pole at the Polo Grounds was only two hundred fifty-eight feet from home plate, a high school poke for a pull hitter like Williams. The double-decked grandstand at Forbes Field in Pittsburgh was just three hundred feet away. And Williams salivated at the thought of Ebbets Field.

"Jesus, I'd give a fortune to play a season here," Williams told me after the Sox had played an exhibition with the Dodgers in Brooklyn. "I'd hit seventy home runs."

"Seventy?" Even for Ted that was ambitious. He never hit more than forty-three in a season.

"Hell, it's a line-drive shot right into those low left-field bleachers," he said. "And just a routine fly ball, two hundred and ninety-seven feet over that right-field wall. No wonder Musial hit like hell here. If I played seventy-seven games here every year, I would have broken Ruth's record."

Williams and everybody else wondered what he would have achieved had he not missed those five years—1943, 1944, 1945, 1952, and 1953—when he was in the service. If you figured he averaged thirty homers a year, that would have given him a career total of six hundred seventy-one. In fact, Williams might have hit even more, since he hit seventy-three in the two years before he went off to World War II. And that's not counting the seasons of 1954 and 1955, when he missed a total of two months with a broken collar-bone and divorce problems.

I think that's why Williams became such a fanatical student of the game when he came back. He had so much time to make up for that he felt he couldn't waste an at-bat. He wanted every possible edge he could get, because he had no speed. Cronin had told him early on.

"Two things you're going to regret," Cronin told Williams once over dinner. "That you never played in New York. And that you couldn't run."

As high as his average was—and it was .344 lifetime—it would have been higher if Williams had the speed of the young Mickey Mantle. Williams almost never got an infield hit. If he'd just had one a week in 1941, he would have hit .454.

Williams had to earn every hit he got. That's why his focus at the plate was absolute. I've never seen anybody with such perfect concentration, such incredible intensity. Looking back, Williams wondered how he could have been that way every time at bat, more than five hundred times a season for more than two decades.

It was the challenge, he decided, and the fear. The challenge of proving he was the greatest hitter who ever lived. And the fear of slipping. He'd seen it happen to Jimmie Foxx. In 1938, the year before Williams came up, Foxx had hit fifty home runs, led the league in batting, and was named Most Valuable Player. Four years later, he was out of baseball.

Williams relished a challenge. That's why he loved playing in the All-Star Game, because he got to face those great National League pitchers. And that's why he loved hitting against fastball pitchers like Bob Feller and Allie Reynolds. The faster, the better. He hated going up against guys like Ed Lopat and Stubby Overmire who threw curveballs and off-speed stuff. "Every time I hit against Lopat I thought: What's wrong? I don't feel good up here," Williams told me.

But the fireballers fascinated him. In 1955, Ted called me up to ask me about Cleveland's hot new rookie. Williams had been going through a rough divorce and had missed the first month of the season.

"How good is this kid Score? I've heard a lot about him."

"Ted, he's wicked," I told him. "Boy, can he throw hard. I think he's the fastest pitcher in baseball right now."

"How's he come in on you?" Williams wanted to know.

"Overhand."

"He's not sidearm?"

"No," I assured him. "He's overhand."

"That's good," Williams said. "Goddamn, I can't wait to hit against him."

I'm sure he called thirty other guys, asking them the same thing: Tell me about him. What's he got?

Well, the first time Williams faced Score, he went four-for-five. He killed him. "I don't understand how he hit me that hard," Score said in the clubhouse afterward.

Williams loved bucking the odds, the steeper, the better. That's why he insisted on hitting to right even after many clubs went to the Boudreau shift, which was designed to make him go to the opposite field.

Lou Boudreau, who managed the Indians, dreamed up the shift in 1946. He moved everybody but the left-fielder to the right of second base and dared Williams to punch balls through the crowd.

Williams wasn't upset about it. In fact, he said he would have done the same thing himself. For a while, he confounded the shift by tapping singles to left. Finally, Williams said the hell with it and began ripping balls at all those people in right.

"If you'd beaten the shift," I told him once. "You'd have hit .400 again."

Williams shook his head. "I'm right on top of the plate," he said. "I would have had to drop back to hit the pitch on the outside corner and poke it into left field, and that might have bothered my natural swing. Besides, the fans don't pay to see me hit singles to the opposite field."

I think Williams was actually honored by the idea of the shift. He liked the idea that people had to go to extraordinary lengths to stop him, and he enjoyed solving the puzzle.

Williams was that way when it came to fishing, too. The

tougher the fish was to find or to land, the more it excited him.

Once we were down in Mexico in a place called Paz Maya, doing a show for *American Sportsman*. We were looking for permit, which is a real trophy fish in the tropics. It's a big pompano, with a black tail waving in the air, but it comes in on the shallow-water flats and feeds like a bonefish. Well, the first day we saw quite a few permit, but we didn't catch any.

"What do you think?" I asked Williams after we came in that night.

"Ahh, we'll get 'em," he assured me. "I'll figure it out."

That was Ted. He loved to figure things out. The only thing he couldn't figure out was how to hit those cunny-thumb pitchers.

We didn't get a permit on the next day, either. We made quite a few casts but the fish would spook or something else would happen. So my head cameraman came to see me.

"Curt, I gotta tell you. If we don't get any tomorrow, we've gotta scrub the show," he said. "Because we need at least three days' production."

And Williams could only stay six days.

"Listen, we're in a little trouble here," I told Ted the next morning. "I've got my own money on the table for this shoot. If we don't get any fish this morning . . ."

"Bet you five hundred bucks we get a permit this morning," he told me. "What do you say? Want to bet me?"

I started to bet him, hoping I would lose and he would save the show. But Ted was always so confident about everything, I decided against it.

Well, we didn't get any permit that morning, either. Now it was lunchtime and my producer and cameraman poled over in their skiff.

"Getting to be cutoff time," they told me. "Something better happen this afternoon."

Of course, Williams was listening to all this.

"I'll tell you what," he said. "Goddamn, I'll bet you a thousand dollars I get a permit by two o'clock."

Well, about one-thirty he caught a nice permit and we got it on film. I caught one right after him, and we ended up catching three or four that afternoon. Then we went right into production, which

Ted hated. He hated the dialogue and the close-ups of the hands and face, all that after-the-fact stuff you have to do for TV. He wanted to fish. And fishing came as naturally to Williams as hitting did.

People ask me who was the greatest fisherman I ever had on my twenty years of *American Sportsman*. No question, it was Williams. From marlin to salmon to bass to bonefish, he was the most versatile I ever saw. He enjoyed the nuances of every kind of fishing and he was a fountain of knowledge. You could ask him anything.

And if you knew something he didn't, he'd pepper you with questions. "What trout streams do you like out in Wyoming?" he'd ask me. "What's the best time of year to go? What are the best flies? Why do you use those?"

One day when we were in Washington, my phone rang around nine in the morning.

"Hey, I just read in the paper that they're having the national fly-casting distance tournament over at the Reflecting Pool today," Williams told me. "What do you say we go and look around?"

When we got there, all of these platforms were sticking out above the pool. Guys with baskets holding extra line strapped around their bellies were practicing. Well, one of them recognized Williams and invited him up to take a shot at it.

"Naww, I don't want to bother you," Ted told him.

"C'mon, it'd be an honor," the guy assured him.

So Williams went up on the platform, took a couple of test casts, then—boom!—that line shot out of that basket. They measured it and the distance was a hundred and seventy or eighty feet, only six feet short of the guy who ended up winning. And here's Williams, who didn't even practice and was using a strange rod.

Ted never lacked for confidence, I'll say that for him. After he read *The Old Man and The Sea*, Williams said that he never would have sat in that rowboat as long as Hemingway's old man did. He insisted he would have caught his marlin in twenty-five minutes.

"Name me a guy who's a better fisherman than I am," Williams challenged Jack Fadden, the old Red Sox trainer, one day. "Nobody can fly-fish as good as I can. I'm a great big-game fisherman. I'm a great spin fisherman. Name one guy who's a better all-around fisherman than me."

Well, Fadden knew just how to deflate Williams. That's why Williams loved him.

"Theodore, I know somebody who caught more fish in one minute than you have in your whole life," Fadden told him

"Yeah, who?"

"Our Lord Jesus Christ," Fadden crowed.

"Aww, I'll give you that one," Williams grumbled. "But name me another."

Ted's ego got him a reputation among the Boston writers as a prima donna. But that wasn't how baseball people viewed him. Williams was demanding of himself and highly opinionated. But I never saw him argue with an umpire, show up a manager, or knock another ballplayer. The only guy he ever put down or got mad at was himself.

If an umpire called him out on a close pitch, he'd never gripe about it. "Gee, I thought that ball was outside," Williams might say, softly. Then he'd walk back to the dugout. He had respect for any umpire who'd made it to the majors. He always said that the good ones could call a pitch within an inch ninety-five percent of the time.

Everyone wrote what a wild, undisciplined guy Williams was and wondered how anybody could manage him. But the truth was that Williams had six managers—from Cronin to Billy Jurges—and never gave any of them any trouble. He'd been a Marine, so he respected authority. And his favorite manager—Joe McCarthy—was the toughest disciplinarian in the game.

"How do you think you'll get along with Williams?" someone asked McCarthy after the Sox hired him in 1948. McCarthy had made the Yankees wear neckties on the road and Williams hated neckties. So people thought they'd be at each other's throats before long.

"Any manager who can't get along with a .400 hitter should have his head examined," McCarthy said.

Cronin, who was involved with the Red Sox for all of Williams's years in Boston, said that Ted never missed a plane, train, or bus.

Williams was a model ballplayer. He rarely disagreed with the front office over money and never held out. Yawkey would send Williams a contract during the off-season, and Williams would go up to Boston to talk it over.

"What do you think of the contract?" Yawkey would ask him.

"Pretty good," Williams would reply. "Of course, I had a hell of a year last year."

"We know you did," Yawkey would say with a nod.

Even after Williams had signed, Yawkey wanted to make sure he was satisfied.

"Are you sure you're happy now? This is what you want?"

"Yup," Williams would say. They'd shake hands and Williams would go back to Florida until it was time for spring training.

Ted always thought he was treated fairly. In fact, before his final year in 1960, he sent his contract back to Yawkey with a note saying that he didn't deserve the hundred and twenty-five thousand dollars and wanted to take a thirty-five-thousand-dollar cut.

The year before, Williams had ruptured a disk in his neck— probably from those violent swings he used to take—and it all but ruined him as a batter. He could barely turn his head to look at the pitcher.

Well, Ted had struggled through a miserable season. He started out by going one-for-twenty-two and ended up batting only .254— the only time he was ever under .300. He hit only ten homers and drove in only forty-three runs.

Yawkey had actually wanted him to retire after that. Williams was forty-one now, and Yawkey didn't want him looking like an old washed-up fighter who didn't know when to hang up the gloves.

But Ted insisted on playing one more season and he ended up batting .316 and having the highest ratio of home runs to at-bats of his career. He'd been ashamed of that .254 and those ten homers— hell, Williams used to hit ten in batting practice. "Old T.S.W. doesn't have bad years," he'd once boasted to the press.

Williams wanted to go out hitting .300 and he wanted five hundred career home runs. Going into the 1960 season, he was eight shy. Well, by June he knew he was having a year worth quitting on, so he made the announcement. Teddy Ballgame would retire at the end of the season.

Probably five hundred thousand people will swear to you that they were inside Fenway to see Williams's final game. Actually, there were only about ten thousand seats filled. It was a raw, gray, dismal day in the final week of September. Who wanted to see the seventh-place Sox play a meaningless game against the Orioles?

But since it was the last home date for the Sox and Williams had already announced his retirement, they had a brief farewell ceremony beforehand. John Collins, the mayor, gave Williams a silver Paul Revere bowl, the same memento City Hall has given to a hundred thousand other people.

"As we all know," I told the crowd, "this is the final home game for—in my opinion and most of yours—the greatest hitter who ever lived. Ted Williams. Twenty years ago, a skinny kid from San Diego came to the Red Sox camp . . ."

I went on to tell about the numbers and the records—the batting titles, the Most Valuable Player awards, the All-Star appearances, the .406 season. "But what set Ted Williams apart," I said, "was his incredible pride. Every day he played, he tried to make himself better. He wanted to become the greatest hitter who ever lived—and I believe he did. Pride is what made him great. He's a thoroughbred, a champion of sports."

After the crowd had finished cheering, Ted pulled me aside. "Goddamn it," he growled, "that's the nicest thing anybody's ever said about me. I want a copy."

"There is no copy." I shrugged. "It was all ad-libbed."

Well, everyone was looking for Williams to hit one out. But he walked and flied to center in his first two trips to the plate. Then he hit a long ball to right that looked like it might be gone. But Al Pilarcik hauled it in with his back against the bullpen wall.

"Damn, I hit the living hell out of that one," Williams said when he got back to the dugout. "I really stung it. If that one didn't go out, nothing is going to go out today."

Williams had one final chance in the eighth. But the lights were on by now and it was drizzling. So the conditions weren't exactly promising.

The crowd began cheering as soon as Willie Tasby, the leadoff hitter, emerged. They knew that Williams, the on-deck man, would be out within seconds.

When he finally stepped into the box, the fans gave him a standing ovation that lasted a full two minutes. People said that Jack Fisher, who was born the year that Williams came into the league, grooved a pitch for him as a tribute. But he didn't.

Fisher wanted to deliver a fastball, low and away on a one-and-one count. But the pitch sailed up and in and Williams put it on top of the Boston bullpen roof, four hundred feet away. Then he circled the bases quickly, his head down, went into the dugout, and wouldn't come out.

"Ladies and gentlemen," I told the radio audience, "Ted Williams had just hit a home run in the last at-bat of his career."

Years later, somebody asked me about that. "There were still two games left in the season," he said. "How could you have known it was Williams's last at-bat?"

Because Johnny Orlando, the Sox clubhouse man and Williams's close friend, had told me so before the game. Ted had a bad cold, so he'd gone to see Yawkey for permission to skip the final series in New York.

"I think this is going to be the Kid's last game," Orlando had told me.

Well, the crowd went nuts—*We want Ted! We want Ted!*—trying to seduce Williams from the dugout for a bow. But he wouldn't come out. "Gods do not answer letters," mused John Updike in "Hubs Fans Bid Kid Adieu", his famous account of the game, which appeared in *The New Yorker.*

Williams thought his career had ended with the homer. Pinky Higgins, the manager, had already told Carroll Hardy to go in for Williams at the top of the ninth. Then Higgins changed his mind.

"Williams, left field," he barked. But as soon as Williams sprinted out of the dugout, Higgins sent Hardy after him. He wanted Williams to hear one final roar before the era ended.

Epilogue:
That Innocence Vanished

Ted Williams's last home run marked the end of an era in American sports. When he hit his first, twenty-one years earlier, there were only sixteen big-league teams. They traveled by train, played in the afternoon, and used only white players. By 1960, baseball had changed forever.

For fifty years, no franchises changed cities. Then, within five years in the fifties, the Braves, Browns, Athletics, Dodgers, and Giants all had moved. There had never been a franchise west of St. Louis. Now both San Francisco and Los Angeles had one. So the days of taking the Super Chief were over. Clubs had to fly.

Trains could no longer take you where baseball was going—at least not overnight. The Senators moved to Minnesota. The National League put a franchise in Houston, and the American League added one in Los Angeles. Americans had been on the move since the war had ended. Their sports teams had to follow. They also had to adapt to the country's changing habits.

Americans no longer had the leisure time to watch ball games during weekdays. When Williams first came up in 1939, only twenty-one night games were played in the entire American League. The year he retired, the Red Sox alone played nineteen.

Even though attendance was growing—twenty million people went to major-league games in 1960, more than double the prewar figure—fewer Americans now considered baseball their favorite sport. They'd been seduced by professional football. They liked the speed of the game, and its violent collisions. Baseball, with all that dead time between pitches, had become too slow for their tastes.

Football had always been a Saturday game in the country's mind, played on college campuses. But by the sixties, that had changed. Attendance at the NFL's Sunday games had tripled in a decade. The turning point was the 1958 championship game at Yankee Stadium, where the Colts beat the Giants in overtime. It wasn't so much that the game itself was close and dramatic, but that it was on national television. Everybody in the country saw it—or so it seemed.

In just ten years, the number of television sets in America had soared from one million to fifty million. TV wasn't just a novelty, a plaything anymore. It was a necessity, as much a part of the house as the stove or refrigerator. And pro football was the perfect sport for TV.

It might not have seemed that way, with twenty-two guys on the field and substitutes running in and out of the game on every play. You might have thought all that hustle-bustle would be too complicated for the viewer, but actually, football was made for the medium.

The game was played on a hundred-yard rectangle in brief, explosive bursts. The action itself was easy to follow and there was lots of it. The camera could come down and narrow in on the quarterback taking the snap, then broaden out for wide shots of running plays and receivers going downfield. So everything was covered.

Unlike baseball, which was played in innings, football was played in minutes. So it fit neatly into a time slot, which was tremendously important to the networks. And the pro game was played on Sunday afternoons, when the networks had little else to show.

That's why the American Football League, which played its first game a few weeks before Williams hit his final homer, was destined to be a success. It was tailor-made for television. Its eight original cities—Boston, New York, Buffalo, Houston, Dallas, Denver, Los Angeles, and Oakland—weren't chosen by accident. They were large cities, most of them bypassed by the NFL, and they were all in major TV markets.

The most important thing the new league's owners did was sign a five-year deal with ABC right away, then made their league as attractive to TV as possible. AFL players wore their names on the back of their jerseys, so that viewers could identify them at a glance. The league used the two-point conversion, so that fewer games would end in ties. And AFL offenses were built around great passers like George Blanda, Jack Kemp, and Frank Tripucka, so there was lots of scoring. NFL people laughed at the AFL at the beginning, calling it the Almost Football League, but exactly a decade later, the NFL merged with it.

If football was the game of the sixties, it's because TV made it so. And the man who revolutionized the way TV covered football was a young redheaded producer named Roone Arledge. I first met him in 1960, when I was broadcasting the college Game of the Week for ABC. ABC had given up showing college football in the fifties because they'd lost money on it. The reason, as Arledge saw it, was because the network had brought the game to the fan. He decided to bring the fan to the game, to put him right on the sideline.

So Arledge doubled the number of cameras in the stadium. He used shoulder minicams to get close-ups of players and coaches on the sidelines and fans in the stands. He went with big shotgun microphones that could pick up the quaterback's signals and the crashing and grunting in the line. He used videotape to play back highlights at halftime and after the game.

All that seems obvious now, but it was unheard of back then. Television was coming out of its old small-screen, black-and-white days and bringing sports with it. If radio had helped make the twenties the Golden Age of Sports, TV did the same for the sixties. Except now the fan at home no longer had to use his imagination. TV put him right in the game.

A sport could become more popular just by being on television. That's how powerful the medium was. If it was on TV, it was important. Arledge understood that before anyone else did.

Roone and I used to room together on the road when we were doing the college games. One night, before the Penn State–

Syracuse game, I was lying down working on my charts, memorizing the roster numbers. Roone was on the other bed, scribbling on a legal pad.

"What are you doing?" I asked him. "Taking notes?"

"I'm putting down some ideas for a new sports show," he said. "Once football's over, we really don't have anything for the winter. So I'm thinking about a program that would go all over the world, doing offbeat sports. I don't want to copy Dave Garroway's *Wide, Wide World*. So we'll call it *Wide World of Sports*."

"What kind of stuff would you show?" I wondered.

"Skiing, Australian football, log rolling. A lot of kooky things," Roone said. "What do you think?"

I shook my head. "It'll never go."

Well, *Wide World* took off like a rocket and it's still on the air, thirty years later. Ironically, my son, Curt, Jr., is now the show's executive producer. I thought it wouldn't last, but I was wrong.

It was a new era; the forties seemed a million years ago. The sight of Jackie Robinson in a big-league uniform had been a cultural shock in 1947. By 1960, there were more than fifty black players in the majors.

By 1960, it seemed odd that there had ever been a time when rosters were lily white. Ten years earlier, the NBA had no blacks. Now its two most dominant players—Bill Russell and Wilt Chamberlain—were black. By 1965, so were seven of the ten starters in the NBA All-Star Game.

By 1958, the best running back in the NFL was a black man—Cleveland's Jim Brown. In 1961, a black player—Ernie Davis of Syracuse—won the Heisman Trophy, college football's top award.

The old order was beginning to crumble. The Yankees, who won five straight pennants at the beginning of the sixties, finished sixth in 1965 and didn't win another pennant until 1976, the year baseball went to free agency.

One by one, the college football dynasties came apart. Except for one magic season with Pete Dawkins in 1958, Army was never the same after its cribbing scandal. Notre Dame didn't have a winning season between 1958 and 1964, when Ara Parseghian turned the program around. Oklahoma, which won forty-seven straight in the fifties, didn't win another national championship until 1974.

The new powerhouses were schools like Alabama, Southern Cal, Texas, Arkansas, and Nebraska.

It had become tougher and tougher for the smaller schools to stay competitive. Two-platoon football meant twice as many scholarships, twice as much of everything. The day when a Rice, a Texas Christian, a Syracuse, or a service academy could win a national title had passed. College football had become a big business, favoring schools with big stadiums and big budgets.

America was in the midst of a sports explosion, especially among the pros. Leagues expanded, split into more divisions, and spawned rival leagues. As late as 1957, the NBA still had three of its eight franchises in the state of New York. By 1964, the league had outgrown the smaller cities. The Lakers had moved from Minneapolis to Los Angeles, the Nats from Syracuse to Philadelphia, the Royals from Rochester to Cincinnati, the Pistons from Fort Wayne to Detroit.

In 1961, there hadn't been a market for a second professional basketball league; Abe Saperstein's ABL folded after a year. But by 1967, the ABA was able to take root in eleven cities. Four of its teams—New York, Denver, San Antonio, and Indiana—ended up as NBA franchises.

For twenty-five years, the National Hockey League had only six teams, all of them northeast of Chicago. In 1967, the league doubled, as franchises popped up in unlikely places like Oakland, Los Angeles, and St. Louis.

The NCAA basketball tournament, which had only eight teams in 1949, had grown to twenty-five by 1960. And by the mid-sixties, one team owned the title—UCLA. Their best player, a seven-footer named Lew Alcindor, had gone to high school in New York.

No longer was it assumed that you'd play for a school in your home state. Anybody could play anywhere. A kid from Philadelphia could switch on his TV, see UCLA winning by twenty points, and decide he wanted to be a Bruin. That was tough for the old-time coaches like Hank Iba and Adolph Rupp, who'd never been big on recruiting, especially out of state.

But you couldn't count on winning with homegrown kids anymore, and you couldn't count on winning just with white players. That became obvious in 1966, when Texas Western's all-black team beat Rupp's all-white Kentucky team for the NCAA title.

Recruiting had become as important as coaching—maybe more important. And with recruiting—and the excesses that went with it—came the loss of whatever illusions were left in American sports. More schools than ever went on probation for violating the rules— for forging transcripts, for giving kids cars and cash. But the lure of success—the money and publicity that came with championships— made cheating seem worth the risk.

Maybe all of that had been going on when I was growing up in Wyoming. Maybe we weren't hearing about it, or maybe we just didn't want to believe it. I don't know if life was simpler in America during the thirties and forties, but it certainly seemed more innocent.

That innocence vanished, piece by piece, during the fifties. By the time Ted Williams stepped to the plate for the last time, he was a shadow from a bygone season.

Bibliography

Allen, Maury. *You Could Look It Up*. New York: Times Books, 1979.

Auerbach, Arnold. *Basketball for the Player, the Fan and the Coach*. New York: Simon & Schuster, 1975.

Auerbach, Red, and Joe Fitzgerald. *Red Auerbach*. New York: Putnam, 1977.

Baldassaro, Lawrence, ed. *The Ted Williams Reader*. New York: Simon & Schuster, 1991.

Cousy, Bob, and Edward Linn. *The Last Loud Roar*. Englewood Cliffs, NJ: Prentice-Hall, 1964.

Eskenazi, Gerald. *Bill Veeck: A Baseball Legend*. New York: McGraw-Hill, 1988.

Goldstein, Richard. *Spartan Seasons*. New York: Macmillan, 1980.

Gowdy, Curt, and Al Hirshberg. *Cowboy at the Mike*. New York: Doubleday, 1966.

Hirshberg, Al. *What's the Matter with the Red Sox?* New York: Dodd, Mead, 1973.

Jenkins, Dan. *Saturday's America*. Boston: Little, Brown, 1970.

Jennison, Christopher. *Wait 'Til Next Year*. New York: Norton, 1974.

Keith, Harold. *Forty-seven Straight*. Norman, OK: University of Oklahoma Press, 1984.

Marsh, Irving, and Edward Ehre. ed. *Best Sports Stories, 1945.* New York: Dutton, 1946.

Marsh, Irving, and Edward Ehre, ed. *Best Sports Stories, 1947.* New York: Dutton, 1947.

McKenzie, Michael. *Oklahoma State University: History-Making Basketball.* Marceline, MO: Walsworth, 1992.

Newhouse, Dave. *Heismen: After the Glory.* St. Louis: Sporting News, 1985.

Padwe, Sandy. *Basketball's Hall of Fame.* Englewood Cliffs, NJ: Prentice-Hall, 1970.

Paige, LeRoy (Satchel). *Maybe I'll Pitch Forever.* Garden City, NY: Doubleday, 1962.

Piersall, Jimmy, and Al Hirshberg. *Fear Strikes Out.* Boston: Little, Brown, 1955.

Pope, Edwin. *Football's Greatest Coaches.* Atlanta: Tupper and Love, 1955.

Rowan, Carl. *Wait Till Next Year.* New York: Random House, 1960.

Seidel, Michael. *Ted Williams—A Baseball Life.* Chicago: Contemporary Books, 1991.

Shannon, Bill, and George Kalinsky. *The Ballparks.* New York: Hawthorn Books, 1975.

Smith, Red. *To Absent Friends.* New York: Atheneum, 1982.

Sullivan, George. *Picture History of the Boston Celtics.* Indianapolis: Bobbs-Merrill, 1981.

Sullivan, George. *Picture History of the Boston Red Sox.* Indianapolis: Bobbs-Merrill, 1979.

Sullivan, George, and John Powers. *Yankees: An Illustrated History.* Englewood Cliffs, NJ: Prentice-Hall, 1982.

Switzer, Barry, and Bud Shrake. *Bootlegger's Boy.* New York: Morrow, 1990.

Twombly, Wells. *Shake Down the Thunder.* Radnor, PA: Chilton, 1974.

Index